Roman Catholic Missal
Catholic Sunday & Daily Mass Reading
2024, Year B

A Year of Daily Catholic Mass Readings

& Sacred Observances

For The First Quarter 2024

Book 1 of 4

Liturgical Calendar 2024 - Quarter 1

January | February | March

2024 Jan 1 Mon: MARY, MOTHER OF GOD S (Octave of Christmas). No obligation this year to attend Mass.

Nm 6: 22-27/ Ps 67: 2-3. 5. 6. 8 (2a)/ Gal 4: 4-7/ Lk 2: 16-21

2024 Jan 2 Tue: Basil the Great and Gregory Nazianzen, bps, drs M

1 Jn 2: 22-28/ Ps 98: 1. 2-3ab. 3cd-4/ Jn 1: 19-28

2024 Jan 3 Wed: Christmas Weekday/ Holy Name of Jesus

1 Jn 2: 29 -- 3: 6/ Ps 98: 1. 3cd-4. 5-6/ Jn 1: 29-34

2024 Jan 4 Thu: Elizabeth Ann Seton, r M

1 Jn 3: 7-10/ Ps 98: 1. 7-8. 9/ Jn 1: 35-42

2024 Jan 5 Fri: John Neumann, bp M

1 Jn 3: 11-21/ Ps 100: 1b-2. 3. 4. 5/ Jn 1: 43-51

2024 Jan 6 Sat: Christmas Weekday/ Andre Bessette, r

1 Jn 5: 5-13/ Ps 147: 12-13. 14-15. 19-20/ Mk 1: 7-11 or Lk 3: 23-38

<u>2024 Jan 7 SUN: EPIPHANY OF THE LORD S</u>

Is 60: 1-6/ Ps 72: 1-2. 7-8. 10-11. 12-13/ Eph 3: 2-3a. 5-6/ Mt 2: 1-12

2024 Jan 8 Mon: BAPTISM OF THE LORD F

Is 55: 1-11 or 1 Jn 5: 1-9/ Is 12: 2-3. 4bcd. 5-6 (3)/ Mk 1: 7-11

2024 Jan 9 Tue: Ordinary Weekday

When the Baptism of the Lord occurs on Monday of the First Week in Ordinary Time (e.g. this year), the readings assigned to Monday may be joined to those of Tuesday so that the opening of each book will be read. Monday's readings: 1 Sm 1: 1-8/ Ps 116: 12-13. 14-17. 18-19/ Mk 1: 14-20. Tuesday's readings: 1 Sm 1: 9-20/ 1 Sm 2: 1. 4-5. 6-7. 8abcd/ Mk 1: 21-28

2024 Jan 10 Wed: Ordinary Weekday

1 Sm 3: 1-10. 19-20/ Ps 40: 2 and 5. 7-8a. 8b-9. 10/ Mk 1: 29-39

2024 Jan 11 Thu: Ordinary Weekday

1 Sm 4: 1-11/ Ps 44: 10-11. 14-15. 24-25/ Mk 1: 40-45

2024 Jan 12 Fri: Ordinary Weekday

1 Sm 8: 4-7. 10-22a/ Ps 89: 16-17. 18-19/ Mk 2: 1-12

2024 Jan 13 Sat: Ordinary Weekday/ BVM/ Hilary, bp, dr

1 Sm 9: 1-4. 17-19; 10: 1/ Ps 21: 2-3. 4-5. 6-7/ Mk 2: 13-17

<u>2024 Jan 14 SUN: SECOND SUNDAY IN ORDINARY TIME</u>

1 Sm 3: 3b-10. 19/ Ps 40: 2. 4. 7-8. 8-9. 10 (8a. 9a)/ 1 Cor 6: 13c-15a. 17-20/ Jn 1: 35-42

2024 Jan 15 Mon: Ordinary Weekday

1 Sm 15: 16-23/ Ps 50: 8-9. 16bc-17. 21 and 23/ Mk 2: 18-22

2024 Jan 16 Tue: Ordinary Weekday

1 Sm 16: 1-13/ Ps 89: 20. 21-22. 27-28/ Mk 2: 23-28

2024 Jan 17 Wed: Anthony, ab M

1 Sm 17: 32-33. 37. 40-51/ Ps 144: 1b. 2. 9-10/ Mk 3: 1-6

2024 Jan 18 Thu: Ordinary Weekday

1 Sm 18: 6-9; 19: 1-7/ Ps 56: 2-3. 9-10a. 10b-11. 12-13/ Mk 3: 7-12

2024 Jan 19 Fri: Ordinary Weekday

1 Sm 24: 3-21/ Ps 57: 2. 3-4. 6 and 11/ Mk 3: 13-19

2024 Jan 20 Sat: Ordinary Weekday/ BVM/ Fabian, pp, mt/ Sebastian, mt

2 Sm 1: 1-4. 11-12. 19. 23-27/ Mk 3: 20-21

2024 Jan 21 SUN: THIRD SUNDAY IN ORDINARY TIME

Jon 3: 1-5. 10/ Ps 25: 4-5. 6-7. 8-9 (4a)/ 1 Cor 7: 29-31/ Mk 1: 14-20

2024 Jan 22 Mon: Day of Prayer for the Legal Protection of Unborn Children M

2 Sm 5: 1-7. 10/ Ps 89: 20. 21-22. 25-26/ Mk 3: 22-30

2024 Jan 23 Tue: Ordinary Weekday/ Vincent of Saragossa, d, mt/ Marianne Cope, v

2 Sm 6: 12b-15. 17-19/ Ps 24: 7. 8. 9. 10/ Mk 3: 31-35

2024 Jan 24 Wed: Francis de Sales, bp, rf, dr M

2 Sm 7: 4-17/ Ps 89: 4-5. 27-28. 29-30/ Mk 4: 1-20

2024 Jan 25 Thu: Conversion of Paul, ap F

Acts 22: 3-16 or Acts 9: 1-22/ Ps 117: 1bc. 2/ Mk 16: 15-18

2024 Jan 26 Fri: Timothy and Titus, bps M

2 Tm 1: 1-8 or Ti 1: 1-5/ Ps 96: 1-2a. 2b-3. 7-8a. 10/ Mk 4: 26-34

2024 Jan 27 Sat: Ordinary Weekday/ BVM/ Angela Merici, v, rf

2 Sm 12: 1-7a. 10-17/ Ps 51: 12-13. 14-15. 16-17/ Mk 4: 35-41

2024 Jan 28 SUN: FOURTH SUNDAY IN ORDINARY TIME

Dt 18: 15-20/ Ps 95: 1-2. 6-7. 7-9 (8)/ 1 Cor 7: 32-35/ Mk 1: 21-28

2024 Jan 29 Mon: Ordinary Weekday

2 Sm 15: 13-14. 30; 16: 5-13/ Ps 3: 2-3. 4-5. 6-7/ Mk 5: 1-20

2024 Jan 30 Tue: Ordinary Weekday

2 Sm 18: 9-10. 14b. 24-25a. 30 -- 19: 3/ Ps 86: 1-2. 3-4. 5-6/ Mk 5: 21-43

2024 Jan 31 Wed: John Bosco, p, rf M

2 Sm 24: 2. 9-17/ Ps 32: 1-2. 5. 6. 7/ Mk 6: 1-6

2024 Feb 1 Thu: Ordinary Weekday

1 Kgs 2: 1-4. 10-12/ 1 Chr 29: 10. 11ab. 11d-12a. 12bcd/ Mk 6: 7-13

2024 Feb 2 Fri: PRESENTATION OF THE LORD F

Mal 3: 1-4/ Ps 24: 7. 8. 9. 10/ Heb 2: 14-18/ Lk 2: 22-40

2024 Feb 3 Sat: Ordinary Weekday/ BVM/ Blase, bp, mt/ Ansgar, bp, ms

1 Kgs 3: 4-13/ Ps 119: 9. 10. 11. 12. 13. 14/ Mk 6: 30-34

2024 Feb 4 SUN: FIFTH SUNDAY IN ORDINARY TIME

Jb 7: 1-4. 6-7/ Ps 147: 1-2. 3-4. 5-6/ 1 Cor 9: 16-19. 22-23/ Mk 1: 29-39

2024 Feb 5 Mon: Agatha, v, mt M

1 Kgs 8: 1-7. 9-13/ Ps 132: 6-7. 8-10/ Mk 6: 53-56

2024 Feb 6 Tue: Paul Miki, p, mt, & co., mts M

1 Kgs 8: 22-23. 27-30/ Ps 84: 3. 4. 5 and 10. 11/ Mk 7: 1-13

2024 Feb 7 Wed: Ordinary Weekday

1 Kgs 10: 1-10/ Ps 37: 30-31. 39-40/ Mk 7: 14-23

2024 Feb 8 Thu: Ordinary Weekday/ Jerome Emiliani, p, rf/ Josephine Bakhita, v

1 Kgs 11: 4-13/ Ps 106: 3-4. 35-36. 37 and 40/ Mk 7: 24-30

2024 Feb 9 Fri: Ordinary Weekday

1 Kgs 11: 29-32; 12: 19/ Ps 81: 10-11ab. 12-13. 14-15/ Mk 7: 31-37

2024 Feb 10 Sat: Scholastica, v, r M

1 Kgs 12: 26-32; 13: 33-34/ Ps 106: 6-7ab. 19-20. 21-22/ Mk 8: 1-10

2024 Feb 11 SUN: SIXTH SUNDAY IN ORDINARY TIME

Lv 13: 1-2. 44-46/ Ps 32: 1-2. 5. 11 (7)/ 1 Cor 10: 31 -- 11: 1/ Mk 1: 40-45

2024 Feb 12 Mon: Ordinary Weekday

Jas 1: 1-11/ Ps 119: 67. 68. 71. 72. 75. 76/ Mk 8: 11-13

2024 Feb 13 Tue: Ordinary Weekday

Jas 1: 12-18/ Ps 94: 12-13a. 14-15. 18-19/ Mk 8: 14-21

2024 Feb 14 Wed: Ash Wednesday. Begin Lenten preparation for the Easter Triduum. NOT a holy day of obligation. Day of fast (ages 18-59) and abstinence from meat (age 14 and up).

Jl 2: 12-18/ Ps 51: 3-4. 5-6ab. 12-13. 14 and 17/ 2 Cor 5: 20 -- 6:2/ Mt 6: 1-6. 16-18

2024 Feb 15 Thu: Thursday after Ash Wednesday

Dt 30: 15-20/ Ps 1: 1-2. 3. 4 and 6/ Lk 9: 22-25

2024 Feb 16 Fri: Friday after Ash Wednesday. Day of abstinence from meat (age 14 and up).

Is 58: 1-9a/ Ps 51: 3-4. 5-6ab. 18-19/ Mt 9: 14-15

2024 Feb 17 Sat: Saturday after Ash Wednesday/ Seven Founders of the Order of Servites, rs

Is 58: 9b-14/ Ps 86: 1-2. 3-4. 5-6/ Lk 5: 27-32

<u>2024 Feb 18 SUN: FIRST SUNDAY OF LENT</u>

Gn 9: 8-15/ Ps 25: 4-5. 6-7. 8-9/ 1 Pt 3: 18-22/ Mk 1: 12-15

2024 Feb 19 Mon: Lenten Weekday

Lv 19: 1-2. 11-18/ Ps 19: 8. 9. 10. 15/ Mt 25: 31-46

2024 Feb 20 Tue: Lenten Weekday

Is 55: 10-11/ Ps 34: 4-5. 6-7. 16-17. 18-19/ Mt 6: 7-15

2024 Feb 21 Wed: Lenten Weekday/ Peter Damian, bp, dr

Jon 3: 1-10/ Ps 51: 3-4. 12-13. 18-19/ Lk 11: 29-32

2024 Feb 22 Thu: Chair of Peter, ap F

1 Pt 5: 1-4/ Ps 23: 1-3a. 4. 5. 6/ Mt 16: 13-19

2024 Feb 23 Fri: Lenten Weekday/ Polycarp, bp, mt.   Day of abstinence from meat (age 14 and up).

Ez 18: 21-28/ Ps 130: 1-2. 3-4. 5-7a. 7bc-8/ Mt 5: 20-26

2024 Feb 24 Sat: Lenten Weekday

Dt 26: 16-19/ Ps 119: 1-2. 4-5. 7-8/ Mt 5: 43-48

2024 Feb 25 SUN: SECOND SUNDAY OF LENT

Gn 22: 1-2. 9a. 10-13. 15-18/ Ps 116: 10. 15. 16-17. 18-19/ Rom 8: 31b-34/ Mk 9:2-10

2024 Feb 26 Mon: Lenten Weekday

Dn 9: 4b-10/ Ps 79: 8. 9. 11 and 13/ Lk 6: 36-38

2024 Feb 27 Tue: Lenten Weekday/ Gregory of Narek, ab, dr

Is 1: 10. 16-20/ Ps 50: 8-9. 16bc-17. 21 and 23/ Mt 23: 1-12

2024 Feb 28 Wed: Lenten Weekday

Jer 18: 18-20/ Ps 31: 5-6. 14. 15-16/ Mt 20: 17-28

2024 Feb 29 Thu: Lenten Weekday

Jer 17: 5-10/ Ps 1: 1-2. 3. 4 and 6/ Lk 16: 19-31

2024 Mar 1 Fri: Lenten Weekday. Day of abstinence from meat (age 14 and up).

Gn 37: 3-4. 12-13a. 17b-28a/ Ps 105: 16-17. 18-19. 20-21/ Mt 21: 33-43. 45-46

2024 Mar 2 Sat: Lenten Weekday

Mi 7: 14-15. 18-20/ Ps 103: 1-2. 3-4. 9-10. 11-12/ Lk 15: 1-3. 11-32

<u>2024 Mar 3 SUN: THIRD SUNDAY OF LENT</u> - First Scrutiny of the Elect.

Scrutiny: Ex 17: 3-7/ Ps 95: 1-2. 6-7. 8-9/ Rom 5: 1-2. 5-8/ Jn 4: 5-42. Otherwise: Ex 20: 1-17/ Ps 19: 8. 9. 10. 11/ 1 Cor 1: 22-25/ Jn 2: 13-25

2024 Mar 4 Mon: Lenten Weekday/ Casimir

2 Kgs 5: 1-15b/ Ps 42: 2. 3; 43: 3. 4/ Lk 4: 24-30. Optional for any day this week: Ex 17: 1-7/ Ps 95: 1-2. 6-7ab. 7c-9/ Jn 4: 5-42

2024 Mar 5 Tue: Lenten Weekday

Dn 3: 25. 34-43/ Ps 25: 4-5ab. 6 and 7bc. 8 and 9/ Mt 18: 21-35

2024 Mar 6 Wed: Lenten Weekday

Dt 4:1. 5-9/ Ps 147: 12-13. 15-16. 19-20/ Mt 5: 17-19

2024 Mar 7 Thu: Lenten Weekday/ Perpetua and Felicity, mts

Jer 7: 23-28/ Ps 95: 1-2. 6-7. 8-9/ Lk 11: 14-23

2024 Mar 8 Fri: Lenten Weekday/ John of God, rf. Day of abstinence from meat (age 14 and up).

Hos 14: 2-10/ Ps 81: 6c-8a. 8bc-9. 10-11ab. 14 and 17/ Mk 12: 28-34

2024 Mar 9 Sat: Lenten Weekday/ Frances of Rome, mw, rf

Hos 6: 1-6/ Ps 51: 3-4. 18-19. 20-21ab/ Lk 18: 9-14

<u>2024 Mar 10 SUN: FOURTH SUNDAY OF LENT - Second Scrutiny of the Elect.</u>

Scrutiny: 1 Sm 16: 1b. 6-7. 10-13a/ Ps 23: 1-3a. 3b-4. 5. 6 (1)/ Eph 5: 8-14/ Jn 9:1-41. Otherwise: 2 Chr 36: 14-16. 19-23/ Ps 137: 1-2. 3. 4-5. 6 (6ab)/ Eph 2: 4-10/ Jn 3:14-21

2024 Mar 11 Mon: Lenten Weekday

Is 65: 17-21/ Ps 30: 2 and 4. 5-6. 11-12a and 13b/ Jn 4: 43-54. Optional for any day this week: Mi 7: 7-9/ Ps 27: 1. 7-8a. 8b-9abc. 13-14/ Jn 9: 1-41

2024 Mar 12 Tue: Lenten Weekday

Ez 47: 1-9. 12/ Ps 46: 2-3. 5-6. 8-9/ Jn 5: 1-16

2024 Mar 13 Wed: Lenten Weekday

Is 49: 8-15/ Ps 145: 8-9. 13cd-14. 17-18/ Jn 5: 17-30

2024 Mar 14 Thu: Lenten Weekday

Ex 32: 7-14/ Ps 106: 19-20. 21-22. 23/ Jn 5: 31-47

2024 Mar 15 Fri: Lenten Weekday. Day of abstinence from meat (age 14 and up).

Wis 2: 1a. 12-22/ Ps 34: 17-18. 19-20. 21 and 23/ Jn 7: 1-2. 10. 25-30

2024 Mar 16 Sat: Lenten Weekday

Jer 11: 18-20/ Ps 7: 2-3. 9bc-10. 11-12/ Jn 7: 40-53

<u>2024 Mar 17 SUN: FIFTH SUNDAY OF LENT</u> - <u>Third Scrutiny of the Elect.</u>

Scrutiny: Ez 37: 12-14/ Ps 130: 1-2. 3-4. 5-6. 7-8/ Rom 8: 8-11/ Jn 11: 1-45. Otherwise: Jer 31: 31-34/ Ps 51: 3-4. 12-13. 14-15 (12a)/ Heb 5: 7-9/ Jn 12: 20-33

2024 Mar 18 Mon: Lenten Weekday/ Cyril of Jerusalem, bp, dr

Dn 13: 1-9. 15-17. 19-30. 33-62 or 13: 41c-62/ Ps 23: 1-3a. 3b-4. 5. 6/ Jn 8: 1-11. Optional for any weekday this week: 2 Kgs 4: 18b-21. 32-37/ Ps 17: 1. 6-7. 8b and 15/ Jn 11: 1-45

<u>2024 Mar 19 Tue: JOSEPH, HUSBAND OF MARY S</u>

2 Sm 7: 4-5a. 12-14a. 16/ Ps 89: 2-3. 4-5. 27 and 29/ Rom 4: 13. 16-18. 22/ Mt 1: 16. 18-21. 24a or Lk 2: 41-51a

2024 Mar 20 Wed: Lenten Weekday

Dn 3: 14-20. 91-92. 95/ Dn 3: 52. 53. 54. 55. 56/ Jn 8: 31-42

2024 Mar 21 Thu: Lenten Weekday

Gn 17: 3-9/ Ps 105: 4-5. 6-7. 8-9/ Jn 8: 51-59

2024 Mar 22 Fri: Lenten Weekday. Day of abstinence from meat (age 14 and up).

Jer 20: 10-13/ Ps 18: 2-3a. 3bc-4. 5-6. 7/ Jn 10: 31-42

2024 Mar 23 Sat: Lenten Weekday/ Toribio de Mogrovejo, bp

Ez 37: 21-28/ Jer 31: 10. 11-12abcd. 13/ Jn 11: 45-56

2024 Mar 24 SUN: PALM SUNDAY OF THE LORD'S PASSION

Procession: Mk 11: 1-10 or Jn 12: 12-16. Mass: Is 50: 4-7/ Ps 22: 8-9. 17-18. 19-20. 23-24/ Phil 2: 6-11/ Mk 14: 1 -- 15: 47

2024 Mar 25 Mon: Monday of Holy Week

Is 42: 1-7/ Ps 27: 1. 2. 3. 13-14/ Jn 12: 1-11. Chrism Mass: Is 61: 1-3a. 6a. 8b-9/ Ps 89: 21-22. 25. 27/ Rv 1: 5-8/ Lk 4: 16-21.

2024 Mar 26 Tue: Tuesday of Holy Week

Is 49: 1-6/ Ps 71: 1-2. 3-4a. 5ab-6ab. 15 and 17/ Jn 13: 21-33. 36-38

2024 Mar 27 Wed: Wednesday of Holy Week

Is 50: 4-9a/ Ps 69: 8-10. 21-22. 31 and 33-34/ Mt 26: 14-25

2024 Mar 28 Thu: Holy Thursday. At evening, begin Easter Triduum of the Lord's Passion, Death and Resurrection.

Evening Mass of the Lord's Supper: Ex 12: 1-8. 11-14/ Ps 116: 12-13. 15-16bc. 17-18/Jn 13: 1-15

2024 Mar 29 Fri: Good Friday. Day of fast (ages 18-59) and abstinence from meat (age 14 and up).

Mass is not celebrated today. Celebration of the Lord's Passion: Is 52: 13 -- 53: 12/ Ps 31: 2. 6. 12-13. 15-16. 17. 25/ Heb 4: 14-16; 5: 7-9/ Jn 18: 1 -- 19: 42

2024 Mar 30 Sat: Holy Saturday

Readings for the Easter Vigil, which is an Easter Sunday Mass: Gn 1: 1 -- 2: 2 or 1: 1.26-31a/ Ps 104: 1-2. 5-6. 10. 12. 13-14. 24. 35 or Ps 33: 4-5. 6-7. 12-13. 20-22/ Gn 22: 1-18 or 22: 1-2. 9a. 10-13. 15-18/ Ps 16: 5. 8. 9-10. 11/ Ex 14: 15 -- 15: 1/ Ex 15: 1-2. 3-4. 5-6. 17-18/ Is 54: 5-14/ Ps 30: 2. 4. 5-6. 11-12. 13/ Is 55: 1-11/ Is 12: 2-3. 4. 5-6/ Bar 3: 9-15. 32 -- 4: 4/ Ps 19: 8. 9. 10. 11/ Ez 36: 16-17a. 18-28/ Ps 42: 3. 5; 43: 3. 4 or Is 12: 2-3. 4bcd. 5-6 or Ps 51: 12-13. 14-15. 18-19/ Rom 6: 3-11/ Ps 118: 1-2. 16-17. 22-23/ Mk 16: 1-7

<u>2024 Mar 31 SUN: EASTER SUNDAY - The Resurrection of our Lord and Savior Jesus Christ.</u>

Acts 10: 34a. 37-43/ Ps 118: 1-2. 16-17. 22-23/ Col 3: 1-4 or 1 Cor 5: 6b-8/ Jn 20: 1-9 or Mk 16: 1-7 or, at an afternoon or evening Mass, Lk 24: 13-35

Easter Triduum ends after Evening Prayer.

January 2024

Daily Mass Readings for Monday, 1 January 2024

Mary, Mother of God Solemnity (Octave of Christmas) First Reading: Numbers 6: 22-27 Responsorial Psalm: Psalms 67: 2-3, 5, 6, 8

Second Reading: Galatians 4: 4-7 Alleluia: Hebrews 1: 1-2 Gospel: Luke 2: 16-21 Lectionary: 18

First Reading: Numbers 6: 22-27

And the Lord spoke to Moses, saying: Say to Aaron and his sons: Thus shall you bless the children of Israel, and you shall say to them:
The Lord bless thee, and keep thee.
The Lord shew his face to thee, and have mercy on thee.

The Lord turn his countenance to thee, and give thee peace.
And they shall invoke my name upon the children of Israel, and I will bless them.

Responsorial Psalm: Psalms 67: 2-3, 5, 6, 8

R. (2a) May God bless us in his mercy.

May God have mercy on us, and bless us: may he cause the light of his countenance to shine upon us, and may he have mercy on us. That we may know thy way upon earth: thy salvation in all nations.

R. May God bless us in his mercy.

Let the nations be glad and rejoice: for thou judgest the people with justice, and directest the nations upon earth.

R. May God bless us in his mercy.

Let the people, O God, confess to thee: let all the people give praise to thee: May God bless us: and all the ends of the earth fear him.

R. May God bless us in his mercy.

Second Reading: Galatians 4: 4-7

4 But when the fullness of the time was come, God sent his Son, made of a woman, made under the law:

5 That he might redeem them who were under the law: that we might receive the adoption of sons.

6 And because you are sons, God hath sent the Spirit of his Son into your hearts, crying: Abba, Father.

7 Therefore now he is not a servant, but a son. And if a son, an heir also through God.

Alleluia: Hebrews 1: 1-2 R. Alleluia, alleluia.

1-2 In the past God spoke to our ancestors through the prophets; in these last days, he has spoken to us through the Son.

R. Alleluia, alleluia.

Gospel: Luke 2: 16-21

16 And they came with haste; and they found Mary and Joseph, and the infant lying in the manger.

17 And seeing, they understood of the word that had been spoken to them concerning this child.

18 And all that heard, wondered; and at those things that were told them by the shepherds.

19 But Mary kept all these words, pondering them in her heart.

20 And the shepherds returned, glorifying and praising God, for all the things they had heard and seen, as it was told unto them.

21 And after eight days were accomplished, that the child should be circumcised, his name was called JESUS, which was called by the angel, before he was conceived in the womb.

Daily Mass Readings for Tuesday, 2 January 2024

Basil the Great and Gregory Nazianzen, Bishops, Doctors Obligatory Memorial
First Reading: First John 2: 22-28
Responsorial Psalm: Psalms 98: 1, 2-3ab, 3cd-4

Alleluia: Hebrews 1: 1-2 Gospel: John 1: 19-28 Lectionary: 205

First Reading: First John 2: 22-28

22 Who is a liar, but he who denieth that Jesus is the Christ? This is Antichrist, who denieth the Father, and the Son.
23 Whosoever denieth the Son, the same hath not the Father. He that confesseth the Son, hath the Father also.

24 As for you, let that which you have heard from the beginning, abide in you. If that abide in you, which you have heard from the beginning, you also shall abide in the Son, and in the Father.
25 And this is the promise which he hath promised us, life everlasting.
26 These things have I written to you, concerning them that seduce you.
27 And as for you, let the unction, which you have received from him, abide in you. And you have no need that any man teach you; but as his unction teacheth you of all things, and is truth, and is no lie. And as it hath taught you, abide in him.
28 And now, little children, abide in him, that when he shall appear, we may have confidence, and not be confounded by him at his coming.

Responsorial Psalm: Psalms 98: 1, 2-3ab, 3cd-4

R. (3cd) All the ends of the earth have seen the saving power of God.

1 Sing ye to the Lord anew canticle: because he hath done wonderful things. His right hand hath wrought for him salvation, and his arm is holy.

R. All the ends of the earth have seen the saving power of God.
2 The Lord hath made known his salvation: he hath revealed his justice in the sight of the Gentiles.

3ab He hath remembered his mercy his truth toward the house of Israel. R. All the ends of the earth have seen the saving power of God.

3cd All the ends of the earth have seen the salvation of our God.
4 Sing joyfully to God, all the earth; make melody, rejoice and sing.

R. All the ends of the earth have seen the saving power of God.

Alleluia: Hebrews 1: 1-2 R. Alleluia, alleluia.

1-2 In times, past, God spoke to our ancestors through the prophets: in these last days, he has spoken to us through his Son.

R. Alleluia, alleluia.

Gospel: John 1: 19-28
19 And this is the testimony of John, when the Jews sent from Jerusalem priests and Levites to him, to ask him: Who art thou?

20 And he confessed, and did not deny: and he confessed: I am not the Christ.

21 And they asked him: What then? Art thou Elias? And he said: I am not. Art thou the prophet? And he answered: No.

22 They said therefore unto him: Who art thou, that we may give an answer to them that sent us? What sayest thou of thyself?

23 He said: I am the voice of one crying out in the wilderness, make straight the way of the Lord, as said the prophet Isaias.

24 And they that were sent, were of the Pharisees.

25 And they asked him, and said to him: Why then dost thou baptize, if thou be not Christ, nor Elias, nor the prophet?

26 John answered them, saying: I baptize with water; but there hath stood one in the midst of you, whom you know not.

27 The same is he that shall come after me, who is preferred before me: the latchet of whose shoe I am not worthy to loose.

28 These things were done in Bethania, beyond the Jordan, where John was baptizing.

Daily Mass Readings for Wednesday, 3 January 2024

Christmas Weekday/ Holy Name of Jesus First Reading: First John 2: 29 – 3: 6 Responsorial Psalm: Psalms 98: 1, 3cd-4, 5-6 Alleluia: John 1: 14a, 12a Gospel: John 1: 29-34 Lectionary: 206

First Reading: First John 2: 29 – 3: 6

29 If you know, that he is just, know ye, that every one also, who doth justice, is born of him.
3:1 Behold what manner of charity the Father hath bestowed upon us, that we should be called, and should be the sons of God. Therefore, the world knoweth not us, because it knew not him.

2 Dearly beloved, we are now the sons of God; and it hath not yet appeared what we shall be. We know, that, when he shall appear, we shall be like to him: because we shall see him as he is.
3 And every one that hath this hope in him, sanctifieth himself, as he also is holy.

4 Whosoever committeth sin committeth also iniquity; and sin is iniquity.
5 And you know that he appeared to take away our sins, and in him there is no sin.
6 Whosoever abideth in him, sinneth not; and whosoever sinneth, hath not seen him, nor known him.

Responsorial Psalm: Psalms 98: 1, 3cd-4, 5-6

R. (3cd) All the ends of the earth have seen the saving power of God.

1 Sing ye to the Lord a new canticle: because he hath done wonderful things. His right hand hath wrought for him salvation, and his arm is holy.

R. All the ends of the earth have seen the saving power of God.
3cd All the ends of the earth have seen the salvation of our God.
4 Sing joyfully to God, all the earth; make melody, rejoice and sing.

R. All the ends of the earth have seen the saving power of God.
5 Sing praise to the Lord on the harp, on the harp, and with the voice of a psalm:

6 With long trumpets, and sound of comet. Make a joyful noise before the Lord our king:

R. All the ends of the earth have seen the saving power of God.

Alleluia: John 1: 14a, 12a R. Alleluia, alleluia.

14a, 12a The Word of God became flesh and dwelt among us. To those who accepted him he gave power to become the children of God.

R. Alleluia, alleluia.

Gospel: John 1: 29-34

29 The next day, John saw Jesus coming to him, and he saith: Behold the Lamb of God, behold him who taketh away the sin of the world.
30 This is he, of whom I said: After me there cometh a man, who is preferred before me: because he was before me.
31 And I knew him not, but that he may be made manifest in Israel, therefore am I come baptizing with water.
32 And John gave testimony, saying: I saw the Spirit coming down, as a dove from heaven, and he remained upon him.

33 And I knew him not; but he who sent me to baptize with water, said to me: He upon whom thou shalt see the Spirit descending, and remaining upon him, he it is that baptizeth with the Holy Ghost.
34 And I saw, and I gave testimony, that this is the Son of God.

Daily Mass Readings for Thursday, 4 January 2024

Elizabeth Ann Seton, Religious Obligatory Memorial First Reading: First John 3: 7-10 Responsorial Psalm: Psalms 98: 1, 7-8, 9 Alleluia: Hebrews 1: 1-2
Gospel: John 1: 35-42
Lectionary: 207

First Reading: First John 3: 7-10

7 Little children, let no man deceive you. He that doth justice is just, even as he is just.
8 He that committeth sin is of the devil: for the devil sinneth from the beginning. For this purpose, the Son of God appeared, that he might destroy the works of the devil.

9 Whosoever is born of God, committeth not sin: for his seed abideth in him, and he can not sin, because he is born of God.
10 In this the children of God are manifest, and the children of the devil. Whosoever is not just, is not of God, nor he that loveth not his brother.

Responsorial Psalm: Psalms 98: 1, 7-8, 9

R. (3cd) All the ends of the earth have seen the saving power of God.
1 Sing ye to the Lord a new canticle: because he hath done wonderful things. His right hand hath wrought for him salvation, and his arm is holy.

R. All the ends of the earth have seen the saving power of God.
7 Let the sea be moved and the fulness thereof: the world and they that dwell therein.
8 The rivers shall clap their hands, the mountains shall rejoice together

R. All the ends of the earth have seen the saving power of God.
9 At the presence of the Lord: because he cometh to judge the earth. He shall judge the world with justice, and the people with equity.

R. All the ends of the earth have seen the saving power of God.

Alleluia: Hebrews 1: 1-2 R. Alleluia, alleluia.

1-2 In the past God spoke to our ancestors through the prophets: in these last days, he has spoken to us through the Son.

R. Alleluia, alleluia.

Gospel: John 1: 35-42

35 The next day again John stood, and two of his disciples.
36 And beholding Jesus walking, he saith: Behold the Lamb of God.
37 And the two disciples heard him speak, and they followed Jesus.
38 And Jesus turning, and seeing them following him, saith to them: What seek you? Who said to him, Rabbi, (which is to say, being interpreted, Master,) where dwellest thou?
39 He saith to them: Come and see. They came, and saw where he abode, and they stayed with him that day: now it was about the tenth hour.
40 And Andrew, the brother of Simon Peter, was one of the two who had heard of John, and followed him.
41 He findeth first his brother Simon, and saith to him: We have found the Messias, which is, being interpreted, the Christ.
42 And he brought him to Jesus. And Jesus looking upon him, said: Thou art Simon the son of Jona: thou shalt be called Cephas, which is interpreted Peter.

Daily Mass Readings for Friday, 5 January 2024

John Neumann, Bishop Obligatory Memorial First Reading: First John 3: 11-21 Responsorial Psalm: Psalms 100: 1b-2, 3, 4, 5 Gospel: John 1: 43-51 Lectionary: 208

First Reading: First John 3: 11-21

11 For this is the declaration, which you have heard from the beginning, that you should love one another.
12 Not as Cain, who was of the wicked one, and killed his brother. And wherefore did he kill him? Because his own works were wicked: and his brother's just.

13 Wonder not, brethren, if the world hate you.
14 We know that we have passed from death to life, because we love the brethren. He that loveth not, abideth in death.
15 Whosoever hateth his brother is a murderer. And you know that no murderer hath eternal life abiding in himself.
16 In this we have known the charity of God, because he hath laid down his life for us: and we ought to lay down our lives for the brethren.
17 He that hath the substance of this world, and shall see his brother in need, and shall shut up his bowels from him: how doth the charity of God abide in him?

18 My little children, let us not love in word, nor in tongue, but in deed, and in truth.
19 In this we know that we are of the truth: and in his sight shall persuade our hearts.

20 For if our heart reprehend us, God is greater than our heart, and knoweth all things.
21 Dearly beloved, if our heart do not reprehend us, we have confidence towards God:

Responsorial Psalm: Psalms 100: 1b-2, 3, 4, 5

R. (2a) Let all the earth cry out to God with joy.
1b-2 Sing joyfully to God, all the earth: serve ye the Lord with gladness. Come in before his presence with exceeding great joy.

R. Let all the earth cry out to God with joy.

3 Know ye that the Lord he is God: he made us, and not we ourselves. We are his people and the sheep of his pasture.

R. Let all the earth cry out to God with joy.

4 Go ye into his gates with praise, into his courts with hymns: and give glory to him. Praise ye his name:

R. Let all the earth cry out to God with joy.

5 For the Lord is sweet, his mercy endureth for ever, and his truth to generation and generation.

R. Let all the earth cry out to God with joy.

Alleluia
R. Alleluia, alleluia.

A holy day has dawned upon us. Come, you nations, and adore the Lord. Today a great light has come upon the earth.

R. Alleluia, alleluia.

Gospel: John 1: 43-51

43 On the following day, he would go forth into Galilee, and he findeth Philip. And Jesus saith to him: Follow me.
44 Now Philip was of Bethsaida, the city of Andrew and Peter.
45 Philip findeth Nathanael, and saith to him: We have found him of whom Moses in the law, and the prophets did write, Jesus the son of Joseph of Nazareth.

46 And Nathanael said to him: Can any thing of good come from Nazareth? Philip saith to him: Come and see.
47 Jesus saw Nathanael coming to him: and he saith of him: Behold an Israelite indeed, in whom there is no guile.

48 Nathanael saith to him: Whence knowest thou me? Jesus answered, and said to him: Before that Philip called thee, when thou wast under the fig tree, I saw

thee.

49 Nathanael answered him, and said: Rabbi, thou art the Son of God, thou art the King of Israel.

50 Jesus answered, and said to him: Because I said unto thee, I saw thee under the fig tree, thou believest: greater things than these shalt thou see.

51 And he saith to him: Amen, amen I say to you, you shall see the heaven opened, and the angels of God ascending and descending upon the Son of man

Daily Mass Readings for Saturday, 6 January 2024

Christmas Weekday/ André Bessette, Religious **First Reading:** *First John 5: 5-13* **Responsorial Psalm:** *Psalms 147: 12-13, 14-15, 19-20* **Alleluia:** *Mark 9: 7*
Gospel: *Mark 1: 7-11 or Luke 3: 23-38* **Lectionary:** *209*

First John 5: 5-13

5 Who is First Reading he that overcometh the world, but he that believeth that Jesus is the Son of God?
6 This is he that came by water and blood, Jesus Christ: not by water only, but by water and blood. And it is the Spirit which testifieth, that Christ is the truth.

7 And there are three who give testimony in heaven, the Father, the Word, and the Holy Ghost. And these three are one.
8 And there are three that give testimony on earth: the spirit, and the water, and the blood: and these three are one.

9 If we receive the testimony of men, the testimony of God is greater. For this is the testimony of God, which is greater, because he hath testified of his Son.
10 He that believeth in the Son of God, hath the testimony of God in himself. He that believeth not the Son, maketh him a liar: because he believeth not in the testimony which God hath testified of his Son.

11 And this is the testimony, that God hath given to us eternal life. And this life is in his Son.
12 He that hath the Son, hath life. He that hath not the Son, hath not life.
13 These things I write to you, that you may know that you have eternal life, you who believe in the name of the Son of God.

Responsorial Psalm: Psalms 147: 12-13, 14-15, 19-20

R. (12a) Praise the Lord, Jerusalem. or

R. Alleluia.
12 Praise the Lord, O Jerusalem: praise thy God, O Sion.

13 Because he hath strengthened the bolts of thy gates, he hath blessed thy children within thee.

R. Praise the Lord, Jerusalem. or
R. Alleluia.

14 Who hath placed peace in thy borders: and filleth thee with the fat of corn.
15 Who sendeth forth his speech to the earth: his word runneth swiftly.

R. Praise the Lord, Jerusalem.

or

R. Alleluia.

19 Who declareth his word to Jacob: his justices and his judgments to Israel.
20 He hath not done in like manner to every nation: and his judgments he hath

not made manifest to them. Alleluia.

R. Praise the Lord, Jerusalem. or
R. Alleluia.

Alleluia: Mark 9: 7 R. Alleluia, alleluia.

7 The heavens were opened and the voice of the Father thundered: This is my beloved Son. Listen to him.

R. Alleluia, alleluia.

Gospel: Mark 1: 7-11 or Luke 3: 23-38

7 John the Baptist preached, saying: There cometh after me one mightier than I, the latchet of whose shoes I am not worthy to stoop down and loose.
8 I have baptized you with water; but he shall baptize you with the Holy Ghost.

9 And it came to pass, in those days, Jesus came from Nazareth of Galilee, and was baptized by John in the Jordan.
10 And forthwith coming up out of the water, he saw the heavens opened, and the Spirit as a dove descending, and remaining on him.

11 And there came a voice from heaven: Thou art my beloved Son; in thee I am well pleased.

Or 23 Jesus himself was beginning about the age of thirty years; being (as it was supposed) the son of Joseph, who was of Heli, who was of Mathat,
24 Who was of Levi, who was of Melchi, who was of Janne, who was of Joseph,

25 Who was of Mathathias, who was of Amos, who was of Nahum, who was of Hesli, who was of Nagge,
26 Who was of Mahath, who was of Mathathias, who was of Semei, who was of Joseph, who was of Juda,

27 Who was of Joanna, who was of Reza, who was of Zorobabel, who was of Salathiel, who was of Neri,
28 Who was of Melchi, who was of Addi, who was of Cosan, who was of Helmadan, who was of Her,

29 Who was of Jesus, who was of Eliezer, who was of Jorim, who was of Mathat, who was of Levi,
30 Who was of Simeon, who was of Judas, who was of Joseph, who was of Jona, who was of Eliakim,

31 Who was of Melea, who was of Menna, who was of Mathatha, who was of Nathan, who was of David,

32 Who was of Jesse, who was of Obed, who was of Booz, who was of Salmon, who was of Naasson,
33 Who was of Aminadab, who was of Aram, who was of Esron, who was of Phares, who was of Judas,

34 Who was of Jacob, who was of Isaac, who was of Abraham, who was of Thare, who was of Nachor,
35 Who was of Sarug, who was of Ragau, who was of Phaleg, who was of Heber, who was of Sale,

36 Who was of Cainan, who was of Arphaxad, who was of Sem, who was of Noe, who was of Lamech,
37 Who was of Mathusale, who was of Henoch, who was of Jared, who was of Malaleel, who was of Cainan,

38 Who was of Henos, who was of Seth, who was of Adam, who was of God.

Daily Mass Readings for Sunday, 7 January 2024

Epiphany of the Lord Solemnity
First Reading: Isaiah 60: 1-6 Responsorial Psalm: Psalms 72: 1-2, 7-8, 10-11, 12-13 Second Reading: Ephesians 3: 2-3a, 5-6 Alleluia: Matthew 2: 2 Gospel: Matthew 2: 1-12
Lectionary: 20

First Reading: Isaiah 60: 1-6

1 Arise, be enlightened, O Jerusalem: for thy light is come, and the glory of the Lord is risen upon thee.
2 For behold darkness shall cover the earth, and a mist the people: but the Lord shall arise upon thee, and his glory shall be seen upon thee.

3 And the Gentiles shall walk in thy light, and kings in the brightness of thy rising.

4 Lift up thy eyes round about, and see: all these are gathered together, they are come to thee: thy sons shall come from afar, and thy daughters shall rise up at thy side.
5 Then shalt thou see, and abound, and thy heart shall wonder and be enlarged, when the multitude of the sea shall be converted to thee, the. strength of the Gentiles shall come to thee.

6 The multitude of camels shall cover thee, the dromedaries of Madian and Epha: all they from Saba shall come, bringing gold and frankincense: and shewing forth praise to the Lord.

Responsorial Psalm: Psalms 72: 1-2, 7-8, 10-11, 12-13

R. (11) Lord, every nation on earth will adore you.

1-2 Give to the king thy judgment, O God: and to the king's son thy justice: To judge thy people with justice, and thy poor with judgment.

R. Lord, every nation on earth will adore you.

7 In his days shall justice spring up, and abundance of peace, till the moon be taken sway.

8 And he shall rule from sea to sea, and from the river unto the ends of the earth.

R. Lord, every nation on earth will adore you.

10 The kings of Tharsis and the islands shall offer presents: the kings of the Arabians and of Saba shall bring gifts:

11 And all kings of the earth shall adore him: all nations shall serve him. R. Lord, every nation on earth will adore you.

12 For he shall deliver the poor from the mighty: and the needy that had no helper.

13 He shall spare the poor and needy: and he shall save the souls of the poor.

R. Lord, every nation on earth will adore you.

Second Reading: Ephesians 3: 2-3a, 5-6

2 If yet you have heard of the dispensation of the grace of God which is given me towards you:
3a How that, according to revelation, the mystery has been made known to me.

5 Which in other generations was not known to the sons of men, as it is now revealed to his holy apostles and prophets in the Spirit:
6 That the Gentiles should be fellow heirs, and of the same body, and co-partners of his promise in Christ Jesus, by the gospel:

Alleluia: Matthew 2: 2 R. Alleluia, alleluia.

2 We saw his star at its rising and have come to do him homage.

R. Alleluia, alleluia.

Gospel: Matthew 2: 1-12

1 When Jesus therefore was born in Bethlehem of Juda, in the days of king Herod, behold, there came wise men from the east to Jerusalem.
2 Saying, Where is he that is born king of the Jews? For we have seen his star in the east, and are come to adore him.

3 And king Herod hearing this, was troubled, and all Jerusalem with him.

4 And assembling together all the chief priests and the scribes of the people, he inquired of them where Christ should be born.

5 But they said to him: In Bethlehem of Juda. For so it is written by the prophet:

6 And thou Bethlehem the land of Juda art not the least among the princes of Juda: for out of thee shall come forth the captain that shall rule my people Israel.

7 Then Herod, privately calling the wise men, learned diligently of them the time of the star which appeared to them;

8 And sending them into Bethlehem, said: Go and diligently inquire after the child, and when you have found him, bring me word again, that I also may come to adore him.

9 Who having heard the king, went their way; and behold the star which they had seen in the east, went before them, until it came and stood over where the child was.

10 And seeing the star they rejoiced with exceeding great joy.

11 And entering into the house, they found the child with Mary his mother, and falling down they adored him; and opening their treasures, they offered him gifts; gold, frankincense, and myrrh.

12 And having received an answer in sleep that they should not return to Herod, they went back another way into their country.

Daily Mass Readings for Monday, 8 January 2024

Baptism of the Lord Feast
First Reading: Isaiah 55: 1-11
Responsorial Psalm: Isaiah 12: 2-3, 4bcd, 5-6
Second Reading: First John 5: 1-9
Alleluia: John 1: 29
Gospel: Mark 1: 7-11
Lectionary: 21
First Reading: Isaiah 55: 1-11

1 All you that thirst, come to the waters: and you that have no money make haste, buy, and eat: come ye, buy wine and milk without money, and without any price.

2 Why do you spend money for that which is not breed, and your labour for that which doth not satisfy you? Hearken diligently to me, and eat that which is good, and your soul shall be delighted in fatness.

3 Incline your ear and come to me: hear and your soul shall live, and I will make an everlasting covenant with you, the faithful mercies of David.

4 Behold I have given him for a witness to the people, for a leader and a master to the Gentiles.

5 Behold thou shalt call a nation, which thou knewest not: and the nations that knew not thee shall run to thee, because of the Lord thy God, and for the Holy One of Israel, for he hath glorified thee.

6 Seek ye the Lord, while he may be found: call upon him, while he is near.

7 Let the wicked forsake his way, and the unjust man his thoughts, and let him return to the Lord, and he will have mercy on him, and to our God: for he is bountiful to forgive.

8 For my thoughts are not your thoughts: nor your ways my ways, saith the Lord.

9 For as the heavens are exalted above the earth, so are my ways exalted above your ways, and my thoughts above your thoughts.

10 And as the rain and the snow come down from heaven, and return no more thither, but soak the earth, and water it, and make it to spring, and give seed to the sower, and bread to the eater:

11 So shall my word be, which shall go forth from my mouth: it shall not return to me void, but it shall do whatsoever I please, and shall prosper in the things for which I sent it.

Responsorial Psalm: Isaiah 12: 2-3, 4bcd, 5-6
R. (3) You will draw water joyfully from the springs of salvation.

2 Behold, God is my saviour, I will deal confidently, and will not fear: O because the Lord is my strength, and my praise, and he is become my salvation.

3 You shall draw waters with joy out of the saviour's fountains: R. You will draw water joyfully from the springs of salvation.

4bcd Praise ye the Lord, and call upon his name: make his works known among the people: remember that his name is high.

R. You will draw water joyfully from the springs of salvation.

5 Sing ye to the Lord, for he hath done great things: shew this forth in all the earth.

6 Rejoice, and praise, O thou habitation of Sion: for great is he that is in the midst of thee, the Holy One of Israel.

R. You will draw water joyfully from the springs of salvation.

Second Reading: First John 5: 1-9
1 Whosoever believeth that Jesus is the Christ, is born of God. And every one that loveth him who begot, loveth him also who is born of him.

2 In this we know that we love the children of God: when we love God, and keep his commandments.

3 For this is the charity of God, that we keep his commandments: and his commandments are not heavy.

4 For whatsoever is born of God, overcometh the world: and this is the victory which overcometh the world, our faith.

5 Who is he that overcometh the world, but he that believeth that Jesus is the Son of God?

6 This is he that came by water and blood, Jesus Christ: not by water only, but by water and blood. And it is the Spirit which testifieth, that Christ is the truth.

7 And there are three who give testimony in heaven, the Father, the Word, and the Holy Ghost. And these three are one.

8 And there are three that give testimony on earth: the spirit, and the water, and the blood: and these three are one.

9 If we receive the testimony of men, the testimony of God is greater. For this is the testimony of God, which is greater, because he hath testified of his Son.

Alleluia: John 1: 29 R. Alleluia, alleluia.

29 John saw Jesus approaching him, and said: Behold the Lamb of God who takes away the sin of the world.

R. Alleluia, alleluia.

Gospel: Mark 1: 7-11
7 And he preached, saying: There cometh after me one mightier than I, the latchet of whose shoes I am not worthy to stoop down and loose.

8 I have baptized you with water; but he shall baptize you with the Holy Ghost.

9 And it came to pass, in those days, Jesus came from Nazareth of Galilee, and was baptized by John in the Jordan.

10 And forthwith coming up out of the water, he saw the heavens opened, and the Spirit as a dove descending, and remaining on him.

11 And there came a voice from heaven: Thou art my beloved Son; in thee I am well pleased.

Daily Mass Readings for Tuesday, 9 January 2024

Ordinary Weekday
First Reading: First Samuel 1: 9-20
Responsorial Psalm: First Samuel 2: 1, 4-5, 6-7, 8abcd
Alleluia: First Thessalonians 2: 13
Gospel: Mark 1: 21-28
Lectionary: 306

First Reading: First Samuel 1: 9-20

9 So Anna arose after she had eaten and drunk in Silo: And Heli the priest sitting upon a stool, before the door of the temple of the Lord:

10 As Anna had her heart full of grief, she prayed to the Lord, shedding many tears,

11 And she made a vow, saying: O Lord, of hosts, if thou wilt look down on the affliction of thy servant, and wilt be mindful of me, and not forget thy handmaid, and wilt give to thy servant a man child: I will give him to the Lord all the days of his life, and no razor shall come upon his head.

12 And it came to pass, as she multiplied prayers before the Lord, that Heli observed her mouth.

13 Now Anna spoke in her heart, and only her lips moved, but her voice was not heard at all. Heli therefore thought her to be drunk,

14 And said to her: How long wilt thou, be drunk? digest a little the wine, of which thou hast taken too much.

15 Anna answering, said: Not so, my lord: for I am an exceeding unhappy woman, and have drunk neither wine nor any strong drink, but I have poured out my soul before the Lord.

16 Count not thy handmaid for one of the daughters of Belial: for out of the abundance of my sorrow and grief have I spoken till now.

17 Then Heli said to her: Go in peace: and the God of Israel grant thee thy petition, which thou hast asked of him.

18 And she said: Would to God thy handmaid may find grace in thy eyes. So the woman went on her way, and ate, and her countenance was no more changed.

19 And they rose in the morning, and worshipped before the Lord: and they returned, and came into their house at Ramatha. And Elcana knew Anna his wife: and the Lord remembered her.

20 And it came to pass when the time was come about, Anna conceived and bore a son, and called his name Samuel: because she had asked him of the Lord.

Responsorial Psalm: First Samuel 2: 1, 4-5, 6-7, 8abcd R. (1) My heart exults in the Lord, my Savior.

1 My heart hath rejoiced in the Lord, and my horn is exalted in my God: my mouth is enlarged over my enemies: because I have joyed in thy salvation.

R. My heart exults in the Lord, my Savior.

4 The bow of the mighty is overcome, and the weak are girt with strength.

5 They that were full before have hired out themselves for bread: and the hungry are filled, so that the barren hath borne many: and she that had many children is weakened.

R. My heart exults in the Lord, my Savior.

6 The Lord killeth and maketh alive, he bringeth down to hell and bringeth back again.

7 The Lord maketh poor and maketh rich, he humbleth and he exalteth. R. My heart exults in the Lord, my Savior.

8abcd He raiseth up the needy from the dust, and lifteth up the poor from the dunghill: that he may sit with princes, and hold the throne of glory.

R. My heart exults in the Lord, my Savior.

Alleluia: First Thessalonians 2: 13 R. Alleluia, alleluia.

13 Receive the word of God, not as the word of men, but as it truly is, the word of God.

R. Alleluia, alleluia.

Gospel: Mark 1: 21-28

21 And they entered into Capharnaum, and forthwith upon the sabbath days going into the synagogue, he taught them.

22 And they were astonished at his doctrine. For he was teaching them as one having power, and not as the scribes.

23 And there was in their synagogue a man with an unclean spirit; and he cried out,

24 Saying: What have we to do with thee, Jesus of Nazareth? art thou come to destroy us? I know who thou art, the Holy One of God.

25 And Jesus threatened him, saying: Speak no more, and go out of the man.

26 And the unclean spirit tearing him, and crying out with a loud voice, went out of him.

27 And they were all amazed, insomuch that they questioned among themselves, saying: What thing is this? what is this new doctrine? for with power he commandeth even the unclean spirits, and they obey him.

28 And the fame of him was spread forthwith into all the country of Galilee.

Daily Mass Readings for Wednesday, 10 January 2024

Ordinary Weekday
First Reading: First Samuel 3: 1-10, 19-20
Responsorial Psalm: Psalms 40: 2 and 5, 7-8a, 8b-9, 10
Alleluia: John 10: 27
Gospel: Mark 1: 29-39
Lectionary: 307
First Reading: First Samuel 3: 1-10, 19-20
1 Now the child Samuel ministered to the Lord before Heli, and the word of the Lord was precious in those days, there was no manifest vision.

2 And it came to pass one day when Heli lay in his place, and his eyes were grown dim, that he could not see:

3 Before the lamp of God went out, Samuel slept in the temple of the Lord, where the ark of God was.

4 And the Lord called Samuel. And he answered: Here am I.

5 And he ran to Heli and said: Here am I: for thou didst call me. He said: I did not call: go back and sleep. And he went and slept.

6 And the Lord called Samuel again. And Samuel arose and went to Heli, and said: Here am I: for thou calledst me. He answered: I did not call thee, my son: return and sleep.

7 Now Samuel did not yet know the Lord, neither had the word of the Lord been revealed to him.

8 And the Lord called Samuel again the third time. And he arose up and went to Heli.

9 And said: Here am I: for thou didst call me. Then Heli understood that the Lord called the child, and he said to Samuel: Go, and sleep: and if he shall call thee any more, thou shalt say: Speak, Lord, for thy servant heareth. So Samuel went and slept in his place.

10 And the Lord came and stood: and he called, as he had called the other times: Samuel, Samuel. And Samuel said: Speak, Lord, for thy servant heareth.

19 And Samuel grew, and the Lord was with him, and not one of his words fell to the ground.

20 And all Israel from Dan to Bersabee, knew that Samuel was a faithful prophet of the Lord.

Responsorial Psalm: Psalms 40: 2 and 5, 7-8a, 8b-9, 10 R. (8a and 9a) Here am I, Lord; I come to do your will.

2 With expectation I have waited for the Lord, and he was attentive to me.

5 Blessed is the man whose trust is in the name of the Lord; and who hath not had regard to vanities, and lying follies.

R. Here am I, Lord; I come to do your will.

7 Sacrifice and oblation thou didst not desire; but thou hast pierced ears for me. Burnt offering and sin offering thou didst not require:

8a Then said I, Behold I come.
R. Here am I, Lord; I come to do your will. 8b In the head of the book it is written of me

9 That I should do thy will: O my God, I have desired it, and thy law in the midst of my heart.

R. Here am I, Lord; I come to do your will.

10 I have declared thy justice in a great church, lo, I will not restrain my lips: O Lord, thou knowest it.

R. Here am I, Lord; I come to do your will.

Alleluia: John 10: 27 R. Alleluia, alleluia.

27 My sheep hear my voice: and I know them, and they follow me. R. Alleluia, alleluia.
Gospel: Mark 1: 29-39

29 And immediately going out of the synagogue they came into the house of Simon and Andrew, with James and John.

30 And Simon's wife's mother lay in a fit of a fever: and forthwith they tell him of her.

31 And coming to her, he lifted her up, taking her by the hand; and immediately the fever left her, and she ministered unto them.

32 And when it was evening, after sunset, they brought to him all that were ill and that were possessed with devils.

33 And all the city was gathered together at the door.

34 And he healed many that were troubled with divers diseases; and he cast out many devils, and he suffered them not to speak, because they knew him.

35 And rising very early, going out, he went into a desert place: and there he prayed.

36 And Simon, and they that were with him, followed after him.
37 And when they had found him, they said to him: All seek for thee.

38 And he saith to them: Let us go into the neighbouring towns and cities, that I may preach there also; for to this purpose am I come.

39 And he was preaching in their synagogues, and in all Galilee, and casting out devils.

Daily Mass Readings for Thursday, 11 January 2024

Ordinary Weekday
First Reading: First Samuel 4: 1-11
Responsorial Psalm: Psalms 44: 10-11, 14-15, 24-25
Alleluia: Matthew 4: 23
Gospel: Mark 1: 40-45
Lectionary: 308
First Reading: First Samuel 4: 1-11

1 And it came to pass in those days, that the Philistines gathered themselves together to fight: and Israel went out to war against the Philistines, and camped by the Stone of help. And the Philistines came to Aphec,

2 And put their army in array against Israel. And when they had joined battle, Israel turned their backs to the Philistines, and there was slain in that fight here and there in the fields about four thousand men.

3 And the people returned to the camp: and the ancients of Israel said: Why hath the Lord defeated us today before the Philistines? Let us fetch unto us the ark of the covenant of the Lord from Silo, and let it come in the midst of us, that it may save us from the hand of our enemies.

4 So the people sent to Silo, and they brought from thence the ark of the covenant of the Lord of hosts sitting upon the cherubims: and the two sons of Heli, Ophni and Phinees, were with the ark of the covenant of God.

5 And when the ark of the covenant of the Lord was come into the camp, all Israel shouted with a great shout, and the earth rang again.

6 And the Philistines heard the noise of the shout, and they said: What is this noise of a great shout in the camp of the Hebrews? And they understood that the ark of the Lord was come into the camp.

7 And the Philistines were afraid, saying: God is come into the camp. And sighing, they said:

8 Woe to us: for there was no such great joy yesterday and the day before: Woe to us. Who shall deliver us from the hand of these high gods? these are the gods that struck Egypt with all the plagues in the desert.

9 Take courage and behave like men, ye Philistines: lest you come to be servants to the Hebrews, as they have served you: take courage and fight.

10 So the Philistines fought, and Israel was overthrown, and every man fled to his own dwelling: and there was an exceeding great slaughter; for there fell of Israel thirty thousand footmen.

11 And the ark of God was taken: and the two sons of Heli, Ophni and Phinees, were slain.

Responsorial Psalm: Psalms 44: 10-11, 14-15, 24-25 R. (27b) Redeem us, Lord, because of your mercy.

10 But now thou hast cast us off, and put us to shame: and thou, O God, wilt not go out with our armies.

11 Thou hast made us turn our back to our enemies: and they that hated us plundered for themselves.

R. Redeem us, Lord, because of your mercy.

14 Thou hast made us a reproach to our neighbours, a scoff and derision to them that are round about us.

15 Thou hast made us a byword among the Gentiles: a shaking of the head among the people.

R. Redeem us, Lord, because of your mercy.

24-25 Why turnest thou face away? and forgettest our want and our trouble? For our soul is humbled down to the dust: our belly cleaveth to the earth.

R. Redeem us, Lord, because of your mercy.

Alleluia: Matthew 4: 23 R. Alleluia, alleluia.

23 Jesus preached the Gospel of the Kingdom and cured every disease among the people.

R. Alleluia, alleluia.

Gospel: Mark 1: 40-45

40 And there came a leper to him, beseeching him, and kneeling down said to him: If thou wilt, thou canst make me clean.

41 And Jesus having compassion on him, stretched forth his hand; and touching him, saith to him: I will. Be thou made clean.

42 And when he had spoken, immediately the leprosy departed from him, and he was made clean.

43 And he strictly charged him, and forthwith sent him away.

44 And he saith to him: See thou tell no one; but go, shew thyself to the high priest, and offer for thy cleansing the things that Moses commanded, for a testimony to them.

45 But he being gone out, began to publish and to blaze abroad the word: so that he could not openly go into the city, but was without in desert places: and they flocked to him from all sides.

Daily Mass Readings for Friday, 12 January 2024

Ordinary Weekday
First Reading: First Samuel 8: 4-7, 10-22a
Responsorial Psalm: Psalms 89: 16-17, 18-19
Alleluia: Luke 7: 16
Gospel: Mark 2: 1-12
Lectionary: 309
First Reading: First Samuel 8: 4-7, 10-22a
4 Then all the ancients of Israel being assembled, came to Samuel to Ramatha.

5 And they said to him: Behold thou art old, and thy sons walk not in thy ways: make us a king, to judge us, as all nations have.

6 And the word was displeasing in the eyes of Samuel, that they should say: Give us a king, to judge us. And Samuel prayed to the Lord.

7 And the Lord said to Samuel: Hearken to the voice of the people in all that they say to thee. For they have not rejected thee, but me, that I should not reign over them.

10 Then Samuel told all the words of the Lord to the people that had desired a king of him,

11 And said: This will be the right of the king, that shall reign over you: He will take your sons, and put them in his chariots, and will make them his horsemen, and his running footmen to run before his chariots,

12 And he will appoint of them to be his tribunes, and centurions, and to plough his fields, and to reap his corn, and to make him arms and chariots.

13 Your daughters also he will take to make him ointments, and to be his cooks, and bakers.

14 And he will take your fields, and your vineyards, and your best oliveyards, and give them to his servants.

15 Moreover he will take the tenth of your corn, and of the revenues of your vineyards, to give his eunuchs and servants.

16 Your servants also and handmaids, and your goodliest young men, and your asses he will take away, and put them to his work.

17 Your flocks also he will tithe, and you shall be his servants.

18 And you shall cry out in that day from the face of the king, whom you have chosen to yourselves. and the Lord will not hear you in that day, because you desired unto yourselves a king.

19 But the people would not hear the voice of Samuel, and they said: Nay: but there shall be a king over us.

20 And we also will be like all nations: and our king shall judge us, and go out before us, and tight our battles for us.

21 And Samuel heard all the words of the people, and rehearsed them in the ears of the Lord.

22a And the Lord said to Samuel: Hearken to their voice, and make them a king.

Responsorial Psalm: Psalms 89: 16-17, 18-19
R. (2) For ever I will sing the goodness of the Lord.

16 Blessed is the people that knoweth jubilation. They shall walk, O Lord, in the light of thy countenance:

17 And in thy name they shall rejoice all the day, and in thy justice they shall be exalted.

R. For ever I will sing the goodness of the Lord.

18 For thou art the glory of their strength: and in thy good pleasure shall our horn be exalted.

19 For our protection is of the Lord, and of our king the holy one of Israel.

R. For ever I will sing the goodness of the Lord.

Alleluia: Luke 7: 16 R. Alleluia, alleluia.

16 A great prophet has arisen in our midst and God has visited his people. R. Alleluia, alleluia.

Gospel: Mark 2: 1-12
1 And again he entered into Capharnaum after some days.

2 And it was heard that he was in the house, and many came together, so that there was no room; no, not even at the door; and he spoke to them the word.

3 And they came to him, bringing one sick of the palsy, who was carried by four.

4 And when they could not offer him unto him for the multitude, they uncovered the roof where he was; and opening it, they let down the bed wherein the man sick of the palsy lay.

5 And when Jesus had seen their faith, he saith to the sick of the palsy: Son, thy sins are forgiven thee.

6 And there were some of the scribes sitting there, and thinking in their hearts:

7 Why doth this man speak thus? he blasphemeth. Who can forgive sins, but God only?

8 Which Jesus presently knowing in his spirit, that they so thought within themselves, saith to them: Why think you these things in your hearts?

9 Which is easier, to say to the sick of the palsy: Thy sins are forgiven thee; or to say: Arise, take up thy bed, and walk?

10 But that you may know that the Son of man hath power on earth to forgive sins, (he saith to the sick of the palsy,)

11 I say to thee: Arise, take up thy bed, and go into thy house.

12 And immediately he arose; and taking up his bed, went his way in the sight of all; so that all wondered and glorified God, saying: We never saw the like.

Daily Mass Readings for Saturday, 13 January 2024

Ordinary Weekday/ Optional Memorial of the Blessed Virgin Mary/ Hilary, Bishop, Doctor
First Reading: First Samuel 9: 1-4, 17-19; 10: 1
Responsorial Psalm: Psalms 21: 2-3, 4-5, 6-7

Alleluia: Luke 4: 18
Gospel: Mark 2: 13-17
Lectionary: 310
First Reading: First Samuel 9: 1-4, 17-19; 10: 1
1 Now I there was a man of Benjamin whose name was Cis, the son of Abiel, the son of Seror, the son of Bechorath, the son of Aphia, the son of a man of Jemini, valiant and strong.

2 And he had a son whose name was Saul, a choice and goodly man, and there was not among the children of Israel a goodlier person than he: from his shoulders and upward he appeared above all the people.

3 And the asses of Cis, Sauls father, were lost: and Cis said to his son Saul: Take one of the servants with thee, and arise, go, and seek the asses. And when they had passed through mount Ephraim,

4 And through the land of Salisa, and had not found them, they passed also through the land of Salim, and they were not there: and through the land of Jemini, and found them not.

17 And when Samuel saw Saul, the Lord said to him: Behold the man, of whom I spoke to thee, this man shall reign over my people.

18 And Saul came to Samuel in the midst of the gate and said: Tell me, I pray thee, where is the house of the seer?

19 And Samuel answered Saul, saying: I am the seer, go up before me to the high place, that you may eat with me today, and I will let thee go in the morning: and tell thee all that is in thy heart.

10:1 And Samuel took a little vial of oil and poured it upon his head, and kissed him, and said: Behold, the Lord hath anointed thee to be prince over his inheritance, and thou shalt deliver his people out of the hands of their enemies, that are round about them. And this shall be a sign unto thee, that God hath anointed thee to be prince.

Responsorial Psalm: Psalms 21: 2-3, 4-5, 6-7 R. (2a) Lord, in your strength the king is glad.

2 In thy strength, O Lord, the king shall joy; and in thy salvation he shall rejoice exceedingly.

3 Thou hast given him his heart's desire: and hast not withholden from him the will of his lips.

R. Lord, in your strength the king is glad.

4 For thou hast prevented him with blessings of sweetness: thou hast set on his head a crown of precious stones.

5 He asked life of thee: and thou hast given him length of days for ever and ever.

R. Lord, in your strength the king is glad.

6 His glory is great in thy salvation: glory and great beauty shalt thou lay upon him.

7 For thou shalt give him to be a blessing for ever and ever: thou shalt make him joyful in gladness with thy countenance.

R. Lord, in your strength the king is glad.

Alleluia: Luke 4: 18 R. Alleluia, alleluia.

18 The Lord sent me to bring glad tidings to the poor and to proclaim liberty to captives.

R. Alleluia, alleluia.

Gospel: Mark 2: 13-17
13 And he went forth again to the sea side; and all the multitude came to him, and he taught them.

14 And when he was passing by, he saw Levi the son of Alpheus sitting at the receipt of custom; and he saith to him: Follow me. And rising up, he followed him.

15 And it came to pass, that as he sat at meat in his house, many publicans and sinners sat down together with Jesus and his disciples. For they were many, who also followed him.

16 And the scribes and the Pharisees, seeing that he ate with publicans and sinners, said to his disciples: Why doth your master eat and drink with publicans and sinners?

17 Jesus hearing this, saith to them: They that are well have no need of a physician, but they that are sick. For I came not to call the just, but sinners.

Daily Mass Readings for Sunday, 14 January 2024

Second Sunday in Ordinary Time
First Reading: First Samuel 3: 3b-10, 19
Responsorial Psalm: Psalms 40: 2, 4ab, 7-8a, 8b-9, 10
Second Reading: First Corinthians 6: 13c-15a, 17-20
Alleluia: John 1: 41, 17b
Gospel: John 1: 35-42
Lectionary: 65
First Reading: First Samuel 3: 3b-10, 19
3b Samuel slept in the temple of the Lord, where the ark of God was.

4 And the Lord called Samuel. And he answered: Here am I.

5 And he ran to Heli and said: Here am I: for thou didst call me. He said: I did not call: go back and sleep. And he went and slept.

6 And the Lord called Samuel again. And Samuel arose and went to Heli, and said: Here am I: for thou calledst me. He answered: I did not call thee, my son: return and sleep.

7 Now Samuel did not yet know the Lord, neither had the word of the Lord been revealed to him.

8 And the Lord called Samuel again the third time. And he arose up and went to Heli.

9 And said: Here am I: for thou didst call me. Then Heli understood that the Lord called the child, and he said to Samuel: Go, and sleep: and if he shall call thee any more, thou shalt say: Speak, Lord, for thy servant heareth. So Samuel went and slept in his place.

10 And the Lord came and stood: and he called, as he had called the other times: Samuel, Samuel. And Samuel said: Speak, Lord, for thy servant heareth.

19 And Samuel grew, and the Lord was with him, and not one of his words fell to the ground.

Responsorial Psalm: Psalms 40: 2, 4ab, 7-8a, 8b-9, 10 R. (8a and 9a) Here am I, Lord; I come to do your will.

2 With expectation I have waited for the Lord, and he was attentive to me. 4ab And he put a new canticle into my mouth, a song to our God.

R. Here am I, Lord; I come to do your will.

7 Sacrifice and oblation thou didst not desire; but thou hast pierced ears for me. Burnt offering and sin offering thou didst not require:

8a Then said I, Behold I come.

R. Here am I, Lord; I come to do your will.

8b In the head of the book it is written of me

9 That I should do thy will: O my God, I have desired it, and thy law in the midst of my heart.

R. Here am I, Lord; I come to do your will.

10 I have declared thy justice in a great church, lo, I will not restrain my lips: O Lord, thou knowest it.

R. Here am I, Lord; I come to do your will.

Second Reading: First Corinthians 6: 13c-15a, 17-20
13c The body is not for fornication, but for the Lord, and the Lord for the body.

14 Now God hath both raised up the Lord, and will raise us up also by his power.

15a Know you not that your bodies are the members of Christ? 17 But he who is joined to the Lord, is one spirit.

18 Fly fornication. Every sin that a man doth, is without the body; but he that committeth fornication, sinneth against his own body.

19 Or know you not, that your members are the temple of the Holy Ghost, who is in you, whom you have from God; and you are not your own?

20 For you are bought with a great price. Glorify and bear God in your body.

Alleluia: John 1: 41, 17b R. Alleluia, alleluia.

41, 17b We have found the Messiah: Jesus Christ, who brings us truth and grace.

R. Alleluia, alleluia.

Gospel: John 1: 35-42
35 The next day again John stood, and two of his disciples.

36 And beholding Jesus walking, he saith: Behold the Lamb of God.

37 And the two disciples heard him speak, and they followed Jesus.

38 And Jesus turning, and seeing them following him, saith to them: What seek you? Who said to him, Rabbi, (which is to say, being interpreted, Master,) where dwellest thou?

39 He saith to them: Come and see. They came, and saw where he abode, and they stayed with him that day: now it was about the tenth hour.

40 And Andrew, the brother of Simon Peter, was one of the two who had heard of John, and followed him.

41 He findeth first his brother Simon, and saith to him: We have found the Messias, which is, being interpreted, the Christ.

42 And he brought him to Jesus. And Jesus looking upon him, said: Thou art Simon the son of Jona: thou shalt be called Cephas, which is interpreted Peter

Daily Mass Readings for Monday, 15 January 2024

Ordinary Weekday
First Reading: First Samuel 15: 16-23
Responsorial Psalm: Psalms 50: 8-9, 16bc-17, 21 and 23
Alleluia: Hebrews 4: 12
Gospel: Mark 2: 18-22
Lectionary: 311
First Reading: First Samuel 15: 16-23

16 And Samuel said to Saul: Suffer me, and I will tell thee what the Lord hath said to me this night. And he said to him: Speak.

17 And Samuel said: When thou wast a little one in thy own eyes, wast thou not made the head of the tribes of Israel? And the Lord anointed thee to be king over Israel.

18 And the Lord sent thee on the way, and said: Go, and kill the sinners of Amalec, and thou shalt fight against them until thou hast utterly destroyed them.

19 Why then didst thou not hearken to the voice of the Lord: but hast turned to the prey, and hast done evil in the eyes of the Lord.

20 And Saul said to Samuel: Yea I have hearkened to the voice of the Lord, and have walked in the way by which the Lord sent me, and have brought Agag the king of Amalec, and Amalec I have slain.

21 But the people took of the spoils sheep and oxen, as the firstfruits of those things that were slain, to offer sacrifice to the Lord their God in Galgal.

22 And Samuel said: Doth the Lord desire holocausts and victims, and not rather that the voice of the Lord should be obeyed? For obedience is better

than sacrifices: and to hearken rather than to offer the fat of rams.

23 Because it is like the sin of witchcraft, to rebel: and like the crime of idolatry, to refuse to obey. Forasmuch therefore as thou hast rejected the word of the Lord, the Lord hath also rejected thee from being king.

Responsorial Psalm: Psalms 50: 8-9, 16bc-17, 21 and 23
R. (23b) To the upright I will show the saving power of God.

8 I will not reprove thee for thy sacrifices: and thy burnt offerings are always in my sight.

9 I will not take calves out of thy house: nor he goats out of thy flocks.
R. To the upright I will show the saving power of God.
16bc Why dost thou declare my justices, and take my covenant in thy mouth?
17 Seeing thou hast hated discipline: and hast cast my words behind thee.

R. To the upright I will show the saving power of God.

21 These things hast thou done, and I was silent. Thou thoughtest unjustly that I should be like to thee: but I will reprove thee, and set before thy face.

23 The sacrifice of praise shall glorify me: and there is the way by which I will shew him the salvation of God.

R. To the upright I will show the saving power of God.

Alleluia: Hebrews 4: 12 R. Alleluia, alleluia.

12 The word of God is living and effective, able to discern reflections and thoughts of the heart.

R. Alleluia, alleluia.

Gospel: Mark 2: 18-22
18 And the disciples of John and the Pharisees used to fast; and they come and say to him: Why do the disciples of John and of the Pharisees fast; but thy disciples do not fast?

19 And Jesus saith to them: Can the children of the marriage fast, as long as the bridegroom is with them? As long as they have the bridegroom with them, they cannot fast.

20 But the days will come when the bridegroom shall be taken away from them; and then they shall fast in those days.

21 No man seweth a piece of raw cloth to an old garment: otherwise the new piecing taketh away from the old, and there is made a greater rent.

22 And no man putteth new wine into old bottles: otherwise the wine will burst the bottles, and both the wine will be spilled, and the bottles will be lost. But new wine must be put into new bottles

Daily Mass Readings for Tuesday, 16 January 2024

Ordinary Weekday
First Reading: First Samuel 16: 1-13 Responsorial Psalm: Psalms 89: 20, 21-22, 27-28 Alleluia: Ephesians 1: 17-18
Gospel: Mark 2: 23-28
Lectionary: 312
First Reading: First Samuel 16: 1-13

1 And the Lord said to Samuel: How long wilt thou mourn for Saul, whom I have rejected from reigning over Israel? fill thy horn with oil, and come, that I may send thee to Isai the Bethlehemite: for I have provided me a king among his sons.

2 And Samuel said: How shall I go? for Saul will hear of it, and he will kill me. And the Lord said: Thou shalt take with thee a calf of the herd, and thou shalt say: I am come to sacrifice to the Lord.

3 And thou shalt call Isai to the sacrifice, and I will shew thee what thou art to do, and thou shalt anoint him whom I shall shew to thee.

4 Then Samuel did as the Lord had said to him. And he came to Bethlehem, and the ancients of the city wondered, and meeting him, they said: Is thy coming hither peaceable?

5 And he said: It is peaceable: I am come to offer sacrifice to the Lord, be ye sanctified, and come with me to the sacrifice. And he sanctified Isai and his sons, and called them to the sacrifice.

6 And when they were come in, he saw Eliab, and said: Is the Lord's anointed before him?

7 And the Lord said to Samuel: Look not on his countenance, nor on the height of his stature: because I have rejected him, nor do I judge according to the look of man: for man seeth those things that appear, but the Lord beholdeth the heart.

8 And Isai called Abinadab, and brought him before Samuel. And he said: Neither hath the Lord chosen this.

9 And Isai brought Samma, and he said of him: Neither hath the Lord chosen this.

10 Isai therefore brought his seven sons before Samuel: and Samuel said to Isai: The Lord hath not chosen any one of these.

11 And Samuel said to Isai: Are here all thy sons? He answered: There remaineth yet a young one, who keepeth the sheep. And Samuel said to Isai: Send, and fetch him, for we will not sit down till he come hither.

12 He sent therefore and brought him Now he was ruddy and beautiful to behold, and of a comely face. And the Lord said: Arise, and anoint him, for this is he.

13 Then Samuel took the horn of oil, and anointed him in the midst of his brethren: and the spirit of the Lord came upon David from that day forward: and Samuel rose up, and went to Ramatha.

Responsorial Psalm: Psalms 89: 20, 21-22, 27-28 R. (21a) I have found David, my servant.

20 Then thou spokest in a vision to thy saints, and saidst: I have laid help upon one that is mighty, and have exalted one chosen out of my people.

R. I have found David, my servant.

21 I have found David my servant: with my holy oil I have anointed him.

22 For my hand shall help him: and my arm shall strengthen him.

R. I have found David, my servant.

27 He shall cry out to me: Thou art my father: my God, and the support of my salvation.

28 And I will make him my firstborn, high above the kings of the earth. R. I have found David, my servant.

Alleluia: Ephesians 1: 17-18 R. Alleluia, alleluia.

17-18 May the Father of our Lord Jesus Christ enlighten the eyes of our hearts, that we may know what is the hope that belongs to our call.

R. Alleluia, alleluia.

Gospel: Mark 2: 23-28
23 And it came to pass again, as the Lord walked through the corn fields on the sabbath, that his disciples began to go forward, and to pluck the ears of corn.

24 And the Pharisees said to him: Behold, why do they on the sabbath day that which is not lawful?

25 And he said to them: Have you never read what David did when he had need, and was hungry himself, and they that were with him?

26 How he went into the house of God, under Abiathar the high priest, and did eat the loaves of proposition, which was not lawful to eat but for the priests, and gave to them who were with him?

27 And he said to them: The sabbath was made for man, and not man for the sabbath.

28 Therefore the Son of man is Lord of the sabbath also.

Daily Mass Readings for Wednesday, 17 January 2024

Anthony, Abbot Obligatory Memorial
First Reading: First Samuel 17: 32-33, 37, 40-51

Responsorial Psalm: Psalms 144: 1b, 2, 9-10 Alleluia: Matthew 4: 23
Gospel: Mark 3: 1-6
Lectionary: 313

First Reading: First Samuel 17: 32-33, 37, 40-51
32 And when he was brought to him, he said to him: Let not any man's heart be dismayed in him: I thy servant will go, and will fight against the Philistine.

33 And Saul said to David: Thou art not able to withstand this Philistine, nor to fight against him: for thou art but a boy, but he is a warrior from his youth.

37 And David said: The Lord who delivered me out of the paw of the lion, and out of the paw of the bear, he will deliver me out of the hand of this Philistine. And Saul said to David: Go, and the Lord be with thee.

40 And he took his staff, which he had always in his hands: and chose him five smooth stones out of the brook, and put them into the shepherd's scrip, which he had with him, and he took a sling in his hand, and went forth against the Philistine.

41 And the Philistine came on, and drew nigh against David, and his armourbearer before him.

42 And when the Philistine looked, and beheld David, he despised him. For he was a young man, ruddy, and of a comely countenance.

43 And the Philistine said to David: Am I a dog, that thou comest to me with a staff? And the Philistine cursed David by his gods.

44 And he said to David: Come to me, and I will give thy flesh to the birds of the air, and to the beasts of the earth.

45 And David said to the Philistine: Thou comest to me with a sword, and with a spear, and with a shield: but I come to thee in the name of the Lord of hosts, the God of the armies of Israel, which thou hast defied.

46 This day, and the Lord will deliver thee into my hand, and I will slay thee, and take away thy head from thee: and I will give the carcasses of the army of the Philistines this day to the birds of the air, and to the beasts of the earth: that all the earth may know that there is a God in Israel.

47 And all this assembly shall know, that the Lord saveth not with sword and spear: for it is his battle, and he will deliver you into our hands.

48 And when the Philistine arose and was coming, and drew nigh to meet David, David made haste, and ran to the fight to meet the Philistine.

49 And he put his hand into his scrip, and took a stone, and cast it with the sling, and fetching it about struck the Philistine in the forehead: and the stone was fixed in his forehead, and he fell on his face upon the earth.

50 And David prevailed over the Philistine, with a sling and a stone, and he struck, and slew the Philistine. And as David had no sword in his hand,

51 He ran, and stood over the Philistine, and took his sword, and drew it out of the sheath, and slew him, and cut off his head. And the Philistines seeing that their champion was dead, fled away.

Responsorial Psalm: Psalms 144: 1b, 2, 9-10 R. (1) Blessed be the Lord, my Rock!

1 Blessed be the Lord my God, who teacheth my hands to fight, and my fingers to war.

R. Blessed be the Lord, my Rock!

2 My mercy, and my refuge: my support, and my deliverer: My protector, and I have hoped in him: who subdueth my people under me.

R. Blessed be the Lord, my Rock!

9 To thee, O God, I will sing a new canticle: on the psaltery and an instrument of ten strings I will sing praises to thee.

10 Who givest salvation to kings: who hast redeemed thy servant David from the malicious sword.

R. Blessed be the Lord, my Rock!

Alleluia: Matthew 4: 23 R. Alleluia, alleluia.

23 Jesus preached the Gospel of the Kingdom and cured every disease among the people.

R. Alleluia, alleluia.

Gospel: Mark 3: 1-6
1 And he entered again into the synagogue, and there was a man there who had a withered hand.

2 And they watched him whether he would heal on the sabbath days; that they might accuse him.

3 And he said to the man who had the withered hand: Stand up in the midst.

4 And he saith to them: Is it lawful to do good on the sabbath days, or to do evil? to save life, or to destroy? But they held their peace.

5 And looking round about on them with anger, being grieved for the blindness of their hearts, he saith to the man: Stretch forth thy hand. And he stretched it forth: and his hand was restored unto him.

6 And the Pharisees going out, immediately made a consultation with the Herodians against him, how they might destroy him

Daily Mass Readings for Thursday, 18 January 2024

Ordinary Weekday
First Reading: First Samuel 18: 6-9; 19: 1-7
Responsorial Psalm: Psalms 56: 2-3, 9-10a, 10b-12, 13-14
Alleluia: Second Timothy 1: 10
Gospel: Mark 3: 7-12
Lectionary: 314
First Reading: First Samuel 18: 6-9; 19: 1-7

6 Now when David returned, after be slew the Philistine, the women came out of all the cities of Israel, singing and dancing, to meet king Saul, with timbrels of joy, and cornets.

7 And the women sung as they played, and they said: I Saul slew his thousands, and David his ten thousands.

8 And Saul was exceeding angry, and this word was displeasing in his eyes, and he said: They have given David ten thousands, and to me they have given but a thousand; what can he have more but the kingdom?

9 And Saul did not look on David with a good eye from that day and forward.

19:1 And Saul spoke to Jonathan his son and to all his servants, that they should kill David. But Jonathan the son of Saul loved David exceedingly.

2 And Jonathan told David, saying: Saul my father seeketh to kill thee: wherefore look to thyself, I beseech thee, in the morning, and thou shalt abide in a secret place and shalt be hid.

3 And I will go out and stand beside my father in the field where thou art: and I will speak of thee to my father, and whatsoever I shall see, I will tell thee.

4 And Jonathan spoke good things of David to Saul his father: and said to him: Sin not, O king, against thy servant, David, because he hath not sinned against thee, and his works are very good towards thee.

5 And he put his life in his hand, and slew the Philistine, and the Lord wrought great salvation for all Israel. Thou sawest it and didst rejoice. Why therefore wilt thou sin against innocent blood by killing David, who is without fault?

6 And when Saul heard this he was appeased with the words of Jonathan, and swore: As the Lord liveth he shall not be slain.

7 Then Jonathan called David and told him all these words: and Jonathan brought in David to Saul, and he was before him, as he had been yesterday and the day before.

Responsorial Psalm: Psalms 56: 2-3, 9-10a, 10b-12, 13-14 R. (5b) In God I trust; I shall not fear.

2 Have mercy on me, O God, for man hath trodden me under foot; all the day long he hath afflicted me fighting against me.

3 My enemies have trodden on me all the day long; for they are many that make war against me.

R. In God I trust; I shall not fear.

9 I have declared to thee my life: thou hast set my tears in thy sight, As also in thy promise.

10a Then shall my enemies be turned back. In what day soever I shall call upon thee.

R. In God I trust; I shall not fear.

10b Behold I know thou art my God.

11 In God will I praise the word, in the Lord will I praise his speech.

12 In God have I hoped, I will not fear what man can do to me.

R. In God I trust; I shall not fear.

13 In me, O God, are vows to thee, which I will pay, praises to thee:

14 Because thou hast delivered my soul from death, my feet from falling: that I may please in the sight of God, in the light of the living.

R. In God I trust; I shall not fear.

Alleluia: Second Timothy 1: 10 R. Alleluia, alleluia.

10 Our Savior Jesus Christ has destroyed death and brought life to light through the Gospel.

R. Alleluia, alleluia.

Gospel: Mark 3: 7-12
7 But Jesus retired with his disciples to the sea; and a great multitude followed him from Galilee and Judea,

8 And from Jerusalem, and from Idumea, and from beyond the Jordan. And they about Tyre and Sidon, a great multitude, hearing the things which he did, came to him.

9 And he spoke to his disciples that a small ship should wait on him because of the multitude, lest they should throng him.

10 For he healed many, so that they pressed upon him for to touch him, as many as had evils.

11 And the unclean spirits, when they saw him, fell down before him: and they cried, saying:

12 Thou art the Son of God. And he strictly charged them that they should not make him known.

Daily Mass Readings for Friday, 19 January 2024

Ordinary Weekday
First Reading: First Samuel 24: 3-21
Responsorial Psalm: Psalms 57: 2, 3-4, 6 and 11
Alleluia: Second Corinthians 5: 19
Gospel: Mark 3: 13-19
Lectionary: 315
First Reading: First Samuel 24: 3-21

3 Saul therefore took three thousand chosen men out of all Israel, and went out to seek after David, and his men, even upon the most craggy rocks, which are accessible only to wild goats.

4 And he came to the sheepcotes, which were in his way. And there was a cave, into which Saul went, to ease nature: now David and his men lay hid in the inner part of the cave.

5 And the servants of David said to him: Behold the day, of which the Lord said to thee: I will deliver thy enemy unto thee, that thou mayest do to him as it shall seem good in thy eyes. Then David arose, and secretly cut off the hem of Saul's robe.

6 After which David's heart struck him, because he had cut off the hem of Saul's robe.

7 And he said to his men: The Lord be merciful unto me, that I may do no such thing to my master the Lord's anointed, as to lay my hand upon him, because he is the Lord's anointed.

8 And David stopped his men with his words, and suffered them not to rise against Saul. But Saul rising up out of the cave, went on his way.

9 And David also rose up after him: and going out of the cave cried after Saul, saying: My lord the king. And Saul looked behind him: and David bowing himself down to the ground, worshipped,

10 And said to Saul: Why dost thou hear the words of men that say David seeketh thy hurt?

11 Behold this day thy eyes have seen, that the Lord hath delivered thee into my hand, in the cave, and I had a thought to kill thee, but my eye hath spared thee. For I said: I will not put out my hand against my lord, because he is the Lord's anointed.

12 Moreover see and know, O my father, the hem of thy robe in my hand, that when I cut, off the hem of thy robe, I would not put out my hand against thee. Reflect, and see, that there is no evil in my hand, nor iniquity, neither have I sinned against thee: but thou liest in wait for my life, to take it away.

13 The Lord judge between me and thee, and the Lord revenge me of thee: but my hand shall not be upon thee.

14 As also it is said in the old proverb: From the wicked shall wickedness come forth: therefore my hand shall not be upon thee. After whom dost thou come out, O king of Israel?

15 After whom dost thou pursue? After a dead dog, after a flea.

16 Be the Lord judge, and judge between me and thee, and see, and judge my cause, and deliver me out of thy hand.

17 And when David had made an end of speaking these words to Saul, Saul said: Is this thy voice, my son David? And Saul lifted up his voice, and wept.

18 And he said to David: Thou art more just than I: for thou hast done good to me, and I have rewarded thee with evil.

19 And thou hast shewn this day what good things thou hast done to me: how the Lord delivered me into thy hand, and thou hast not killed me.

20 For who when he hath found his enemy, will let him go well away? But the Lord reward thee for this good turn, for what thou hast done to me this day.

21 And now as I know that thou shalt surely be king, and have the kingdom of Israel in thy hand:

Responsorial Psalm: Psalms 57: 2, 3-4, 6 and 11 R. (2a) Have mercy on me, God, have mercy.

2 Have mercy on me, O God, have mercy on me: for my soul trusteth in thee. And in the shadow of thy wings will I hope, until iniquity pass away.

R. Have mercy on me, God, have mercy.

3 I will cry to God the most High; to God who hath done good to me.

4 He hath sent from heaven and delivered me: he hath made them a reproach that trod upon me. God hath sent his mercy and his truth,

R. Have mercy on me, God, have mercy.

6 Be thou exalted, O God, above the heavens, and thy glory above all the earth.

11 For thy mercy is magnified even to the heavens: and thy truth unto the clouds.

R. Have mercy on me, God, have mercy. Alleluia: Second Corinthians 5: 19 R. Alleluia, alleluia.

19 God was reconciling the world to himself in Christ, and entrusting to us the message of reconciliation. R. Alleluia, alleluia.

Gospel: Mark 3: 13-19
13 And going up into a mountain, he called unto him whom he would himself: and they came to him.

14 And he made that twelve should be with him, and that he might send them to preach.

15 And he gave them power to heal sicknesses, and to cast out devils. 16 And to Simon he gave the name Peter:

17 And James the son of Zebedee, and John the brother of James; and he named them Boanerges, which is, The sons of thunder:

18 And Andrew and Philip, and Bartholomew and Matthew, and Thomas and James of Alpheus, and Thaddeus, and Simon the Cananean:

19 And Judas Iscariot, who also betrayed him.

Daily Mass Readings for Saturday, 20 January 2024

Ordinary Weekday/ Optional Memorial of the Blessed Virgin Mary/ Fabian, Pope, Martyr/ Sebastian, Martyr
First Reading: Second Samuel 1: 1-4, 11-12, 19, 23-27
Responsorial Psalm: Psalms 80: 2-3, 5-7

Alleluia: Acts 16: 14b
Gospel: Mark 3: 20-21
Lectionary: 316
First Reading: Second Samuel 1: 1-4, 11-12, 19, 23-27
1 Now it came to pass, after Saul was dead, that David returned from the slaughter of the Amalecites, and abode two days in Siceleg.

2 And on the third day, there appeared a man who came out of Saul's camp, with his garments rent, and dust strewed on his head: and when he came to David, he fell upon his face, and adored.

3 And David said to him: From whence comest thou? And he said to him: I am fled out of the camp of Israel.

4 And David said unto him: What is the matter that is come to pass? tell me. He said: The people are fled from the battle, and many of the people are fallen and dead: moreover Saul and Jonathan his son are slain.

11 Then David took hold of his garments and rent them, and likewise all the men that were with him.

12 And they mourned, and wept, and fasted until evening for Saul, and for Jonathan his son, and for the people of the Lord, and for the house of Israel, because they were fallen by the sword.

19 The illustrious of Israel are slain upon thy mountains: how are the valiant fallen?

23 Saul and Jonathan, lovely, and comely in their life, even in death they were not divided: they were swifter than eagles, stronger than lions.

24 Ye daughters of Israel, weep over Saul, who clothed you with scarlet in delights, who gave ornaments of gold for your attire.

25 How are the valiant fallen in battle? Jonathan slain in the high places?

26 I grieve for thee, my brother Jonathan: exceeding beautiful, and amiable to me above the love of women. As the mother loveth her only son, so did I love thee.

27 How are the valiant fallen, and the weapons of war perished? Responsorial Psalm: Psalms 80: 2-3, 5-7

R. (4b) Let us see your face, Lord, and we shall be saved.

2 Give ear, O thou that rulest Israel: thou that leadest Joseph like a sheep. Thou that sittest upon the cherubims, shine forth

3 Before Ephraim, Benjamin, and Manasses. Stir up thy might, and come to save us.

R. Let us see your face, Lord, and we shall be saved.

5 O Lord God of hosts, how long wilt thou be angry against the prayer of thy servant?

6 How long wilt thou feed us with the bread of tears: and give us for our drink tears in measure?

7 Thou hast made us to be a contradiction to our neighbours: and our enemies have scoffed at us.

R. Let us see your face, Lord, and we shall be saved.

Alleluia: Acts 16: 14b R. Alleluia, alleluia.

14b Open our hearts, O Lord, to listen to the words of your Son. R. Alleluia, alleluia.

Gospel: Mark 3: 20-21
20 And they come to a house, and the multitude cometh together again, so that they could not so much as eat bread.

21 And when his friends had heard of it, they went out to lay hold on him. For they said: He is become mad.

Daily Mass Readings for Sunday, 21 January 2024

Third Sunday in Ordinary Time
First Reading: Jonah 3: 1-5, 10
Responsorial Psalm: Psalms 25: 4-5, 6-7, 8-9
Second Reading: First Corinthians 7: 29-31
Alleluia: Mark 1: 15
Gospel: Mark 1: 14-20
Lectionary: 68
First Reading: Jonah 3: 1-5, 10
1 And the word of the Lord came to Jonas the second time, saying:

2 Arise, and go to Ninive the great city: and preach in it the preaching that I bid thee.

3 And Jonas arose, and went to Ninive, according to the word of the Lord: now Ninive was a great city of three days' journey.

4 And Jonas began to enter into the city one day's journey: and he cried, and said: Yet forty days, and Ninive shall be destroyed.

5 And the men of Ninive believed in God: and they proclaimed a fast, and put on sackcloth from the greatest to the least.

10 And God saw their works, that they were turned from their evil way: and God had mercy with regard to the evil which he had said that he would do to them, and he did it not.

Responsorial Psalm: Psalms 25: 4-5, 6-7, 8-9 R. (4a) Teach me your ways, O Lord.

4 Let all them be confounded that act unjust things without cause. shew, O Lord, thy ways to me, and teach me thy paths.

5 Direct me in thy truth, and teach me; for thou art God my Saviour; and on thee have I waited all the day long.

R. Teach me your ways, O Lord.

6 Remember, O Lord, thy bowels of compassion; and thy mercies that are from the beginning of the world.

7 The sins of my youth and my ignorances do not remember. According to thy mercy remember thou me: for thy goodness' sake, O Lord.

R. Teach me your ways, O Lord.

8 The Lord is sweet and righteous: therefore he will give a law to sinners in the way.

9 He will guide the mild in judgment: he will teach the meek his ways.

R. Teach me your ways, O Lord.

Second Reading: First Corinthians 7: 29-31
29 This therefore I say, brethren; the time is short; it remaineth, that they also who have wives, be as if they had none;

30 And they that weep, as though they wept not; and they that rejoice, as if they rejoiced not; and they that buy, as though they possessed not;

31 And they that use this world, as if they used it not: for the fashion of this world passeth away.

Alleluia: Mark 1: 15 R. Alleluia, alleluia.

15 The kingdom of God is at hand. Repent and believe in the Gospel. R. Alleluia, alleluia.

Gospel: Mark 1: 14-20
14 And after that John was delivered up, Jesus came into Galilee, preaching the gospel of the kingdom of God,

15 And saying: The time is accomplished, and the kingdom of God is at hand: repent, and believe the gospel.

16 And passing by the sea of Galilee, he saw Simon and Andrew his brother, casting nets into the sea (for they were fishermen).

17 And Jesus said to them: Come after me, and I will make you to become fishers of men.

18 And immediately leaving their nets, they followed him.

19 And going on from thence a little farther, he saw James the son of Zebedee, and John his brother, who also were mending their nets in the ship:

20 And forthwith he called them. And leaving their father Zebedee in the ship with his hired men, they followed him.

Daily Mass Readings for Monday, 22 January 2024

Day of Prayer for the Legal Protection of Unborn Children Obligatory Memorial
First Reading: Second Samuel 5: 1-7, 10
Responsorial Psalm: Psalms 89: 20, 21-22, 25-26

Alleluia: Second Timothy 1: 10
Gospel: Mark 3: 22-30
Lectionary: 317
First Reading: Second Samuel 5: 1-7, 10
1 Then all the tribes of Israel came to David in Hebron, saying: Behold we are thy bone and thy flesh.

2 Moreover yesterday also and the day before, when Saul was king over us, thou wast he that did lead out and bring in Israel: and the Lord said to thee: Thou shalt feed my people Israel, and thou shalt be prince over Israel.

3 The ancients also of Israel came to the king to Hebron, and king David made a league with them in Hebron before the Lord: and they anointed David to be king over Israel.

4 David was thirty years old when he began to reign, and he reigned forty years.

5 In Hebron he reigned over Juda seven years and six months: and in Jerusalem he reigned three and thirty years over all Israel and Juda.

6 And the king and all the men that were with him went to Jerusalem to the Jebusites the inhabitants of the land: and they said to David: Thou shalt not come in hither unless thou take away the blind and the lame that say: David shall not come in hither.

7 But David took the castle of Sion, the same is the city of David.

10 And he went on prospering and growing up, and the Lord God of hosts was with him.

Responsorial Psalm: Psalms 89: 20, 21-22, 25-26
R. (25a) My faithfulness and my mercy shall be with him.

20 Then thou spokest in a vision to thy saints, and saidst: I have laid help upon one that is mighty, and have exalted one chosen out of my people.

R. My faithfulness and my mercy shall be with him.

21 I have found David my servant: with my holy oil I have anointed him.

22 For my hand shall help him: and my arm shall strengthen him.

R. My faithfulness and my mercy shall be with him.

25 And my truth and my mercy shall be with him: and in my name shall his horn be exalted.

26 And I will set his hand in the sea; and his right hand in the rivers. R. My faithfulness and my mercy shall be with him.

Alleluia: Second Timothy 1: 10 R. Alleluia, alleluia.

10 Our Savior Jesus Christ has destroyed death and brought life to light through the Gospel.

R. Alleluia, alleluia.

Gospel: Mark 3: 22-30
22 And the scribes who were come down from Jerusalem, said: He hath Beelzebub, and by the prince of devils he casteth out devils.

23 And after he had called them together, he said to them in parables: How can Satan cast out Satan?

24 And if a kingdom be divided against itself, that kingdom cannot stand. 25 And if a house be divided against itself, that house cannot stand.

26 And if Satan be risen up against himself, he is divided, and cannot stand, but hath an end.

27 No man can enter into the house of a strong man and rob him of his goods, unless he first bind the strong man, and then shall he plunder his house.

28 Amen I say to you, that all sins shall be forgiven unto the sons of men, and the blasphemies wherewith they shall blaspheme:

29 But he that shall blaspheme against the Holy Ghost, shall never have forgiveness, but shall be guilty of an everlasting sin.

30 Because they said: He hath an unclean spirit.

Daily Mass Readings for Tuesday, 23 January 2024

Ordinary Weekday/ Vincent of Saragossa, Deacon, Martyr/ Marianne Cope, Virgin
First Reading: Second Samuel 6: 12b-15, 17-19
Responsorial Psalm: Psalms 24: 7, 8, 9, 10

Alleluia: Matthew 11: 25
Gospel: Mark 3: 31-35
Lectionary: 318
First Reading: Second Samuel 6: 12b-15, 17-19

12b David went, and brought away the ark of God out of the house of Obededom into the city of David with joy. And there were with David seven choirs, and calves for victims.

13 And when they that carried the ark of the Lord had gone six paces, he sacrificed an ox and a ram:

14 And David danced with all his might before the Lord: and David was girded with a linen ephod.

15 And David and all the house of Israel brought the ark of the covenant of the Lord with joyful shouting, and with sound of trumpet.

17 And they brought the ark of the Lord, and set it in its place in the midst of the tabernacle, which David had pitched for it: and David offered holocausts, and peace offerings before the Lord.

18 And when he had made an end of offering holocausts and peace offerings, he blessed the people in the name of the Lord of hosts.

19 And he distributed to all the multitude of Israel both men and women, to every one, a cake of bread, and a piece of roasted beef, and fine flour fried with oil: and all the people departed every one to his house.

Responsorial Psalm: Psalms 24: 7, 8, 9, 10
R. (8) Who is this king of glory? It is the Lord!

7 Lift up your gates, O ye princes, and be ye lifted up, O eternal gates: and the King of Glory shall enter in.

R. Who is this king of glory? It is the Lord!

8 Who is this King of Glory? the Lord who is strong and mighty: the Lord mighty in battle.

R. Who is this king of glory? It is the Lord!

9 Lift up your gates, O ye princes, and be ye lifted up, O eternal gates: and the King of Glory shall enter in.

R. Who is this king of glory? It is the Lord!

10 Who is this King of Glory? the Lord of hosts, he is the King of Glory.

R. Who is this king of glory? It is the Lord!

Alleluia: Matthew 11: 25 R. Alleluia, alleluia.

25 Blessed are you, Father, Lord of heaven and earth; you have revealed to little ones the mysteries of the Kingdom.

R. Alleluia, alleluia.

Gospel: Mark 3: 31-35
31 And his mother and his brethren came; and standing without, sent unto him, calling him.

32 And the multitude sat about him; and they say to him: Behold thy mother and thy brethren without seek for thee.

33 And answering them, he said: Who is my mother and my brethren?

34 And looking round about on them who sat about him, he saith: Behold my mother and my brethren.

35 For whosoever shall do the will of God, he is my brother, and my sister, and mother.

Daily Mass Readings for Wednesday, 24 January 2024

Francis De Sales, Bishop, Religious Founder, Doctor Obligatory Memorial
First Reading: Second Samuel 7: 4-17
Responsorial Psalm: Psalms 89: 4-5, 27-28, 29-30
Gospel: Mark 4: 1-20

Lectionary: 319
First Reading: Second Samuel 7: 4-17
4 But it came to pass that night, that the word of the Lord came to Nathan, saying:

5 Go, and say to my servant David: Thus saith the Lord: Shalt thou build me a house to dwell in?

6 Whereas I have not dwelt in a house from the day that I brought the children of Israel out of the land of Egypt even to this day: but have walked in a tabernacle, and in a tent.

7 In all the places that I have gone through with all the children of Israel, did ever I speak a word to any one of the tribes of Israel, whom I commanded to

feed my people Israel, saying: Why have you not built me a house of cedar?

8 And now thus shalt thou speak to my servant David: Thus saith the Lord of hosts: a I took thee out of the pastures from following the sheep to be ruler over my people Israel:

9 And I have been with thee wheresoever thou hast walked, and have slain all thy enemies from before thy face: and I have made thee a great man, like unto the name of the great ones that are on the earth.

10 And I will appoint a place for my people Israel, and I will plant them, and they shall dwell therein, and shall be disturbed no more: neither shall the children of iniquity afflict them any more as they did before,

11 From the day that I appointed judges over my people Israel: and I will give thee rest from all thy enemies. And the Lord foretelleth to thee, that the Lord will make thee a house.

12 And when thy days shall be fulfilled, and thou shalt sleep with thy fathers, I will raise up thy seed after thee, which shall proceed out of thy bowels, and I will establish his kingdom.

13 He shall build a house to my name, and I will establish the throne of his kingdom for ever.

14 I will be to him a father, and he shall be to me a son: and if he commit any iniquity, I will correct him with the rod of men, and with the stripes of the children of men.

15 But my mercy I will not take away from him, as I took it from Saul, whom I removed from before my face.

16 And thy house shall be faithful, and thy kingdom for ever before thy face, and thy throne shall be firm for ever.

17 According to all these words and according to all this vision, so did Nathan speak to David.

Responsorial Psalm: Psalms 89: 4-5, 27-28, 29-30
R. (29a) For ever I will maintain my love for my servant.

4 I have made a covenant with my elect: I have sworn to David my servant:

5 Thy seed will I settle for ever. And I will build up thy throne unto generation and generation.

R. For ever I will maintain my love for my servant.

27 He shall cry out to me: Thou art my father: my God, and the support of my salvation.

28 And I will make him my firstborn, high above the kings of the earth.

R. For ever I will maintain my love for my servant.

29 I will keep my mercy for him for ever: and my covenant faithful to him.

30 And I will make his seed to endure for evermore: and his throne as the days of heaven.

R. For ever I will maintain my love for my servant.

Alleluia
R. Alleluia, alleluia.

The seed is the word of God, Christ is the sower; all who come to him will live for ever.

R. Alleluia, alleluia.

Gospel: Mark 4: 1-20
1 And again he began to teach by the sea side; and a great multitude was gathered together unto him, so that he went up into a ship, and sat in the sea;

and all the multitude was upon the land by the sea side.

2 And he taught them many things in parables, and said unto them in his doctrine:

3 Hear ye: Behold, the sower went out to sow.

4 And whilst he sowed, some fell by the way side, and the birds of the air came and ate it up.

5 And other some fell upon stony ground, where it had not much earth; and it shot up immediately, because it had no depth of earth.

6 And when the sun was risen, it was scorched; and because it had no root, it withered away.

7 And some fell among thorns; and the thorns grew up, and choked it, and it yielded no fruit.

8 And some fell upon good ground; and brought forth fruit that grew up, and increased and yielded, one thirty, another sixty, and another a hundred.

9 And he said: He that hath ears to hear, let him hear.

10 And when he was alone, the twelve that were with him asked him the parable.

11 And he said to them: To you it is given to know the mystery of the kingdom of God: but to them that are without, all things are done in parables:

12 That seeing they may see, and not perceive; and hearing they may hear, and not understand: lest at any time they should be converted, and their sins should be forgiven them.

13 And he saith to them: Are you ignorant of this parable? and how shall you know all parables?

14 He that soweth, soweth the word.

15 And these are they by the way side, where the word is sown, and as soon as they have heard, immediately Satan cometh and taketh away the word that was sown in their hearts.

16 And these likewise are they that are sown on the stony ground: who when they have heard the word, immediately receive it with joy.

17 And they have no root in themselves, but are only for a time: and then when tribulation and persecution ariseth for the word they are presently scandalized.

18 And others there are who are sown among thorns: these are they that hear the word,

19 And the cares of the world, and the deceitfulness of riches, and the lusts after other things entering in choke the word, and it is made fruitless.

20 And these are they who are sown upon the good ground, who hear the word, and receive it, and yield fruit, the one thirty, another sixty, and another a hundred.

Daily Mass Readings for Thursday, 25 January 2024

Conversion of Paul, Apostle Feast
First Reading: Acts 22: 3-16 or Acts 9: 1-22 Responsorial Psalm: Psalms 117: 1bc, 2 Alleluia: John 15: 16
Gospel: Mark 16: 15-18
Lectionary: 519

First Reading: Acts 22: 3-16 or Acts 9: 1-22
3 And he saith: I am a Jew, born at Tarsus in Cilicia, but brought up in this city, at the feet of Gamaliel, taught according to the truth of the law of the fathers, zealous for the law, as also all you are this day:

4 Who persecuted this way unto death, binding and delivering into prisons both men and women.

5 As the high priest doth bear me witness, and all the ancients: from whom also receiving letters to the brethren, I went to Damascus, that I might bring them bound from thence to Jerusalem to be punished.

6 And it came to pass, as I was going, and drawing nigh to Damascus at midday, that suddenly from heaven there shone round about me a great light:

7 And falling on the ground, I heard a voice saying to me: Saul, Saul, why persecutest thou me?

8 And I answered: Who art thou, Lord? And he said to me: I am Jesus of Nazareth, whom thou persecutest.

9 And they that were with me, saw indeed the light, but they heard not the voice of him that spoke with me.

10 And I said: What shall I do, Lord? And the Lord said to me: Arise, and go to Damascus; and there it shall be told thee of all things that thou must do.

11 And whereas I did not see for the brightness of that light, being led by the hand by my companions, I came to Damascus.

12 And one Ananias, a man according to the law, having testimony of all the Jews who dwelt there,

13 Coming to me, and standing by me, said to me: Brother Saul, look up. And I the same hour looked upon him.

14 But he said: The God of our fathers hath preordained thee that thou shouldst know his will, and see the Just One, and shouldst hear the voice from his mouth.

15 For thou shalt be his witness to all men, of those things which thou hast seen and heard.

16 And now why tarriest thou? Rise up, and be baptized, and wash away thy sins, invoking his name.

Or

1 And Saul, as yet breathing out threatenings and slaughter against the disciples of the Lord, went to the high priest,

2 And asked of him letters to Damascus, to the synagogues: that if he found any men and women of this way, he might bring them bound to Jerusalem.

3 And as he went on his journey, it came to pass that he drew nigh to Damascus; and suddenly a light from heaven shined round about him.

4 And falling on the ground, he heard a voice saying to him: Saul, Saul, why persecutest thou me?

5 Who said: Who art thou, Lord? And he: I am Jesus whom thou persecutest. It is hard for thee to kick against the goad.

6 And he trembling and astonished, said: Lord, what wilt thou have me to do?

7 And the Lord said to him: Arise, and go into the city, and there it shall be told thee what thou must do. Now the men who went in company with him, stood amazed, hearing indeed a voice, but seeing no man.

8 And Saul arose from the ground; and when his eyes were opened, he saw nothing. But they leading him by the hands, brought him to Damascus.

9 And he was there three days, without sight, and he did neither eat nor drink.

10 Now there was a certain disciple at Damascus, named Ananias. And the Lord said to him in a vision: Ananias. And he said: Behold I am here, Lord.

11 And the Lord said to him: Arise, and go into the street that is called Stait, and seek in the house of Judas, one named Saul of Tarsus. For behold he prayeth.

12 (And he saw a man named Ananias coming in, and putting his hands upon him, that he might receive his sight.)

13 But Ananias answered: Lord, I have heard by many of this man, how much evil he hath done to thy saints in Jerusalem.

14 And here he hath authority from the chief priests to bind all that invoke thy name.

15 And the Lord said to him: Go thy way; for this man is to me a vessel of election, to carry my name before the Gentiles, and kings, and the children of Israel.

16 For I will shew him how great things he must suffer for my name's sake.

17 And Ananias went his way, and entered into the house. And laying his hands upon him, he said: Brother Saul, the Lord Jesus hath sent me, he that appeared to thee in the way as thou camest; that thou mayest receive thy sight, and be filled with the Holy Ghost.

18 And immediately there fell from his eyes as it were scales, and he received his sight; and rising up, he was baptized.

19 And when he had taken meat, he was strengthened. And he was with the disciples that were at Damascus, for some days.

20 And immediately he preached Jesus in the synagogues, that he is the Son of God.

21 And all that heard him, were astonished, and said: Is not this he who persecuted in Jerusalem those that called upon this name: and came hither for that intent, that he might carry them bound to the chief priests?

22 But Saul increased much more in strength, and confounded the Jews who dwelt at Damascus, affirming that this is the Christ.

Responsorial Psalm: Psalms 117: 1bc, 2
R. (mark 16:15) Go out to all the world, and tell the Good News.

or

R. Alleluia.

1bc O praise the Lord, all ye nations: praise him, all ye people.

R. Go out to all the world, and tell the Good News.

or

R. Alleluia.

2 For his mercy is confirmed upon us: and the truth of the Lord remaineth for ever.

R. Go out to all the world, and tell the Good News. or
R. Alleluia.

Alleluia: John 15: 16 R. Alleluia, alleluia.

16 I chose you from the world, to go and bear fruit that will last, says the Lord.

R. Alleluia, alleluia.

Gospel: Mark 16: 15-18
15 And he said to them: Go ye into the whole world, and preach the gospel to every creature.

16 He that believeth and is baptized, shall be saved: but he that believeth not shall be condemned.

17 And these signs shall follow them that believe: In my name they shall cast out devils: they shall speak with new tongues.

18 They shall take up serpents; and if they shall drink any deadly thing, it shall not hurt them: they shall lay their hands upon the sick, and they shall recover.

Daily Mass Readings for Friday, 26 January 2024

Timothy and Titus, Bishops Obligatory Memorial First Reading: Second Timothy 1: 1-8 or Titus 1: 1-5 Responsorial Psalm: Psalms 96: 1-2a, 2b-3, 7-8a, 10 Alleluia: Matthew 11: 25
Gospel: Mark 4: 26-34
Lectionary: 520, 321

First Reading: Second Timothy 1: 1-8 or Titus 1: 1-5
1 Paul, an apostle of Jesus Christ, by the will of God, according to the promise of life, which is in Christ Jesus.

2 To Timothy my dearly beloved son, grace, mercy, and peace, from God the Father, and from Christ Jesus our Lord.

3 I give thanks to God, whom I serve from my forefathers with a pure conscience, that without ceasing, I have a remembrance of thee in my prayers, night and day.

4 Desiring to see thee, being mindful of thy tears, that I may be filled with joy,

5 Calling to mind that faith which is in thee unfeigned, which also dwelt first in thy grandmother Lois, and in thy mother Eunice, and I am certain that in thee also.

6 For which cause I admonish thee, that thou stir up the grace of God which is in thee, by the imposition of my hands.

7 For God hath not given us the spirit of fear: but of power, and of love, and of sobriety.

8 Be not thou therefore ashamed of the testimony of our Lord, nor of me his prisoner: but labour with the gospel, according to the power of God,

Or

1 Paul, a servant of God, and an apostle of Jesus Christ, according to the faith of the elect of God and the acknowledging of the truth, which is according to godliness:

2 Unto the hope of life everlasting, which God, who lieth not, hath promised before the times of the world:

3 But hath in due times manifested his word in preaching, which is committed to me according to the commandment of God our Saviour:

4 To Titus my beloved son, according to the common faith, grace and peace from God the Father, and from Christ Jesus our Saviour.

5 For this cause I left thee in Crete, that thou shouldest set in order the things that are wanting, and shouldest ordain priests in every city, as I also appointed thee:

Responsorial Psalm: Psalms 96: 1-2a, 2b-3, 7-8a, 10
R. (3) Proclaim God's marvelous deeds to all the nations.

1 Sing ye to the Lord a new canticle: sing to the Lord, all the earth. 2a Sing ye to the Lord and bless his name.
R. Proclaim God's marvelous deeds to all the nations.
2b Shew forth his salvation from day to day.

3 Declare his glory among the Gentiles: his wonders among all people.

R. Proclaim God's marvelous deeds to all the nations.

7 Bring ye to the Lord, O ye kindreds of the Gentiles, bring ye to the Lord glory and honour:

8a Bring to the Lord glory unto his name.

R. Proclaim God's marvelous deeds to all the nations.

10 Say ye among the Gentiles, the Lord hath reigned. For he hath corrected the world, which shall not be moved: he will judge the people with justice.

R. Proclaim God's marvelous deeds to all the nations.

Alleluia: Matthew 11: 25 R. Alleluia, alleluia.

25 Blessed are you, Father, Lord of heaven and earth; you have revealed to little ones the mysteries of the Kingdom.

R. Alleluia, alleluia.

Gospel: Mark 4: 26-34

26 And he said: So is the kingdom of God, as if a man should cast seed into the earth,

27 And should sleep, and rise, night and day, and the seed should spring, and grow up whilst he knoweth not.

28 For the earth of itself bringeth forth fruit, first the blade, then the ear, afterwards the full corn in the ear.

29 And when the fruit is brought forth, immediately he putteth in the sickle, because the harvest is come.

30 And he said: To what shall we liken the kingdom of God? or to what parable shall we compare it?

31 It is as a grain of mustard seed: which when it is sown in the earth, is less than all the seeds that are in the earth:

32 And when it is sown, it groweth up, and becometh greater than all herbs, and shooteth out great branches, so that the birds of the air may dwell under the shadow thereof.

33 And with many such parables, he spoke to them the word, according as they were able to hear.

34 And without parable he did not speak unto them; but apart, he explained all things to his disciples.

Daily Mass Readings for Saturday, 27 January 2024

Ordinary Weekday/ Optional Memorial of the Blessed Virgin Mary/ Angela Merici, Virgin, Religious Founder
First Reading: Second Samuel 12: 1-7a, 10-17
Responsorial Psalm: Psalms 51: 12-13, 14-15, 16-17

Alleluia: John 3: 16
Gospel: Mark 4: 35-41
Lectionary: 322
First Reading: Second Samuel 12: 1-7a, 10-17
1 And the Lord sent Nathan to David: and when he was come to him, he said to him: There were two men in one city, the one rich, and the other poor.

2 The rich man had exceeding many sheep and oxen.

3 But the poor man had nothing at all but one little ewe lamb, which he had bought and nourished up, and which had grown up in his house together with his children, eating of his bread, and drinking of his cup, and sleeping in his bosom: and it was unto him as a daughter.

4 And when a certain stranger was come to the rich man, he spared to take of his own sheep and oxen, to make a feast for that stranger, who was come to him, but took the poor man's ewe, and dressed it for the man that was come to him.

5 And David's anger being exceedingly kindled against that man, he said to Nathan: As the Lord liveth, the man that hath done this is a child of death.

6 He shall restore the ewe fourfold, because he did this thing, and had no pity.

7a And Nathan said to David: Thou art the man. Thus saith the Lord the God of Israel.

10 Therefore the sword shall never depart from thy house, because thou hast despised me, and hast taken the wife of Urias the Hethite to be thy wife.

11 Thus saith the Lord: Behold, I will raise up evil against thee out of thy own house, and I will take thy wives before thy eyes I and give them to thy neighbour, and he shall lie with thy wives in the sight of this sun.

12 For thou didst it secretly: but I will do this thing in the sight of all Israel, and in the sight of the sun.

13 And David said to Nathan: I have sinned against the Lord. And Nathan said to David: The Lord also hath taken away thy sin: thou shalt not die.

14 Nevertheless, because thou hast given occasion to the enemies of the Lord to blaspheme, for this thing, the child that is born to thee, shall surely die.

15 And Nathan returned to his house. The Lord also struck the child which the wife of Urias had borne to David, and his life was despaired of.

16 And David besought the Lord for the child: and David kept a fast, and going in by himself lay upon the ground.

17 And the ancients of his house came, to make him rise from the ground: but he would not, neither did he eat meat with them.

Responsorial Psalm: Psalms 51: 12-13, 14-15, 16-17 R. (12a) Create a clean heart in me, O God.

12 Create a clean heart in me, O God: and renew a right spirit within my bowels.

13 Cast me not away from thy face; and take not thy holy spirit from me.

R. Create a clean heart in me, O God.

14 Restore unto me the joy of thy salvation, and strengthen me with a perfect spirit.

15 I will teach the unjust thy ways: and the wicked shall be converted to thee.
R. Create a clean heart in me, O God.

16 Deliver me from blood, O God, thou God of my salvation: and my tongue shall extol thy justice.

17 O Lord, thou wilt open my lips: and my mouth shall declare thy praise.

R. Create a clean heart in me, O God.

Alleluia: John 3: 16 R. Alleluia, alleluia.

16 God so loved the world that he gave his only-begotten Son, so that everyone who believes in him might have eternal life.

R. Alleluia, alleluia.

Gospel: Mark 4: 35-41
35 And he saith to them that day, when evening was come: Let us pass over to the other side.

36 And sending away the multitude, they take him even as he was in the ship: and there were other ships with him.

37 And there arose a great storm of wind, and the waves beat into the ship, so that the ship was filled.

38 And he was in the hinder part of the ship, sleeping upon a pillow; and they awake him, and say to him: Master, doth it not concern thee that we perish?

39 And rising up, he rebuked the wind, and said to the sea: Peace, be still. And the wind ceased: and there was made a great calm.

40 And he said to them: Why are you fearful? have you not faith yet?

41 And they feared exceedingly: and they said one to another: Who is this (thinkest thou) that both wind and sea obey him?

Daily Mass Readings for Sunday, 28 January 2024

Fourth Sunday in Ordinary Time
First Reading: Deuteronomy 18: 15-20
Responsorial Psalm: Psalms 95: 1-2, 6-7, 8-9
Second Reading: First Corinthians 7: 32-35
Alleluia: Matthew 4: 16
Gospel: Mark 1: 21-28
Lectionary: 71
First Reading: Deuteronomy 18: 15-20
15 The Lord thy God will raise up to thee a PROPHET of thy nation and of thy brethren like unto me: him thou shalt hear:

16 As thou desiredst of the Lord thy God in Horeb, when the assembly was gathered together, and saidst: Let me not hear any more the voice of the Lord my God, neither let me see any more this exceeding great fire, lest I die.

17 And the Lord said to me: They have spoken all things well.

18 I will raise them up a prophet out of the midst of their brethren like to thee: and I will put my words in his mouth, and he shall speak to them all that I shall command him.

19 And he that will not hear his words, which he shall speak in my name, I will be the revenger.

20 But the prophet, who being corrupted with pride, shall speak in my name things that I did not command him to say, or in the name of strange gods, shall be slain.

Responsorial Psalm: Psalms 95: 1-2, 6-7, 8-9
R. (8) If today you hear his voice, harden not your hearts.

1 Come let us praise the Lord with joy: let us joyfully sing to God our saviour.

2 Let us come before his presence with thanksgiving; and make a joyful noise to him with psalms.

R. If today you hear his voice, harden not your hearts.
6 Come let us adore and fall down: and weep before the Lord that made us.

7 For he is the Lord our God: and we are the people of his pasture and the sheep of his hand.

R. If today you hear his voice, harden not your hearts.

8 Today if you shall hear his voice, harden not your hearts:

9 As in the provocation, according to the day of temptation in the wilderness: where your fathers tempted me, they proved me, and saw my works.

R. If today you hear his voice, harden not your hearts.

Second Reading: First Corinthians 7: 32-35
32 But I would have you to be without solicitude. He that is without a wife, is solicitous for the things that belong to the Lord, how he may please God.

33 But he that is with a wife, is solicitous for the things of the world, how he may please his wife: and he is divided.

34 And the unmarried woman and the virgin thinketh on the things of the Lord, that she may be holy both in body and in spirit. But she that is married thinketh on the things of the world, how she may please her husband.

35 And this I speak for your profit: not to cast a snare upon you; but for that which is decent, and which may give you power to attend upon the Lord, without impediment.

Alleluia: Matthew 4: 16 R. Alleluia, alleluia.

16 The people who sit in darkness have seen a great light; on those dwelling in a land overshadowed by death, light has arisen.

R. Alleluia, alleluia.

Gospel: Mark 1: 21-28
21 And they entered into Capharnaum, and forthwith upon the sabbath days going into the synagogue, he taught them.

22 And they were astonished at his doctrine. For he was teaching them as one having power, and not as the scribes.

23 And there was in their synagogue a man with an unclean spirit; and he cried out,

24 Saying: What have we to do with thee, Jesus of Nazareth? art thou come to destroy us? I know who thou art, the Holy One of God.

25 And Jesus threatened him, saying: Speak no more, and go out of the man.

26 And the unclean spirit tearing him, and crying out with a loud voice, went out of him.

27 And they were all amazed, insomuch that they questioned among themselves, saying: What thing is this? what is this new doctrine? for with power he commandeth even the unclean spirits, and they obey him.

28 And the fame of him was spread forthwith into all the country of Galilee

Daily Mass Readings for Monday, 29 January 2024

Ordinary Weekday
First Reading: Second Samuel 15: 13-14, 30; 16: 5-13
Responsorial Psalm: Psalms 3: 2-3, 4-5, 6-7
Alleluia: Luke 7: 16
Gospel: Mark 5: 1-20
Lectionary: 323
First Reading: Second Samuel 15: 13-14, 30; 16: 5-13
13 And there came a messenger to David, saying: All Israel with their whole heart followeth Absalom.

14 And David said to his servants, that were with him in Jerusalem: Arise and let us flee: for we shall not escape else from the face of Absalom: make haste to go out, lest he come and overtake us, and bring ruin upon us, and smite the city with the edge of the sword.

30 But David went up by the ascent of mount Olivet, going up and weeping, walking barefoot, and with his head covered, and all the people that were with them, went up with their heads covered weeping.

16:5 And king David came as far as Bahurim: and behold there came out from thence a man of the kindred of the house of Saul named Semei, the son of Gera, and coming out he cursed as he went on,

6 And he threw stones at David, and at all the servants of king David: and all the people, and all the warriors walked on the right, and on the left side of the king.

7 And thus said Semei when he cursed the king: Come out, come out, thou man of blood, and thou man of Belial.

8 The Lord hath repaid thee for all the blood of the house of Saul: because thou hast usurped the kingdom in his stead, and the Lord hath given the kingdom into the hand of Absalom thy son: and behold thy evils press upon thee, because thou art a man of blood.

9 And Abisai the son of Sarvia said to the king: Why should this dead dog curse my lord the king? I will go, and cut off his head.

10 And the king said: What have I to do with you, ye sons of Sarvia? Let him alone and let him curse: for the Lord hath bid him curse David: and who is he that shall dare say, why hath he done so?

11 And the king said to Abisai, and to all his servants: Behold my son, who came forth from my bowels, seeketh my life: how much more now a son of Jemini? let him alone that he may curse as the Lord hath bidden him.

12 Perhaps the Lord may look upon my affliction, and the Lord may render me good for the cursing of this day.

13 And David and his men with him went by the way. And Semei by the hill's side went over against him, cursing, and casting stones at him, and scattering earth.

Responsorial Psalm: Psalms 3: 2-3, 4-5, 6-7 R. (8a) Lord, rise up and save me.

2 Why, O Lord, are they multiplied that afflict me? many are they who rise up against me.

3 Many say to my soul: There is no salvation for him in his God.
R. Lord, rise up and save me.
4 But thou, O Lord art my protector, my glory, and the lifter up of my head.

5 I have cried to the Lord with my voice: and he hath heard me from his holy hill.

R. Lord, rise up and save me.

6 I have slept and taken my rest: and I have risen up, because the Lord hath protected me.

7 I will not fear thousands of the people, surrounding me: arise, O Lord; save me, O my God.

R. Lord, rise up and save me.

Alleluia: Luke 7: 16 R. Alleluia, alleluia.

16 A great prophet has arisen in our midst and God has visited his people. R. Alleluia, alleluia.

Gospel: Mark 5: 1-20

1 And they came over the strait of the sea into the country of the Gerasens.

2 And as he went out of the ship, immediately there met him out of the monuments a man with an unclean spirit,

3 Who had his dwelling in the tombs, and no man now could bind him, not even with chains.

4 For having been often bound with fetters and chains, he had burst the chains, and broken the fetters in pieces, and no one could tame him.

5 And he was always day and night in the monuments and in the mountains, crying and cutting himself with stones.

6 And seeing Jesus afar off, he ran and adored him.

7 And crying with a loud voice, he said: What have I to do with thee, Jesus the Son of the most high God? I adjure thee by God that thou torment me not.

8 For he said unto him: Go out of the man, thou unclean spirit.

9 And he asked him: What is thy name? And he saith to him: My name is Legion, for we are many.

10 And he besought him much, that he would not drive him away out of the country.

11 And there was there near the mountain a great herd of swine, feeding.

12 And the spirits besought him, saying: Send us into the swine, that we may enter into them.

13 And Jesus immediately gave them leave. And the unclean spirits going out, entered into the swine: and the herd with great violence was carried headlong into the sea, being about two thousand, and were stifled in the sea.

14 And they that fed them fled, and told it in the city and in the fields. And they went out to see what was done:

15 And they came to Jesus, and they see him that was troubled with the devil, sitting, clothed, and well in his wits, and they were afraid.

16 And they that had seen it, told them, in what manner he had been dealt with who had the devil; and concerning the swine.

17 And they began to pray him that he would depart from their coasts.

18 And when he went up into the ship, he that had been troubled with the devil, began to beseech him that he might be with him.

19 And he admitted him not, but saith to him: Go into thy house to thy friends, and tell them how great things the Lord hath done for thee, and hath had

mercy on thee.

20 And he went his way, and began to publish in Decapolis how great things Jesus had done for him: and all men wondered.

Daily Mass Readings for Tuesday, 30 January 2024

Ordinary Weekday
First Reading: Second Samuel 18: 9-10, 14, 24-25a, 30 – 19: 3 Responsorial
Psalm: Psalms 86: 1-2, 3-4, 5-6
Alleluia: Matthew 8: 17
Gospel: Mark 5: 21-43
Lectionary: 324
First Reading: Second Samuel 18: 9-10, 14, 24-25a, 30 – 19: 3

9 And it happened that Absalom met the servants of David, riding on a mule: and as the mule went under a thick and large oak, his head stuck in the oak: and while he hung between the heaven and the earth, the mule on which he rode passed on.

10 And one saw this and told Joab, saying: I saw Absalom hanging upon an oak.

14 And Joab said: Not as thou wilt, but will set upon him in thy sight. So he took three lances in his hand, and thrust them into the heart of Absalom: and whilst he yet panted for life, sticking on the oak,

24 And David sat between the two gates: and the watchman that was on the top of the gate upon the wall, lifting up his eyes, saw a man running alone.

25a And crying out he told the king: and the king said: If he be alone, there are good tidings in his mouth.

30 And the king said to him: Pass, and stand here.

31 And when he had passed, and stood still, Chusai appeared: and coming up he said: I bring good tidings, my lord, the king, for the Lord hath judged for thee this day from the hand of all that have risen up against thee.

32 And the king said to Chusai: Is the young man Absalom safe? And Chusai answering him, said: Let the enemies of my lord, the king, and all that rise against him unto evil, be as the young man is.

19:1 The king therefore being much moved, went up to the high chamber over the gate, and wept. And as he went he spoke in this manner: My son Absalom,

Absalom my son: would to God that I might die for thee, Absalom my son, my son Absalom.

2 And it was told Joab, that the king wept and mourned for his son:

3 And the victory that day was turned into mourning unto all the people: for the people heard say that day: The king grieveth for his son.

Responsorial Psalm: Psalms 86: 1-2, 3-4, 5-6 R. 91a Listen, Lord, and answer me.

1 Incline thy ear, O Lord, and hear me: for I am needy and poor.

2 Preserve my soul, for I am holy: save thy servant, O my God, that trusteth in thee.

R. Listen, Lord, and answer me.

3 Have mercy on me, O Lord, for I have cried to thee all the day.

4 Give joy to the soul of thy servant, for to thee, O Lord, I have lifted up my soul.

R. Listen, Lord, and answer me.

5 For thou, O Lord, art sweet and mild: and plenteous in mercy to all that call upon thee.

6 Give ear, O Lord, to my prayer: and attend to the voice of my petition. R. Listen, Lord, and answer me.

Alleluia: Matthew 8: 17 R. Alleluia, alleluia.

17 Christ took away our infirmities and bore our diseases. R. Alleluia, alleluia.

Gospel: Mark 5: 21-43
21 And when Jesus had passed again in the ship over the strait, a great multitude assembled together unto him, and he was nigh unto the sea.

22 And there cometh one of the rulers of the synagogue named Jairus: and seeing him, falleth down at his feet.

23 And he besought him much, saying: My daughter is at the point of death, come, lay thy hand upon her, that she may be safe, and may live.

24 And he went with him, and a great multitude followed him, and they thronged him.

25 And a woman who was under an issue of blood twelve years,

26 And had suffered many things from many physicians; and had spent all that she had, and was nothing the better, but rather worse,

27 When she had heard of Jesus, came in the crowd behind him, and touched his garment.

28 For she said: If I shall touch but his garment, I shall be whole.

29 And forthwith the fountain of her blood was dried up, and she felt in her body that she was healed of the evil.

30 And immediately Jesus knowing in himself the virtue that had proceeded from him, turning to the multitude, said: Who hath touched my garments?

31 And his disciples said to him: Thou seest the multitude thronging thee, and sayest thou who hath touched me?

32 And he looked about to see her who had done this.

33 But the woman fearing and trembling, knowing what was done in her, came and fell down before him, and told him all the truth.

34 And he said to her: Daughter, thy faith hath made thee whole: go in peace, and be thou whole of thy disease.

35 While he was yet speaking, some come from the ruler of the synagogue's house, saying: Thy daughter is dead: why dost thou trouble the master any further?

36 But Jesus having heard the word that was spoken, saith to the ruler of the synagogue: Fear not, only believe.

37 And he admitted not any man to follow him, but Peter, and James, and John the brother of James.

38 And they come to the house of the ruler of the synagogue; and he seeth a tumult, and people weeping and wailing much.

39 And going in, he saith to them: Why make you this ado, and weep? the damsel is not dead, but sleepeth.

40 And they laughed him to scorn. But he having put them all out, taketh the father and the mother of the damsel, and them that were with him, and entereth in where the damsel was lying.

41 And taking the damsel by the hand, he saith to her: Talitha cumi, which is, being interpreted: Damsel (I say to thee) arise.

42 And immediately the damsel rose up, and walked: and she was twelve years old: and they were astonished with a great astonishment.

43 And he charged them strictly that no man should know it: and commanded that something should be given her to eat.

Daily Mass Readings for Wednesday, 31 January 2024

John Bosco, Priest, Religious Founder Obligatory Memorial First Reading: Second Samuel 24: 2, 9-17
Responsorial Psalm: Psalms 32: 1-2, 5, 6, 7
Alleluia: John 10: 27

Gospel: Mark 6: 1-6
Lectionary: 325
First Reading: Second Samuel 24: 2, 9-17

2 And the king said to Joab the general of his army: Go through all the tribes of Israel from Dan to Bersabee, and number ye the people that I may know the number of them.

9 And Joab gave up the sum of the number of the people to the king, and there were found of Israel eight hundred thousand valiant men that drew the sword:

and of Juda five hundred thousand fighting men.

10 But David's heart struck him, after the people were numbered: and David said to the Lord: I have sinned very much in what I have done: but I pray thee, O Lord, to take away the iniquity of thy servant, because I have done exceeding foolishly.

11 And David arose in the morning, and the word of the Lord came to Gad the prophet and the seer of David, saying:

12 Go, and say to David: Thus saith the Lord: I give thee thy choice of three things, choose one of them which thou wilt, that I may do it to thee.

13 And when Gad was come to David, he told him, saying: Either seven years of famine shall come to thee in thy land: or thou shalt flee three months before thy adversaries, and they shall pursue thee: or for three days there shall be a pestilence in thy land. Now therefore deliberate, and see what answer I shall return to him that sent me.

14 And David said to Gad: I am in a great strait: but it is better that I should fall into the hands of the Lord (for his mercies are many) than into the hands of men.

15 And the Lord sent a pestilence upon Israel, from the morning unto the time appointed, and there died of the people from Dan to Bersabee seventy thousand men.

16 And when the angel of the Lord had stretched out his hand over Jerusalem to destroy it, the Lord had pity on the affliction, and said to the angel that slew the people: It is enough: now hold thy hand. And the angel of the Lord was by the threshingfloor of Areuna the Jebusite.

17 And David said to the Lord, when he saw the angel striking the people: It is I; I am he that have sinned, I have done wickedly: these that are the sheep, what have they done? let thy hand, I beseech thee, be turned against me, and against my father's house.

Responsorial Psalm: Psalms 32: 1-2, 5, 6, 7 R. (5c) Lord, forgive the wrong I have done.

1 Blessed are they whose iniquities are forgiven, and whose sins are covered.

2 Blessed is the man to whom the Lord hath not imputed sin, and in whose spirit there is no guile.

R. Lord, forgive the wrong I have done.

5 I have acknowledged my sin to thee, and my injustice I have not concealed. I said I will confess against myself my injustice to the Lord: and thou hast forgiven the wickedness of my sin.

R. Lord, forgive the wrong I have done.

6 For this shall every one that is holy pray to thee in a seasonable time. And yet in a flood of many waters, they shall not come nigh unto him.

R. Lord, forgive the wrong I have done.

7 Thou art my refuge from the trouble which hath encompassed me: my joy, deliver me from them that surround me.

R. Lord, forgive the wrong I have done.

Allcluia: John 10: 27 R. Alleluia, alleluia.

27 My sheep hear my voice, says the Lord; I know them, and they follow me.
R. Alleluia, alleluia.
Gospel: Mark 6: 1-6

1 And going out from thence, he went into his own country; and his disciples followed him.

2 And when the sabbath was come, he began to teach in the synagogue: and many hearing him were in admiration at his doctrine, saying: How came this man by all these things? and what wisdom is this that is given to him, and such mighty works as are wrought by his hands?

3 Is not this the carpenter, the son of Mary, the brother of James, and Joseph, and Jude, and Simon? are not also his sisters here with us? And they were scandalized in regard of him.

4 And Jesus said to them: A prophet is not without honor, but in his own country, and in his own house, and among his own kindred.

5 And he could not do any miracles there, only that he cured a few that were sick, laying his hands upon them.

6 And he wondered because of their unbelief, and he went through the villages round about teaching.

February 2024

Daily Mass Readings for Thursday, 1 February 2024

Ordinary Weekday
First Reading: First Kings 2: 1-4, 10-12
Responsorial Psalm: First Chronicles 29: 10, 11ab, 11d-12a, 12bcd Alleluia: Mark 1: 15
Gospel: Mark 6: 7-13
Lectionary: 326
First Reading: First Kings 2: 1-4, 10-12

1 And the days of David drew nigh that he should die, and he charged his son Solomon, saying:

2 I am going the way of all flesh: take thou courage, and shew thyself a man.

3 And keep the charge of the Lord thy God, to walk in his ways, and observe his ceremonies, and his precepts, and judgments, and testimonies, as it is written in the law of Moses: that thou mayest understand all thou dost, and whithersoever thou shalt turn thyself:

4 That the Lord may confirm his words, which he hath spoken of me, saying: If thy children shall take heed to their ways, and shall walk before me in truth, with all their heart, and with all their soul, there shall not be taken away from thee a man on the throne of Israel.

10 So David slept with his fathers, and was buried in the city of David.

11 And the days that David reigned in Israel, were forty years: in Hebron he reigned seven years, in Jerusalem thirty-three.

12 And Solomon sat upon the throne of his father David, and his kingdom was strengthened exceedingly.

Responsorial Psalm: First Chronicles 29: 10, 11ab, 11d-12a, 12bcd R. (12b) Lord, you are exalted over all.

10 Blessed art thou, O Lord the God of Israel, our father from eternity to eternity.

R. Lord, you are exalted over all.
11ab Thine, O Lord, is magnificence, and power, and glory, and victory. R.

Lord, you are exalted over all.
11d O Lord, and thou art above all princes.
12a Thine are riches, and thine is glory, thou hast dominion over all.

R. Lord, you are exalted over all.

12bcd In thy hand is power and might: in thy hand greatness, and the empire of all things.

R. Lord, you are exalted over all.

Alleluia: Mark 1: 15 R. Alleluia, alleluia.

15 The Kingdom of God is at hand; repent and believe in the Gospel. R. Alleluia, alleluia.

Gospel: Mark 6: 7-13
7 And he called the twelve; and began to send them two and two, and gave them power over unclean spirits.

8 And he commanded them that they should take nothing for the way, but a staff only: no scrip, no bread, nor money in their purse,

9 But to be shod with sandals, and that they should not put on two coats.

10 And he said to them: Wheresoever you shall enter into an house, there abide till you depart from that place.

11 And whosoever shall not receive you, nor hear you; going forth from thence, shake off the dust from your feet for a testimony to them.

12 And going forth they preached that men should do penance:

13 And they cast out many devils, and anointed with oil many that were sick, and healed them.

Daily Mass Readings for Friday, 2 February 2024

Presentation of the Lord Feast
First Reading: Malachi 3: 1-4
Responsorial Psalm: Psalms 24: 7, 8, 9, 10
Second Reading: Hebrews 2: 14-18
Alleluia: Luke 2: 32
Gospel: Luke 2: 22-40 or Luke 2: 22-32
Lectionary: 524

First Reading: Malachi 3: 1-4

1 Behold I send my angel, and he shall prepare the way before my face. And presently the Lord, whom you seek, and the angel of the testament, whom you desire, shall come to his temple. Behold he cometh, saith the Lord of hosts.

2 And who shall be able to think of the day of his coming? and who shall stand to see him? for he is like a refining fire, and like the fuller's herb:

3 And he shall sit refining and cleansing the silver, and he shall purify the sons of Levi, and shall refine them as gold, and as silver, and they shall offer sacrifices to the Lord in justice.

4 And the sacrifice of Juda and of Jerusalem shall please the Lord, as in the days of old, and in the ancient years.

Responsorial Psalm: Psalms 24: 7, 8, 9, 10
R. (8) Who is this king of glory? It is the Lord!

7 Lift up your gates, O ye princes, and be ye lifted up, O eternal gates: and the King of Glory shall enter in.

R. Who is this king of glory? It is the Lord!

8 Who is this King of Glory? the Lord who is strong and mighty: the Lord mighty in battle.

R. Who is this king of glory? It is the Lord!

9 Lift up your gates, O ye princes, and be ye lifted up, O eternal gates: and the King of Glory shall enter in.

R. Who is this king of glory? It is the Lord!
10 Who is this King of Glory? the Lord of hosts, he is the King of Glory. R. Who is this king of glory? It is the Lord!
Second Reading: Hebrews 2: 14-18

14 Therefore because the children are partakers of flesh and blood, he also himself in like manner hath been partaker of the same: that, through death, he might destroy him who had the empire of death, that is to say, the devil:

15 And might deliver them, who through the fear of death were all their lifetime subject to servitude.

16 For no where doth he take hold of the angels: but of the seed of Abraham he taketh hold.

17 Wherefore it behoved him in all things to be made like unto his brethren, that he might become a merciful and faithful priest before God, that he might be a propitiation for the sins of the people.

18 For in that, wherein he himself hath suffered and been tempted, he is able to succour them also that are tempted.

Alleluia: Luke 2: 32 R. Alleluia, alleluia.

32 A light of revelation to the Gentiles, and glory for your people Israel. R. Alleluia, alleluia.

Gospel: Luke 2: 22-40 or Luke 2: 22-32
22 And after the days of her purification, according to the law of Moses, were accomplished, they carried him to Jerusalem, to present him to the Lord:

23 As it is written in the law of the Lord: Every male opening the womb shall be called holy to the Lord:

24 And to offer a sacrifice, according as it is written in the law of the Lord, a pair of turtledoves, or two young pigeons:

25 And behold there was a man in Jerusalem named Simeon, and this man was just and devout, waiting for the consolation of Israel; and the Holy Ghost

was in him.

26 And he had received an answer from the Holy Ghost, that he should not see death, before he had seen the Christ of the Lord.

27 And he came by the Spirit into the temple. And when his parents brought in the child Jesus, to do for him according to the custom of the law,

28 He also took him into his arms, and blessed God, and said:

29 Now thou dost dismiss thy servant, O Lord, according to thy word in peace;

30 Because my eyes have seen thy salvation,

31 Which thou hast prepared before the face of all peoples:

32 A light to the revelation of the Gentiles, and the glory of thy people Israel.

33 And his father and mother were wondering at those things which were spoken concerning him.

34 And Simeon blessed them, and said to Mary his mother: Behold this child is set for the fall, and for the resurrection of many in Israel, and for a sign which shall be contradicted;

35 And thy own soul a sword shall pierce, that, out of many hearts, thoughts may be revealed.

36 And there was one Anna, a prophetess, the daughter of Phanuel, of the tribe of Aser; she was far advanced in years, and had lived with her husband seven years from her virginity.

37 And she was a widow until fourscore and four years; who departed not from the temple, by fastings and prayers serving night and day.

38 Now she, at the same hour, coming in, confessed to the Lord; and spoke of him to all that looked for the redemption of Israel.

39 And after they had performed all things according to the law of the Lord, they returned into Galilee, to their city Nazareth.

40 And the child grew, and waxed strong, full of wisdom; and the grace of God was in him.

Or

22 And after the days of her purification, according to the law of Moses, were accomplished, they carried him to Jerusalem, to present him to the Lord:

23 As it is written in the law of the Lord: Every male opening the womb shall be called holy to the Lord:

24 And to offer a sacrifice, according as it is written in the law of the Lord, a pair of turtledoves, or two young pigeons:

25 And behold there was a man in Jerusalem named Simeon, and this man was just and devout, waiting for the consolation of Israel; and the Holy Ghost was in him.

26 And he had received an answer from the Holy Ghost, that he should not see death, before he had seen the Christ of the Lord.

27 And he came by the Spirit into the temple. And when his parents brought in the child Jesus, to do for him according to the custom of the law,

28 He also took him into his arms, and blessed God, and said:

29 Now thou dost dismiss thy servant, O Lord, according to thy word in peace;

30 Because my eyes have seen thy salvation,
31 Which thou hast prepared before the face of all peoples:
32 A light to the revelation of the Gentiles, and the glory of thy people Israel.

Daily Mass Readings for Saturday, 3 February 2024

Ordinary Weekday/ Optional Memorial of the Blessed Virgin Mary/ Blase, Bishop, Martyr/ Ansgar, Bishop, Missionary
First Reading: First Kings 3: 4-13
Responsorial Psalm: Psalms 119: 9, 10, 11, 12, 13, 14
Alleluia: John 10: 27
Gospel: Mark 6: 30-34
Lectionary: 328
First Reading: First Kings 3: 4-13

4 He went therefore to Gabaon, to sacrifice there: for that was the great high place: a thousand victims for holocausts did Solomon offer upon that altar in Gabaon.

5 And the Lord appeared to Solomon in a dream by night, saying: Ask what thou wilt that I should give thee.

6 And Solomon said: Thou hast shewn great mercy to thy servant David my father, even at, he walked before thee in truth, and justice, and an upright heart with thee: and thou hast kept thy great mercy for him, and hast given him a son to sit on his throne, as it is this day.

7 And now, O Lord God, thou hast made thy servant king instead of David my father: and I am but a child, and know not how to go out and come in.

8 And thy servant is in the midst of the people which thou hast chosen, an immense people, which cannot be numbered nor counted for multitude.

9 Give therefore to thy servant an understanding heart, to judge thy people, and discern between good and evil. For who shall be able to judge this people, thy people which is so numerous?

10 And the word was pleasing to the Lord that Solomon had asked such a thing.

11 And the Lord said to Solomon: Because thou hast asked this thing, and hast not asked for thyself long life or riches, nor the lives of thy enemies, but hast asked for thyself wisdom to discern judgment,

12 Behold I have done for thee according to thy words, and have given thee a wise and understanding heart, insomuch that there hath been no one like thee before thee, nor shall arise after thee.

13 Yea and the things also which thou didst not ask, I have given thee: to wit riches and glory, as that no one hath been like thee among the kings in all days heretofore.

Responsorial Psalm: Psalms 119: 9, 10, 11, 12, 13, 14 R. (12b) Lord, teach me your statutes.

9 By what doth a young man correct his way? by observing thy words. R. Lord, teach me your statutes.

10 With my whole heart have I sought after thee: let me not stray from thy commandments.

R. Lord, teach me your statutes.
11 Thy words have I hidden in my heart, that I may not sin against thee.

R. Lord, teach me your statutes.
12 Blessed art thou, O Lord: teach me thy justifications. R. Lord, teach me your statutes.

13 With my lips I have pronounced all the judgments of thy mouth.

R. Lord, teach me your statutes.

14 I have been delighted in the way of thy testimonies, as in all riches.

R. Lord, teach me your statutes.

Alleluia: John 10: 27 R. Alleluia, alleluia.

27 My sheep hear my voice, says the Lord; I know them, and they follow me. R. Alleluia, alleluia.

Gospel: Mark 6: 30-34
30 And the apostles coming together unto Jesus, related to him all things that they had done and taught.

31 And he said to them: Come apart into a desert place, and rest a little. For there were many coming and going: and they had not so much as time to eat.

32 And going up into a ship, they went into a desert place apart.

33 And they saw them going away, and many knew: and they ran flocking thither on foot from all the cities, and were there before them.

34 And Jesus going out saw a great multitude: and he had compassion on them, because they were as sheep not having a shepherd, and he began to teach them many things.

Daily Mass Readings for Sunday, 4 February 2024

Fifth Sunday in Ordinary Time
First Reading: Job 7: 1-4, 6-7
Responsorial Psalm: Psalms 147: 1-2, 3-4, 5-6
Second Reading: First Corinthians 9: 16-19, 22-23
Alleluia: Matthew 8: 17
Gospel: Mark 1: 29-39
Lectionary: 74
First Reading: Job 7: 1-4, 6-7
1 The life of man upon earth is a warfare, and his days are like the days of a hireling.

2 As a servant longeth for the shade, as the hireling looketh for the end of his work;

3 So I also have had empty months, and have numbered to myself wearisome nights.

4 If I lie down to sleep, I shall say: When shall arise? and again I shall look for the evening, and shall be filled with sorrows even till darkness.

6 My days have passed more swiftly than the web is cut by the weaver, and are consumed without any hope.

7 Remember that my life is but wind, and my eyes shall not return to see good things.

Responsorial Psalm: Psalms 147: 1-2, 3-4, 5-6
R. (3a) Praise the Lord, who heals the brokenhearted.

or
R. Alleluia.

1 Praise ye the Lord, because psalm is good: to our God be joyful and comely praise.

2 The Lord buildeth up Jerusalem: he will gather together the dispersed of Israel.

R. Praise the Lord, who heals the brokenhearted.
or
R. Alleluia.
3 Who healeth the broken of heart, and bindeth up their bruises.
4 Who telleth the number of the stars: and calleth them all by their names. R. Praise the Lord, who heals the brokenhearted.

or
R. Alleluia.

5 Great is our Lord, and great is his power: and of his wisdom there is no number.

6 The Lord lifteth up the meek, and bringeth the wicked down even to the ground.

R. Praise the Lord, who heals the brokenhearted. or
R. Alleluia.
Second Reading: First Corinthians 9: 16-19, 22-23

16 For if I preach the gospel, it is no glory to me, for a necessity lieth upon me: for woe is unto me if I preach not the gospel.

17 For if I do this thing willingly, I have a reward: but if against my will, a dispensation is committed to me:

18 What is my reward then? That preaching the gospel, I may deliver the gospel without charge, that I abuse not my power in the gospel.

19 For whereas I was free as to all, I made myself the servant of all, that I might gain the more.

22 To the weak I became weak, that I might gain the weak. I became all things to all men, that I might save all.

23 And I do all things for the gospel's sake: that I may be made partaker thereof.

Alleluia: Matthew 8: 17 R. Alleluia, alleluia.

17 Christ took away our infirmities and bore our diseases. R. Alleluia, alleluia.

Gospel: Mark 1: 29-39

29 And immediately going out of the synagogue they came into the house of Simon and Andrew, with James and John.

30 And Simon's wife's mother lay in a fit of a fever: and forthwith they tell him of her.

31 And coming to her, he lifted her up, taking her by the hand; and immediately the fever left her, and she ministered unto them.

32 And when it was evening, after sunset, they brought to him all that were ill and that were possessed with devils.

33 And all the city was gathered together at the door.

34 And he healed many that were troubled with divers diseases; and he cast out many devils, and he suffered them not to speak, because they knew him.

35 And rising very early, going out, he went into a desert place: and there he prayed.

36 And Simon, and they that were with him, followed after him.
37 And when they had found him, they said to him: All seek for thee.

38 And he saith to them: Let us go into the neighbouring towns and cities, that I may preach there also; for to this purpose am I come.

39 And he was preaching in their synagogues, and in all Galilee, and casting out devils.

Daily Mass Readings for Monday, 5 February 2024

Agatha, Virgin, Martyr Obligatory Memorial First Reading: First Kings 8: 1-7, 9-13 Responsorial Psalm: Psalms 132: 6-7, 8-10 Alleluia: Matthew 4: 23

Gospel: Mark 6: 53-56
Lectionary: 329
First Reading: First Kings 8: 1-7, 9-13

1 Then all the ancients of Israel with the princes of the tribes, and the heads of the families of the children of Israel were assembled to king Solomon in Jerusalem: that they might carry the ark of the covenant of the Lord out of the city of David, that is, out of Sion.

2 And all Israel assembled themselves to king Solomon on the festival day in the month of Ethanim, the same is the seventh month.

3 And all the ancients of Israel came, and the priests took up the ark,

4 And carried the ark of the Lord, and the tabernacle of the covenant, and all the vessels of the sanctuary, that were in the tabernacle: and the priests and the Levites carried them.

5 And king Solomon, and all the multitude of Israel, that were assembled unto him went with him before the ark, and they sacrificed sheep and oxen that could not be counted or numbered.

6 And the priests brought in the ark of the covenant of the Lord into its place, into the oracle of the temple, into the holy of holies under the wings of the cherubims.

7 For the cherubims spread forth their wings over the place of the ark, and covered the art, and the staves thereof above.

9 Now in the ark there was nothing else but the two tables of stone, which Moses put there at Horeb, when the Lord made a covenant with the children of Israel, when they came out of the land of Egypt.

10 And it came to pass, when the priests were come out of the sanctuary, that a cloud filled the house of the Lord,

11 And the priests could not stand to minister because of the cloud: for the glory of the Lord had filled the house of the Lord.

12 Then Solomon said: The Lord said that he would dwell in a cloud.

13 Building I have built a house for thy dwelling, to be thy most firm throne for ever.

Responsorial Psalm: Psalms 132: 6-7, 8-10 R. (8a) Lord, go up to the place of your rest!

6 Behold we have heard of it in Ephrata: we have found it in the fields of the wood.

7 We will go into his tabernacle: We will adore in the place where his feet stood.

R. Lord, go up to the place of your rest!

8 Arise, O Lord, into thy resting place: thou and the ark, which thou hast sanctified.

9 Let thy priests be clothed with justice: and let thy saints rejoice.

10 For thy servant David's sake, turn not away the face of thy anointed.

R. Lord, go up to the place of your rest!

Alleluia: Matthew 4: 23 R. Alleluia, alleluia.

23 Jesus preached the Gospel of the Kingdom and cured every disease among the people.

R. Alleluia, alleluia.

Gospel: Mark 6: 53-56
53 And when they had passed over, they came into the land of Genezareth, and set to the shore.

54 And when they were gone out of the ship, immediately they knew him:

55 And running through that whole country, they began to carry about in beds those that were sick, where they heard he was.

56 And whithersoever he entered, into towns or into villages or cities, they laid the sick in the streets, and besought him that they might touch but the hem of his garment: and as many as touched him were made whole.

Daily Mass Readings for Tuesday, 6 February 2024

Paul Miki, Priest, Martyr, & Companions, Martyrs Obligatory Memorial First Reading: First Kings 8: 22-23, 27-30
Responsorial Psalm: Psalms 84: 3, 4, 5 and 10, 11
Alleluia: Psalms 119: 36, 29b

Gospel: Mark 7: 1-13
Lectionary: 330
First Reading: First Kings 8: 22-23, 27-30
22 And Solomon stood before the altar of the Lord in the sight of the assembly of Israel, and spread forth his hands towards heaven;

23 And said: Lord God of Israel, there is no God like thee in heaven above, or on earth beneath: who keepest covenant and mercy with thy servants that have walked before thee with all their heart.

27 Is it then to be thought that God should indeed dwell upon earth? for if heaven, and the heavens of heavens cannot contain thee, how much less this house which I have built?

28 But have regard to the prayer of thy servant, and to his supplications, O Lord my God: hear the hymn and the prayer, which thy servant prayeth before thee this day:

29 That thy eyes may be open upon this house night and day: upon the house of which thou hast said: My name shall be there: that thou mayest hearken to the prayer, which thy servant prayeth in this place to thee.

30 That thou mayest hearken to the supplication of thy servant and of thy people Israel, whatsoever they shall pray for in this place, and hear them in the place of thy dwelling in heaven; and when thou hearest, shew them mercy.

Responsorial Psalm: Psalms 84: 3, 4, 5 and 10, 11
R. (2) How lovely is your dwelling place, Lord, mighty God!

3 My soul longeth and fainteth for the courts of the Lord. My heart and my flesh have rejoiced in the living God.

R. How lovely is your dwelling place, Lord, mighty God!

4 For the sparrow hath found herself a house, and the turtle a nest for herself where she may lay her young ones: Thy altars, O Lord of hosts, my king and myGod.

R. How lovely is your dwelling place, Lord, mighty God!

5 Blessed are they that dwell in thy house, O Lord: they shall praise thee for ever and ever.

10 Behold, O God our protector: and look on the face of thy Christ. R. How lovely is your dwelling place, Lord, mighty God!

11 For better is one day in thy courts above thousands. I have chosen to be an abject in the house of my God, rather than to dwell in the tabernacles of sinners.

R. How lovely is your dwelling place, Lord, mighty God!

Alleluia: Psalms 119: 36, 29b R. Alleluia, alleluia.

36, 29b Incline my heart, O God, to your decrees; and favor me with your law.

R. Alleluia, alleluia.

Gospel: Mark 7: 1-13
1 And there assembled together unto him the Pharisees and some of the scribes, coming from Jerusalem.

2 And when they had seen some of his disciples eat bread with common, that is, with unwashed hands, they found fault.

3 For the Pharisees, and all the Jews eat not without often washing their hands, holding the tradition of the ancients:

4 And when they come from the market, unless they be washed, they eat not: and many other things there are that have been delivered to them to observe, the washings of cups and of pots, and of brazen vessels, and of beds.

5 And the Pharisees and scribes asked him: Why do not thy disciples walk according to the tradition of the ancients, but they eat bread with common hands?

6 But he answering, said to them: Well did Isaias prophesy of you hypocrites, as it is written: This people honoureth me with their lips, but their heart is far from me.

7 And in vain do they worship me, teaching doctrines and precepts of men.

8 For leaving the commandment of God, you hold the tradition of men, the washing of pots and of cups: and many other things you do like to these.

9 And he said to them: Well do you make void the commandment of God, that you may keep your own tradition.

10 For Moses said: Honour thy father and thy mother; and He that shall curse father or mother, dying let him die.

11 But you say: If a man shall say to his father or mother, Corban, (which is a gift,) whatsoever is from me, shall profit thee.

12 And further you suffer him not to do any thing for his father or mother,

13 Making void the word of God by your own tradition, which you have given forth. And many other such like things you do.

Daily Mass Readings for Wednesday, 7 February 2024

Ordinary Weekday
First Reading: First Kings 10: 1-10
Responsorial Psalm: Psalms 37: 5-6, 30-31, 39-40
Alleluia: John 17: 17b, 17a
Gospel: Mark 7: 14-23
Lectionary: 331
First Reading: First Kings 10: 1-10

1 And the queen of Saba, having; heard of the fame of Solomon in the name of the Lord, came to try him with hard questions.

2 And entering into Jerusalem with a great train, and riches, and camels that carried spices, and an immense quantity of gold, and precious stones, she came to king Solomon, and spoke to him all that she had in her heart.

3 And Solomon informed her of all the things she proposed to him: there was not any word the king was ignorant of, and which he could not answer her.

4 And when the queen of Saba saw all the wisdom of Solomon, and the house which he had built,

5 And the meat of his table, and the apartments of his servants, and the order of his ministers, and their apparel, and the cupbearers, and the holocausts, which he offered in the house of the Lord: she had no longer any spirit in her,

6 And she said to the king: The report is true, which I heard in my own country,

7 Concerning thy words, and concerning thy wisdom. And I did not believe them that told me, till I came myself, and saw with my own eyes, and have found that the half hath not been told me: thy wisdom and thy works, exceed the fame which I heard.

8 Blessed are thy men, and blessed are thy servants, who stand before thee always, and hear thy wisdom.

9 Blessed be the Lord thy God, whom thou hast pleased, and who hath set thee upon the throne of Israel, because the Lord hath loved Israel for ever, and hath appointed thee king, to do judgment and justice.

10 And she gave the king a hundred and twenty talents of gold, and of spices a very great store, and precious stones: there was brought no more such abundance of spices as these which the queen of Saba gave to king Solomon.

Responsorial Psalm: Psalms 37: 5-6, 30-31, 39-40 R. (30a) The mouth of the just murmurs wisdom.

5 Commit thy way to the Lord, and trust in him, and he will do it.

6 And he will bring forth thy justice as the light, and thy judgment as the noonday.

R. The mouth of the just murmurs wisdom.

30 The mouth of the just shall meditate wisdom: and his tongue shall speak judgment.

31 The law of his God is in his heart, and his steps shall not be supplanted. R. The mouth of the just murmurs wisdom.

39 But the salvation of the just is from the Lord, and he is their protector in the time of trouble.

40 And the Lord will help them and deliver them: and he will rescue them from the wicked, and save them, because they have hoped in him.

R. The mouth of the just murmurs wisdom.

Alleluia: John 17: 17b, 17a R. Alleluia, alleluia.

17b, 17a Your word, O Lord, is truth: consecrate us in the truth. R. Alleluia, alleluia.

Gospel: Mark 7: 14-23
14 And calling again the multitude unto him, he said to them: Hear ye me all, and understand.

15 There is nothing from without a man that entering into him, can defile him. But the things which come from a man, those are they that defile a man.

16 If any man have ears to hear, let him hear.

17 And when he was come into the house from the multitude, his disciples asked him the parable.

18 And he saith to them: So are you also without knowledge? understand you not that every thing from without, entering into a man cannot defile him:

19 Because it entereth not into his heart, but goeth into the belly, and goeth out into the privy, purging all meats?

20 But he said that the things which come out from a man, they defile a man.

21 For from within out of the heart of men proceed evil thoughts, adulteries, fornications, murders,

22 Thefts, covetousness, wickedness, deceit, lasciviousness, an evil eye, blasphemy, pride, foolishness.

23 All these evil things come from within, and defile a man.

Daily Mass Readings for Thursday, 8 February 2024

Ordinary Weekday/ Jerome Emiliani, Priest, Religious Founder/ Josephine Bakhita, Virgin
First Reading: First Kings 11: 4-13
Responsorial Psalm: Psalms 106: 3-4, 35-36, 37 and 40

Alleluia: James 1: 21bc
Gospel: Mark 7: 24-30
Lectionary: 332
First Reading: First Kings 11: 4-13

4 And when he was now old, his heart was turned away by women to follow strange gods: and his heart was not perfect with the Lord his God, as was the heart of David his father.

5 But Solomon worshipped Astarthe the goddess of the Sidonians, and Moloch the idol of the ammonites.

6 And Solomon did that which was net pleasing before the Lord, and did not fully follow the Lord, as David his father.

7 Then Solomon built a temple for Chamos the idol of Moab, on the hill that is over against Jerusalem, and for Moloch the idol of the children of Ammon.

8 And he did in this manner for all his wives that were strangers, who burnt incense, and offered sacrifice to their gods.

9 And the Lord was angry with Solomon, because his mind was turned away from the Lord the God of Israel, who had appeared to him twice,

10 And had commanded him concerning this thing, that he should not follow strange gods: but he kept not the things which the Lord commanded him.

11 The Lord therefore said to Solomon: Because thou hast done this, and hast not kept my covenant, and my precepts, which I have commanded thee, I will divide and rend thy kingdom, and will give it to thy servant.

12 Nevertheless in thy days I will not do it, for David thy father's sake: but I will rend it out of the hand of thy son.

13 Neither will I take away the whole kingdom, but I will give one tribe to thy son for the sake of David my servant, and Jerusalem which I have chosen.

Responsorial Psalm: Psalms 106: 3-4, 35-36, 37 and 40 R. (4a) Remember us, O Lord, as you favor your people.

3 Blessed are they that keep judgment, and do justice at all times.

4 Remember us, O Lord, in the favour of thy people: visit us with thy salvation.

R. Remember us, O Lord, as you favor your people.
35 And they were mingled among the heathens, and learned their works:

36 And served their idols, and it became a stumblingblock to them.

R. Remember us, O Lord, as you favor your people.

37 And they sacrificed their sons, and their daughters to devils.

40 And the Lord was exceedingly angry with his people: and he abhorred his inheritance.

R. Remember us, O Lord, as you favor your people.

Alleluia: James 1: 21bc R. Alleluia, alleluia.

21bc Humbly welcome the word that has been planted in you and is able to save your souls.

R. Alleluia, alleluia.

Gospel: Mark 7: 24-30
24 And rising from thence he went into the coasts of Tyre and Sidon: and entering into a house, he would that no man should know it, and he could not be hid.

25 For a woman as soon as she heard of him, whose daughter had an unclean spirit, came in and fell down at his feet.

26 For the woman was a Gentile, a Syrophenician born. And she besought him that he would cast forth the devil out of her daughter.

27 Who said to her: Suffer first the children to be filled: for it is not good to take the bread of the children, and cast it to the dogs.

28 But she answered and said to him: Yea, Lord; for the whelps also eat under the table of the crumbs of the children.

29 And he said to her: For this saying go thy way, the devil is gone out of thy daughter.

30 And when she was come into her house, she found the girl lying upon the bed, and that the devil was gone out.

Daily Mass Readings for Friday, 9 February 2024

Ordinary Weekday
First Reading: First Kings 11: 29-32; 12: 19
Responsorial Psalm: Psalms 81: 10-11ab, 12-13, 14-15
Alleluia: Acts 16: 14b
Gospel: Mark 7: 31-37
Lectionary: 333

First Reading: First Kings 11: 29-32; 12: 19

29 So it came to paste at that time, that Jeroboam went out of Jerusalem, and the prophet Ahias the Silonite, clad with a new garment, found him in the way: and they two were alone in the held.

30 And Ahias taking his new garment, wherewith he was clad, divided it into twelve parts:

31 And he said to Jeroboam: Take to thee ten pieces: for thus saith the Lord the God of Israel: Behold I will rend the kingdom out of the hand of Solomon, and will give thee ten tribes.

32 But one tribe shall remain to him for the sake of my servant David, and Jerusalem the city, which I have chosen out of all the tribes of Israel:

12:19 And Israel revolted from the house of David, unto this day.

Responsorial Psalm: Psalms 81: 10-11ab, 12-13, 14-15 R. (11a and 9a) I am the Lord, your God: hear my voice.

10 There shall be no new god in thee: neither shalt thou adore a strange god.
11ab For I am the Lord thy God, who brought thee out of the land of Egypt. R.
I am the Lord, your God: hear my voice.
12 But my people heard not my voice: and Israel hearkened not to me.

13 So I let them go according to the desires of their heart: they shall walk in their own inventions.

R. I am the Lord, your God: hear my voice.
14 If my people had heard me: if Israel had walked in my ways:

15 I should soon have humbled their enemies, and laid my hand on them that troubled them.

R. I am the Lord, your God: hear my voice.

Alleluia: Acts 16: 14b R. Alleluia, alleluia.

14b Open our hearts, O Lord, to listen to the words of your Son. R. Alleluia, alleluia.

Gospel: Mark 7: 31-37
31 And again going out of the coasts of Tyre, he came by Sidon to the sea of Galilee, through the midst of the coasts of Decapolis.

32 And they bring to him one deaf and dumb; and they besought him that he would lay his hand upon him.

33 And taking him from the multitude apart, he put his fingers into his ears, and spitting, he touched his tongue:

34 And looking up to heaven, he groaned, and said to him: Ephpheta, which is, Be thou opened.

35 And immediately his ears were opened, and the string of his tongue was loosed, and he spoke right.

36 And he charged them that they should tell no man. But the more he charged them, so much the more a great deal did they publish it.

37 And so much the more did they wonder, saying: He hath done all things well; he hath made both the deaf to hear, and the dumb to speak.

Daily Mass Readings for Saturday, 10 February 2024

Scholastica, Virgin, Religious Obligatory Memorial First Reading: First Kings 12: 26-32; 13: 33-34 Responsorial Psalm: Psalms 106: 6-7ab, 19-20, 21-22 Alleluia: Matthew 4: 4b

Gospel: Mark 8: 1-10
Lectionary: 334
First Reading: First Kings 12: 26-32; 13: 33-34

26 And Jeroboam said in his heart: Now shall the kingdom return to the house of David,

27 If this people go up to offer sacrifices in the house of the Lord at Jerusalem: and the heart of this people will turn to their lord Roboam the king of Juda, and they will kill me, and return to him.

28 And finding out a device he made two golden calves, and said to them: Go ye up no more to Jerusalem: Behold thy gods, O Israel, who brought thee out of the land of Egypt.

29 And he set the one in Bethel, and the other in Dan:

30 And this thing became an occasion of sin: for the people went to adore the calf as far as Dan.

31 And he made temples in the high places, and priests of the lowest of the people, who were not of the sons of Levi.

32 And he appointed a feast in the eighth month, on the fifteenth day of the month, after the manner of the feast that was celebrated in Juda. And going up to the altar, he did in like manner in Bethel, to sacrifice to the calves, which he had made: and he placed in Bethel priests of the high places, which he had made.

13:33 After these words Jeroboam came not back from his wicked way: but on the contrary he made of the meanest of the people priests of the high places: whosoever would, he filled his hand, and he was made a priest of the high places.

34 And for this cause did the house of Jeroboam sin, and was cut off and destroyed from the face of the earth.

Responsorial Psalm: Psalms 106: 6-7ab, 19-20, 21-22 R. (4a) Remember us, O Lord, as you favor your people.

6 We have sinned with our fathers: we have acted unjustly, we have wrought iniquity.

7ab Our fathers understood not thy wonders in Egypt.
R. Remember us, O Lord, as you favor your people.
19 They made also a calf in Horeb: and they adored the graven thing.
20 And they changed their glory into the likeness of a calf that eateth grass. R. Remember us, O Lord, as you favor your people.

21 They forgot God, who saved them, who had done great things in Egypt, 22 Wondrous works in the land of Cham: terrible things in the Red Sea.

R. Remember us, O Lord, as you favor your people.

Alleluia: Matthew 4: 4b R. Alleluia, alleluia.

4b One does not live on bread alone, but on every word that comes forth from the mouth of God.

R. Alleluia, alleluia.

Gospel: Mark 8: 1-10
1 In those days again, when there was a great multitude, and had nothing to eat; calling his disciples together, he saith to them:

2 I have compassion on the multitude, for behold they have now been with me three days, and have nothing to eat.

3 And if I shall send them away fasting to their home, they will faint in the way; for some of them came from afar off.

4 And his disciples answered him: From whence can any one fill them here with bread in the wilderness?

5 And he asked them: How many loaves have ye? Who said: Seven.

6 And taking the seven loaves, giving thanks, he broke, and gave to his disciples for to set before them; and they set them before the people.

7 And they had a few little fishes; and he blessed them, and commanded them to be set before them.

8 And they did eat and were filled; and they took up that which was left of the fragments, seven baskets.

9 And they that had eaten were about four thousand; and he sent them away.

10 And immediately going up into a ship with his disciples, he came into the parts of Dalmanutha.

Daily Mass Readings for Sunday, 11 February 2024

Sixth Sunday in Ordinary Time
First Reading: Leviticus 13: 1-2, 44-46 Responsorial Psalm: Psalms 32: 1-2, 5, 11 Second Reading: First Corinthians 10: 31 – 11: 1 Alleluia: Luke 7: 16 Gospel: Mark 1: 40-45
Lectionary: 77
First Reading: Leviticus 13: 1-2, 44-46
1 And the Lord spoke to Moses and Aaron, saying:

2 The man in whose skin or flesh shalt arise a different colour or a blister, or as it were something shining, that is, the stroke of the leprosy, shall be brought to Aaron the priest, or any one of his sons.

44 Now whosoever shall be defiled with the leprosy, and is separated by the judgment of the priest,

45 Shall have his clothes hanging loose, his head bare, his mouth covered with a cloth, and he shall cry out that he is defiled and unclean.

46 All the time that he is a leper and unclean, he shall dwell alone without the camp.

Responsorial Psalm: Psalms 32: 1-2, 5, 11
R. (7) I turn to you, Lord, in time of trouble, and you fill me with the joy of salvation.

1 To David himself, understanding. Blessed are they whose iniquities are forgiven, and whose sins are covered.

2 Blessed is the man to whom the Lord hath not imputed sin, and in whose spirit there is no guile.

R. I turn to you, Lord, in time of trouble, and you fill me with the joy of salvation.

5 I have acknowledged my sin to thee, and my injustice I have not concealed. I said I will confess against myself my injustice to the Lord: and thou hast forgiven the wickedness of my sin.

R. I turn to you, Lord, in time of trouble, and you fill me with the joy of salvation.

11 Be glad in the Lord, and rejoice, ye just, and glory, all ye right of heart.

R. I turn to you, Lord, in time of trouble, and you fill me with the joy of salvation.

Second Reading: First Corinthians 10: 31 – 11: 1
31 Therefore, whether you eat or drink, or whatsoever else you do, do all to the glory of God.

32 Be without offence to the Jews, and to the Gentiles, and to the church of God:

33 As I also in all things please all men, not seeking that which is profitable to myself, but to many, that may be saved.

11:1 Be ye followers of me, as I also am of Christ.

Alleluia: Luke 7: 16 R. Alleluia, alleluia.

16 A great prophet has arisen in our midst, God has visited his people. R. Alleluia, alleluia.

Gospel: Mark 1: 40-45
40 And there came a leper to him, beseeching him, and kneeling down said to him: If thou wilt, thou canst make me clean.

41 And Jesus having compassion on him, stretched forth his hand; and touching him, saith to him: I will. Be thou made clean.

42 And when he had spoken, immediately the leprosy departed from him, and he was made clean.

43 And he strictly charged him, and forthwith sent him away.

44 And he saith to him: See thou tell no one; but go, shew thyself to the high priest, and offer for thy cleansing the things that Moses commanded, for a testimony to them.

45 But he being gone out, began to publish and to blaze abroad the word: so that he could not openly go into the city, but was without in desert places: and they flocked to him from all sides.

Daily Mass Readings for Monday, 12 February 2024 Ordinary Weekday

First Reading: James 1: 1-11
Responsorial Psalm: Psalms 119: 67, 68, 71, 72, 75, 76
Alleluia: John 14: 6
Gospel: Mark 8: 11-13
Lectionary: 335

First Reading: James 1: 1-11

1 James the servant of God, and of our Lord Jesus Christ, to the twelve tribes which are scattered abroad, greeting.

2 My brethren, count it all joy, when you shall fall into divers temptations;

3 Knowing that the trying of your faith worketh patience.

4 And patience hath a perfect work; that you may be perfect and entire, failing in nothing.

5 But if any of you want wisdom, let him ask of God, who giveth to all men abundantly, and upbraideth not; and it shall be given him.

6 But let him ask in faith, nothing wavering. For he that wavereth is like a wave of the sea, which is moved and carried about by the wind.

7 Therefore let not that man think that he shall receive any thing of the Lord.

8 A double minded man is inconstant in all his ways.

9 But let the brother of low condition glory in his exaltation:

10 And the rich, in his being low; because as the flower of the grass shall he pass away.

11 For the sun rose with a burning heat, and parched the grass, and the flower thereof fell off, and the beauty of the shape thereof perished: so also shall the rich man fade away in his ways.

Responsorial Psalm: Psalms 119: 67, 68, 71, 72, 75, 76

R. (77a) Be kind to me, Lord, and I shall live.
67 Before I was humbled I offended; therefore have I kept thy word. R. Be kind to me, Lord, and I shall live.
68 Thou art good; and in thy goodness teach me thy justifications.
R. Be kind to me, Lord, and I shall live.

71 It is good for me that thou hast humbled me, that I may learn thy justifications.

R. Be kind to me, Lord, and I shall live.

72 The law of thy mouth is good to me, above thousands of gold and silver.

R. Be kind to me, Lord, and I shall live.

75 I know, O Lord, that thy judgments are equity: and in thy truth thou hast humbled me.

R. Be kind to me, Lord, and I shall live.

76 O! let thy mercy be for my comfort, according to thy word unto thy servant.

R. Be kind to me, Lord, and I shall live.

Alleluia: John 14: 6 R. Alleluia, alleluia.

6 I am the way and the truth and the life, says the Lord; no one comes to the Father except through me.

R. Alleluia, alleluia.

Gospel: Mark 8: 11-13
11 And the Pharisees came forth, and began to question with him, asking him a sign from heaven, tempting him.

12 And sighing deeply in spirit, he saith: Why doth this generation seek a sign? Amen, I say to you, a sign shall not be given to this generation.

13 And leaving them, he went up again into the ship, and passed to the other side of the water.

Daily Mass Readings for Tuesday, 13 February 2024

Ordinary Weekday
First Reading: James 1: 12-18
Responsorial Psalm: Psalms 94: 12-13a, 14-15, 18-19
Alleluia: John 14: 23
Gospel: Mark 8: 14-21
Lectionary: 336
First Reading: James 1: 12-18

12 Blessed is the man that endureth temptation; for when he hath been proved, he shall receive a crown of life, which God hath promised to them that love him.

13 Let no man, when he is tempted, say that he is tempted by God. For God is not a tempter of evils, and he tempteth no man.

14 But every man is tempted by his own concupiscence, being drawn away and allured.

15 Then when concupiscence hath conceived, it bringeth forth sin. But sin, when it is completed, begetteth death.

16 Do not err, therefore, my dearest brethren.

17 Every best gift, and every perfect gift, is from above, coming down from the Father of lights, with whom there is no change, nor shadow of alteration.

18 For of his own will hath he begotten us by the word of truth, that we might be some beginning of his creatures.

Responsorial Psalm: Psalms 94: 12-13a, 14-15, 18-19 R. (12a) Blessed the man you instruct, O Lord.

12 Blessed is the man whom thou shalt instruct, O Lord: and shalt teach him out of thy law.

13a That thou mayst give him rest from the evil days. R. Blessed the man you instruct, O Lord.

14 For the Lord will not cast off his people: neither will he forsake his own inheritance.

15 Until justice be turned into judgment: and they that are near it are all the upright in heart.

R. Blessed the man you instruct, O Lord.
18 If I said: My foot is moved: thy mercy, O Lord, assisted me.

19 According to the multitude of my sorrows in my heart, thy comforts have given joy to my soul.

R. Blessed the man you instruct, O Lord.

Alleluia: John 14: 23 R. Alleluia, alleluia.

23 Whoever loves me will keep my word, says the Lord; and my Father will love him and we will come to him.

R. Alleluia, alleluia.

Gospel: Mark 8: 14-21
14 And they forgot to take bread; and they had but one loaf with them in the ship.

15 And he charged them, saying: Take heed and beware of the leaven of the Pharisees, and of the leaven of Herod.

16 And they reasoned among themselves, saying: Because we have no bread.

17 Which Jesus knowing, saith to them: Why do you reason, because you have no bread? do you not yet know nor understand? have you still your heart blinded?

18 Having eyes, see you not? and having ears, hear you not? neither do you remember.

19 When I broke the five loaves among five thousand, how many baskets full of fragments took you up? They say to him, Twelve.

20 When also the seven loaves among four thousand, how many baskets of fragments took you up? And they say to him, Seven.

21 And he said to them: How do you not yet understand?

Daily Mass Readings for Wednesday, 14 February 2024

Ash Wednesday, Begin Lenten Preparation for the Easter Triduum, Not a Holy Day of Obligation, Day of Fast (Ages 18-59) and Abstinence from Meat (Age 14 and Up)
First Reading: Joel 2: 12-18
Responsorial Psalm: Psalms 51: 3-4, 5-6ab, 12-13, 14 and 17
Second Reading: Second Corinthians 5: 20 – 6:2
Verse Before the Gospel: Psalms 95: 8
Gospel: Matthew 6: 1-6, 16-18
Lectionary: 219
First Reading: Joel 2: 12-18
12 Now therefore saith the Lord: Be converted to me with all your heart, in fasting, and in weeping, and in mourning.

13 And rend your hearts, and not your garments, and turn to the Lord your God: for he is gracious and merciful, patient and rich in mercy, and ready to repent of the evil.

14 Who knoweth but he will return, and forgive, and leave a blessing behind him, sacrifice and libation to the Lord your God?

15 Blow the trumpet in Sion, sanctify a fast, call a solemn assembly,

16 Gather together the people, sanctify the church, assemble the ancients, gather together the little ones, and them that suck at the breasts: let the bridegroom go forth from his bed, and the bride out of her bride chamber.

17 Between the porch and the altar the priests the Lord's ministers shall weep, and shall say: Spare, O Lord, spare thy people: and give not thy inheritance to reproach, that the heathen should rule over them. Why should they say among the nations: Where is their God?

18 The Lord hath been zealous for his land, and hath spared his people.

Responsorial Psalm: Psalms 51: 3-4, 5-6ab, 12-13, 14 and 17 R. (3a) Be merciful, O Lord, for we have sinned.

3 Have mercy on me, O God, according to thy great mercy. And according to the multitude of thy tender mercies blot out my iniquity.

4 Wash me yet more from my iniquity, and cleanse me from my sin. R. Be merciful, O Lord, for we have sinned.
5 For I know my iniquity, and my sin is always before me.
6ab To thee only have I sinned, and have done evil before thee.

R. Be merciful, O Lord, for we have sinned.

12 Create a clean heart in me, O God: and renew a right spirit within my bowels.

13 Cast me not away from thy face; and take not thy holy spirit from me. R. Be merciful, O Lord, for we have sinned.

14 Restore unto me the joy of thy salvation, and strengthen me with a perfect spirit.

17 O Lord, thou wilt open my lips: and my mouth shall declare thy praise.

R. Be merciful, O Lord, for we have sinned.

Second Reading: Second Corinthians 5: 20 – 6:2
20 For Christ therefore we are ambassadors, God as it were exhorting by us. For Christ, we beseech you, be reconciled to God.

21 Him, who knew no sin, he hath made sin for us, that we might be made the justice of God in him.

6:1 And we helping do exhort you, that you receive not the grace of God in vain.

2 For he saith: In an accepted time have I heard thee; and in the day of salvation have I helped thee. Behold, now is the acceptable time; behold, now is the day of salvation.

Verse Before the Gospel: Psalms 95: 8
8 If today you hear his voice, harden not your hearts.

Gospel: Matthew 6: 1-6, 16-18
1 Take heed that you do not your justice before men, to be seen by them: otherwise you shall not have a reward of your Father who is in heaven.

2 Therefore when thou dost an almsdeed, sound not a trumpet before thee, as the hypocrites do in the synagogues and in the streets, that they may be honoured by men. Amen I say to you, they have received their reward.

3 But when thou dost alms, let not thy left hand know what thy right hand doth.

4 That thy alms may be in secret, and thy Father who seeth in secret will repay thee.

5 And when ye pray, you shall not be as the hypocrites, that love to stand and pray in the synagogues and corners of the streets, that they may be seen by men: Amen I say to you, they have received their reward.

6 But thou when thou shalt pray, enter into thy chamber, and having shut the door, pray to thy Father in secret: and thy Father who seeth in secret will repay thee.

16 And when you fast, be not as the hypocrites, sad. For they disfigure their faces, that they may appear unto men to fast. Amen I say to you, they have received their reward.

17 But thou, when thou fastest anoint thy head, and wash thy face;

18 That thou appear not to men to fast, but to thy Father who is in secret: and thy Father who seeth in secret, will repay thee.

Daily Mass Readings for Thursday, 15 February 2024

Thursday after Ash Wednesday
First Reading: Deuteronomy 30: 15-20
Responsorial Psalm: Psalms 1: 1-2, 3, 4 and 6
Verse Before the Gospel: Matthew 4: 17
Gospel: Luke 9: 22-25
Lectionary: 220
First Reading: Deuteronomy 30: 15-20
15 Consider that I have set before thee this day life and good, and on the other hand death and evil:

16 That thou mayst love the Lord thy God, and walk in his ways, and keep his commandments and ceremonies and judgments, and thou mayst live, and he may multiply thee, and bless thee in the land, which thou shalt go in to possess.

17 But if thy heart be turned away, so that thou wilt not hear, and being deceived with error thou adore strange gods, and serve them:

18 I foretell thee this day that thou shalt perish, and shalt remain but a short time in the land, to which thou shalt pass over the Jordan, and shalt go in to possess it.

19 I call heaven and earth to witness this day, that I have set before you life and death, blessing and cursing. Choose therefore life, that both thou and thy seed may live:

20 And that thou mayst love the Lord thy God, and obey his voice, and adhere to him (for he is thy life, and the length of thy days,) that thou mayst dwell in the land, for which the Lord swore to thy fathers Abraham, Isaac, and Jacob that he would give it them.

Responsorial Psalm: Psalms 1: 1-2, 3, 4 and 6
R. (40: 5a) Blessed are they who hope in the Lord.

1 Blessed is the man who hath not walked in the counsel of the ungodly, nor stood in the way of sinners, nor sat in the chair of pestilence.

2 But his will is in the law of the Lord, and on his law he shall meditate day and night.

R. Blessed are they who hope in the Lord.

3 And he shall be like a tree which is planted near the running waters, which shall bring forth its fruit, in due season. And his leaf shall not fall off: and all whatsoever he shall do shall prosper.

R. Blessed are they who hope in the Lord.

4 Not so the wicked, not so: but like the dust, which the wind driveth from the face of the earth.

6 For the Lord knoweth the way of the just: and the way of the wicked shall perish.

R. Blessed are they who hope in the Lord.

Verse Before the Gospel: Matthew 4: 17
17 Repent, says the Lord; the Kingdom of heaven is at hand.

Gospel: Luke 9: 22-25
22 Saying: The Son of man must suffer many things, and be rejected by the ancients and chief priests and scribes, and be killed, and the third day rise again.

23 And he said to all: If any man will come after me, let him deny himself, and take up his cross daily, and follow me.

24 For whosoever will save his life, shall lose it; for he that shall lose his life for my sake, shall save it.

25 For what is a man advantaged, if he gain the whole world, and lose himself, and cast away himself?

Daily Mass Readings for Friday, 16 February 2024

Friday after Ash Wednesday, Day of Abstinence from Meat (Age 14 and Up)
First Reading: Isaiah 58: 1-9a
Responsorial Psalm: Psalms 51: 3-4, 5-6ab, 18-19
Verse Before the Gospel: Amos 5: 14

Gospel: Matthew 9: 14-15
Lectionary: 221
First Reading: Isaiah 58: 1-9a
1 Cry, cease not, lift up thy voice like a trumpet, and shew my people their wicked doings, and the house of Jacob their sins.

2 For they seek me from day to day, sad desire to know my ways, as a nation that hath done justice, and hath not forsaken the judgment of their God: they ask of me the judgments of justice: they are willing to approach to God.

3 Why have we fasted, and thou hast not regarded: have we humbled our souls, and thou hast not taken notice? Behold in the day of your fast your own will is found, and you exact of all your debtors.

4 Behold you fast for debates and strife. and strike with the fist wickedly. Do not fast as you have done until this day, to make your cry to be heard on high.

5 Is this such a fast as I have chosen: for a man to afflict his soul for a day? is this it, to wind his head about like a circle, and to spread sackcloth and ashes? wilt thou call this a fast, and a day acceptable to the Lord?

6 Is not this rather the fast that I have chosen? loose the bands of wickedness, undo the bundles that oppress, let them that are broken go free, and break

asunder every burden.

7 Deal thy bread to the hungry, and bring the needy and the harbourless into thy house: when thou shalt see one naked, cover him, and despise not thy own flesh.

8 Then shall thy light break forth as the morning, and thy health shall speedily arise, and thy justice shall go before thy face, and the glory of the Lord shall gather thee up.

9a Then shalt thou call, and the Lord shall hear: thou shalt cry, and he shall say, Here I am.

Responsorial Psalm: Psalms 51: 3-4, 5-6ab, 18-19
R. (19b) A heart contrite and humbled, O God, you will not spurn.

3 Have mercy on me, O God, according to thy great mercy. And according to the multitude of thy tender mercies blot out my iniquity.

4 Wash me yet more from my iniquity, and cleanse me from my sin.

R. A heart contrite and humbled, O God, you will not spurn.
5 For I know my iniquity, and my sin is always before me.
6ab To thee only have I sinned, and have done evil before thee. R. A heart contrite and humbled, O God, you will not spurn.

18 For if thou hadst desired sacrifice, I would indeed have given it: with burnt offerings thou wilt not be delighted.

19 A sacrifice to God is an afflicted spirit: a contrite and humbled heart, O God, thou wilt not despise.

R. A heart contrite and humbled, O God, you will not spurn.

Verse Before the Gospel: Amos 5: 14
14 Seek good and not evil so that you may live, and the Lord will be with you.

Gospel: Matthew 9: 14-15
14 Then came to him the disciples of John, saying: Why do we and the Pharisees fast often, but thy disciples do not fast?

15 And Jesus said to them: Can the children of the bridegroom mourn, as long as the bridegroom is with them? But the days will come, when the bridegroom shall be taken away from them, and then they shall fast.

Daily Mass Readings for Saturday, 17 February 2024

Saturday after Ash Wednesday/ Seven Founders of the Order of Servites, Religious Founder
First Reading: Isaiah 58: 9b-14
Responsorial Psalm: Psalms 86: 1-2, 3-4, 5-6
Verse Before the Gospel: Ezekiel 33: 11
Gospel: Luke 5: 27-32
Lectionary: 222
First Reading: Isaiah 58: 9b-14

9b Thus says the Lord: If thou wilt take away the chain out of the midst of thee, and cease to stretch out the finger, and to speak that which profiteth not.

10 When thou shalt pour out thy soul to the hungry, and shalt satisfy the afflicted soul then shall thy light rise up in darkness, and thy darkness shall be as the noonday.

11 And the Lord will give thee rest continually, and will fill thy soul with brightness, and deliver thy bones, and thou shalt be like a watered garden, and like a fountain of water whose waters shall not fail.

12 And the places that have been desolate for ages shall be built in thee: thou shalt raise up the foundations of generation and generation: and thou shalt be called the repairer of the fences, turning the paths into rest.

13 If thou turn away thy foot from the sabbath, from doing thy own will in my holy day, and call the sabbath delightful, and the holy of the Lord glorious, and glorify him, while thou dost not thy own ways, and thy own will is not found: to speak a word:

14 Then shalt thou be delighted in the Lord, and I will lift thee up above the high places of the earth, and will feed thee with the inheritance of Jacob thy father. For the mouth of the Lord hath spoken it.

Responsorial Psalm: Psalms 86: 1-2, 3-4, 5-6
R. (11ab) Teach me your way, O Lord, that I may walk in your truth.

1 A prayer for David himself. Incline thy ear, O Lord, and hear me: for I am needy and poor.

2 Preserve my soul, for I am holy: save thy servant, O my God, that trusteth in thee.

R. Teach me your way, O Lord, that I may walk in your truth.
3 Have mercy on me, O Lord, for I have cried to thee all the day.

4 Give joy to the soul of thy servant, for to thee, O Lord, I have lifted up my soul.

R. Teach me your way, O Lord, that I may walk in your truth.

5 For thou, O Lord, art sweet and mild: and plenteous in mercy to all that call upon thee.

6 Give ear, O Lord, to my prayer: and attend to the voice of my petition. R. Teach me your way, O Lord, that I may walk in your truth.

Verse Before the Gospel: Ezekiel 33: 11
11 I take no pleasure in the death of the wicked man, says the Lord, but rather in his conversion, that he may live.

Gospel: Luke 5: 27-32
27 And after these things he went forth, and saw a publican named Levi, sitting at the receipt of custom, and he said to him: Follow me.

28 And leaving all things, he rose up and followed him.

29 And Levi made him a great feast in his own house; and there was a great company of publicans, and of others, that were at table with them.

30 But the Pharisees and scribes murmured, saying to his disciples: Why do you eat and drink with publicans and sinners?

31 And Jesus answering, said to them: They that are whole, need not the physician: but they that are sick.

32 I came not to call the just, but sinners to penance.

Daily Mass Readings for Sunday, 18 February 2024

First Sunday Of Lent
First Reading: Genesis 9: 8-15
Responsorial Psalm: Psalms 25: 4-5, 6-7, 8-9
Second Reading: First Peter 3: 18-22
Verse Before the Gospel: Matthew 4: 4b
Gospel: Mark 1: 12-15
Lectionary: 23
First Reading: Genesis 9: 8-15
8 Thus also said God to Noe, and to his sons with him,

9 Behold I will establish my covenant with you, and with your seed after you:

10 And with every living soul that is with you, as well in all birds as in cattle and beasts of the earth, that are come forth out of the ark, and in all the beasts of the earth.

11 I will establish my covenant with you, and all flesh shall be no more destroyed with the waters of a flood, neither shall there be from henceforth a flood to waste the earth.

12 And God said: This is the sign of the covenant which I give between me and you, and to every living soul that is with you, for perpetual generations.

13 I will set my bow in the clouds, and it shall be the sign of a covenant between me, and between the earth.

14 And when I shall cover the sky with clouds, my bow shall appear in the clouds:

15 And I will remember my covenant with you, and with every living soul that beareth flesh: and there shall no more be waters of a flood to destroy all flesh.

Responsorial Psalm: Psalms 25: 4-5, 6-7, 8-9
R. (10) Your ways, O Lord, are love and truth to those who keep your covenant.

4 Let all them be confounded that act unjust things without cause. shew, O Lord, thy ways to me, and teach me thy paths.

5 Direct me in thy truth, and teach me; for thou art God my Saviour; and on thee have I waited all the day long.

R. Your ways, O Lord, are love and truth to those who keep your covenant.

6 Remember, O Lord, thy bowels of compassion; and thy mercies that are from the beginning of the world.

7 The sins of my youth and my ignorances do not remember. According to thy mercy remember thou me: for thy goodness' sake, O Lord.

R. Your ways, O Lord, are love and truth to those who keep your covenant.

8 The Lord is sweet and righteous: therefore he will give a law to sinners in the way.

9 He will guide the mild in judgment: he will teach the meek his ways.
R. Your ways, O Lord, are love and truth to those who keep your covenant.

Second Reading: First Peter 3: 18-22
18 Because Christ also died once for our sins, the just for the unjust: that he might offer us to God, being put to death indeed in the flesh, but enlivened in the spirit,

19 In which also coming he preached to those spirits that were in prison:

20 Which had been some time incredulous, when they waited for the patience of God in the days of Noe, when the ark was a building: wherein a few, that is, eight souls, were saved by water.

21 Whereunto baptism being of the like form, now saveth you also: not the putting away of the filth of the flesh, but the examination of a good conscience towards God by the resurrection of Jesus Christ.

22 Who is on the right hand of God, swallowing down death, that we might be made heirs of life everlasting: being gone into heaven, the angels and powers and virtues being made subject to him.

Verse Before the Gospel: Matthew 4: 4b
4b One does not live on bread alone, but on every word that comes forth from the mouth of God.

Gospel: Mark 1: 12-15

12 And immediately the Spirit drove him out into the desert.

13 And he was in the desert forty days and forty nights, and was tempted by Satan; and he was with beasts, and the angels ministered to him.

14 And after that John was delivered up, Jesus came into Galilee, preaching the gospel of the kingdom of God,

15 And saying: The time is accomplished, and the kingdom of God is at hand: repent, and believe the gospel.

Daily Mass Readings for Monday, 19 February 2024

Lenten Weekday
First Reading: Leviticus 19: 1-2, 11-18 Responsorial Psalm: Psalms 19: 8, 9, 10, 15
Verse Before the Gospel: Second Corinthians 6: 2b Gospel: Matthew 25: 31-46
Lectionary: 224
First Reading: Leviticus 19: 1-2, 11-18
1 The Lord spoke to Moses, saying:

2 Speak to all the congregation of the children of Israel, and thou shalt say to them: Be ye holy, because I the Lord your God am holy.

11 You shall not steal. You shall not lie, neither shall any man deceive his neighbour.

12 Thou shalt not swear falsely by my name, nor profane the name of thy God. I am the Lord.

13 Thou shalt not calumniate thy neighbour, nor oppress him by violence. The wages of him that hath been hired by thee shall not abide with thee until the morning.

14 Thou shalt not speak evil of the deaf, nor put a stumblingblock before the blind: but thou shalt fear the Lord thy God, because I am the Lord.

15 Thou shalt not do that which is unjust, nor judge unjustly. Respect not the person of the poor, nor honour the countenance of the mighty. But judge thy neighbour according to justice.

16 Thou shalt not be a detractor nor a whisperer among the people. Thou shalt not stand against the blood of thy neighbour. I am the Lord.

17 Thou shalt not hate thy brother in thy heart, but reprove him openly, lest thou incur sin through him.

18 Seek not revenge, nor be mindful of the injury of thy citizens. Thou shalt love thy friend as thyself. I am the Lord.

Responsorial Psalm: Psalms 19: 8, 9, 10, 15
R. (John 6:63b) Your words, Lord, are Spirit and life.

8 The law of the Lord is unspotted, converting souls: the testimony of the Lord is faithful, giving wisdom to little ones.

R. Your words, Lord, are Spirit and life.

9 The justices of the Lord are right, rejoicing hearts: the commandment of the Lord is lightsome, enlightening the eyes.

R. Your words, Lord, are Spirit and life.

10 The fear of the Lord is holy, enduring for ever and ever: the judgments of the Lord are true, justified in themselves.

R. Your words, Lord, are Spirit and life.

15 And the words of my mouth shall be such as may please: and the meditation of my heart always in thy sight. O Lord, my helper, and my

redeemer.
R. Your words, Lord, are Spirit and life.

Verse Before the Gospel: Second Corinthians 6: 2b
2b Behold, now is a very acceptable time; behold, now is the day of salvation.

Gospel: Matthew 25: 31-46
31 And when the Son of man shall come in his majesty, and all the angels with him, then shall he sit upon the seat of his majesty.

32 And all nations shall be gathered together before him, and he shall separate them one from another, as the shepherd separateth the sheep from the goats:

33 And he shall set the sheep on his right hand, but the goats on his left.

34 Then shall the king say to them that shall be on his right hand: Come, ye blessed of my Father, possess you the kingdom prepared for you from the foundation of the world.

35 For I was hungry, and you gave me to eat; I was thirsty, and you gave me to drink; I was a stranger, and you took me in:

36 Naked, and you covered me: sick, and you visited me: I was in prison, and you came to me.

37 Then shall the just answer him, saying: Lord, when did we see thee hungry, and fed thee; thirsty, and gave thee drink?

38 And when did we see thee a stranger, and took thee in? or naked, and covered thee?

39 Or when did we see thee sick or in prison, and came to thee?

40 And the king answering, shall say to them: Amen I say to you, as long as you did it to one of these my least brethren, you did it to me.

41 Then he shall say to them also that shall be on his left hand: Depart from me, you cursed, into everlasting fire which was prepared for the devil and his angels.

42 For I was hungry, and you gave me not to eat: I was thirsty, and you gave me not to drink.

43 I was a stranger, and you took me not in: naked, and you covered me not: sick and in prison, and you did not visit me.

44 Then they also shall answer him, saying: Lord, when did we see thee hungry, or thirsty, or a stranger, or naked, or sick, or in prison, and did not minister to thee?

45 Then he shall answer them, saying: Amen I say to you, as long as you did it not to one of these least, neither did you do it to me.

46 And these shall go into everlasting punishment: but the just, into life everlasting.

Daily Mass Readings for Tuesday, 20 February 2024

Lenten Weekday
First Reading: Isaiah 55: 10-11
Responsorial Psalm: Psalms 34: 4-5, 6-7, 16-17, 18-19
Verse Before the Gospel: Matthew 4: 4b
Gospel: Matthew 6: 7-15
Lectionary: 225
First Reading: Isaiah 55: 10-11

10 And as the rain and the snow come down from heaven, and return no more thither, but soak the earth, and water it, and make it to spring, and give seed to the sower, and bread to the eater:

11 So shall my word be, which shall go forth from my mouth: it shall not return to me void, but it shall do whatsoever I please, and shall prosper in the things for which I sent it.

Responsorial Psalm: Psalms 34: 4-5, 6-7, 16-17, 18-19 R. (18b) From all their distress God rescues the just.

4 O magnify the Lord with me; and let us extol his name together.

5 I sought the Lord, and he heard me; and he delivered me from all my troubles.

R. From all their distress God rescues the just.

6 Come ye to him and be enlightened: and your faces shall not be confounded.

7 This poor man cried, and the Lord heard him: and saved him out of all his troubles.

R. From all their distress God rescues the just.

16 The eyes of the Lord are upon the just: and his ears unto their prayers.

17 But the countenance of the Lord is against them that do evil things: to cut off the remembrance of them from the earth.

R. From all their distress God rescues the just.

18 The just cried, and the Lord heard them: and delivered them out of all their troubles.

19 The Lord is nigh unto them that are of a contrite heart: and he will save the humble of spirit.

R. From all their distress God rescues the just.

Verse Before the Gospel: Matthew 4: 4b
4b One does not live on bread alone, but on every word that comes forth from the mouth of God.

Gospel: Matthew 6: 7-15
7 And when you are praying, speak not much, as the heathens. For they think that in their much speaking they may be heard.

8 Be not you therefore like to them, for your Father knoweth what is needful for you, before you ask him.

9 Thus therefore shall you pray: Our Father who art in heaven, hallowed be thy name.

10 Thy kingdom come. Thy will be done on earth as it is in heaven. 11 Give us this day our supersubstantial bread.
12 And forgive us our debts, as we also forgive our debtors.
13 And lead us not into temptation. But deliver us from evil. Amen.

14 For if you will forgive men their offences, your heavenly Father will forgive you also your offences.

15 But if you will not forgive men, neither will your Father forgive you your offences.

Daily Mass Readings for Wednesday, 21 February 2024

Lenten Weekday/ Peter Damian, Bishop, Doctor First Reading: Jonah 3: 1-10
Responsorial Psalm: Psalms 51: 3-4, 12-13, 18-19 Verse Before the Gospel: Joel 2: 12-13

Gospel: Luke 11: 29-32

Lectionary: 226
First Reading: Jonah 3: 1-10
1 And the word of the Lord came to Jonas the second time, saying:

2 Arise, and go to Ninive the great city: and preach in it the preaching that I bid thee.

3 And Jonas arose, and went to Ninive, according to the word of the Lord: now Ninive was a great city of three days' journey.

4 And Jonas began to enter into the city one day's journey: and he cried, and said: Yet forty days, and Ninive shall be destroyed.

5 And the men of Ninive believed in God: and they proclaimed a fast, and put on sackcloth from the greatest to the least.

6 And the word came to the king of Ninive; and he rose up out of his throne, and cast away his robe from him, and was clothed with sackcloth, and sat in ashes.

7 And he caused it to be proclaimed and published in Ninive from the mouth of the king and of his princes, saying: Let neither men nor beasts, oxen nor sheep, taste any thing: let them not feed, nor drink water.

8 And let men and beasts be covered with sackcloth, and cry to the Lord with all their strength, and let them turn every one from his evil way, and from the iniquity that is in their hands.

9 Who can tell if God will turn, and forgive: and will turn away from his fierce anger, and we shall not perish?

10 And God saw their works, that they were turned from their evil way: and God had mercy with regard to the evil which he had said that he would do to them, and he did it not.

Responsorial Psalm: Psalms 51: 3-4, 12-13, 18-19

R. (19b) A heart contrite and humbled, O God, you will not spurn.

3 Have mercy on me, O God, according to thy great mercy. And according to the multitude of thy tender mercies blot out my iniquity.

4 Wash me yet more from my iniquity, and cleanse me from my sin.

R. A heart contrite and humbled, O God, you will not spurn.

12 Create a clean heart in me, O God: and renew a right spirit within my bowels.

13 Cast me not away from thy face; and take not thy holy spirit from me. R. A heart contrite and humbled, O God, you will not spurn.

18 For if thou hadst desired sacrifice, I would indeed have given it: with burnt offerings thou wilt not be delighted.

19 A sacrifice to God is an afflicted spirit: a contrite and humbled heart, O God, thou wilt not despise.

R. A heart contrite and humbled, O God, you will not spurn.

Verse Before the Gospel: Joel 2: 12-13
12-13 Even now, says the LORD, return to me with your whole heart for I am gracious and merciful.

Gospel: Luke 11: 29-32
29 And the multitudes running together, he began to say: This generation is a wicked generation: it asketh a sign, and a sign shall not be given it, but the sign of Jonas the prophet.

30 For as Jonas was a sign to the Ninivites; so shall the Son of man also be to this generation.

31 The queen of the south shall rise in the judgment with the men of this generation, and shall condemn them: because she came from the ends of the earth to hear the wisdom of Solomon; and behold more than Solomon here.

32 The men of Ninive shall rise in the judgment with this generation, and shall condemn it; because they did penance at the preaching of Jonas; and behold more than Jonas here.

Daily Mass Readings for Thursday, 22 February 2024

Chair of Peter, Apostle Feast
First Reading: First Peter 5: 1-4
Responsorial Psalm: Psalms 23: 1-3a, 4, 5, 6
Verse Before the Gospel: Matthew 16: 18
Gospel: Matthew 16: 13-19
Lectionary: 535
First Reading: First Peter 5: 1-4

1 The ancients therefore that are among you, I beseech, who am myself also an ancient, and a witness of the sufferings of Christ: as also a partaker of that glory which is to be revealed in time to come:

2 Feed the flock of God which is among you, taking care of it, not by constraint, but willingly, according to God: not for filthy lucre's sake, but voluntarily:

3 Neither as lording it over the clergy, but being made a pattern of the flock from the heart.

4 And when the prince of pastors shall appear, you shall receive a never fading crown of glory.

Responsorial Psalm: Psalms 23: 1-3a, 4, 5, 6
R. (1) The Lord is my shepherd; there is nothing I shall want.

1 The Lord ruleth me: and I shall want nothing.

2 He hath set me in a place of pasture. He hath brought me up, on the water of refreshment:

3a He hath converted my soul.
R. The Lord is my shepherd; there is nothing I shall want.

4 For though I should walk in the midst of the shadow of death, I will fear no evils, for thou art with me. Thy rod and thy staff, they have comforted me.

R. The Lord is my shepherd; there is nothing I shall want.

5 Thou hast prepared a table before me against them that afflict me. Thou hast anointed my head with oil; and my chalice which inebriateth me, how goodly is it!

R. The Lord is my shepherd; there is nothing I shall want.

6 And thy mercy will follow me all the days of my life. And that I may dwell in the house of the Lord unto length of days.

R. The Lord is my shepherd; there is nothing I shall want.

Verse Before the Gospel: Matthew 16: 18
18 You are Peter, and upon this rock I will build my Church; the gates of the netherworld shall not prevail against it.

Gospel: Matthew 16: 13-19
13 And Jesus came into the quarters of Caesarea Philippi: and he asked his disciples, saying: Whom do men say that the Son of man is?

14 But they said: Some John the Baptist, and other some Elias, and others Jeremias, or one of the prophets.

15 Jesus saith to them: But whom do you say that I am?

16 Simon Peter answered and said: Thou art Christ, the Son of the living God.

17 And Jesus answering, said to him: Blessed art thou, Simon Bar-Jona: because flesh and blood hath not revealed it to thee, but my Father who is in heaven.

18 And I say to thee: That thou art Peter; and upon this rock I will build my church, and the gates of hell shall not prevail against it.

19 And I will give to thee the keys of the kingdom of heaven. And whatsoever thou shalt bind upon earth, it shall be bound also in heaven: and whatsoever thou shalt loose upon earth, it shall be loosed also in heaven.

Daily Mass Readings for Friday, 23 February 2024

Lenten Weekday/ Polycarp, Bishop, Martyr, Day of Abstinence from Meat (Age 14 and Up)
First Reading: Ezekiel 18: 21-28
Responsorial Psalm: Psalms 130: 1-2, 3-4, 5-6, 7-8
Verse Before the Gospel: Ezekiel 18: 31
Gospel: Matthew 5: 20-26
Lectionary: 228
First Reading: Ezekiel 18: 21-28

21 But if the wicked do penance for all his sins which he hath committed, and keep all my commandments, and do judgment, and justice, living he shall live, and shall not die.

22 I will not remember all his iniquities that he hath done: in his justice which he hath wrought, he shall live.

23 Is it my will that a sinner should die, saith the Lord God, and not that he should be converted from his ways, and live?

24 But if the just man turn himself away from his justice, and do iniquity according to all the abominations which the wicked man useth to work, shall he live? all his justices which he hath done, shall not be remembered: in the prevarication, by which he hath prevaricated, and in his sin, which he hath committed, in them he shall die.

25 And you have said: The way of the Lord is not right. Hear ye, therefore, O house of Israel: Is it my way that is not right, and are not rather your ways perverse?

26 For when the just turneth himself away from his justice, and committeth iniquity, he shall die therein: in the injustice that he hath wrought he shall die.

27 And when the wicked turneth himself away from his wickedness, which he hath wrought, and doeth judgment, and justice: he shall save his soul alive.

28 Because he considereth and turneth away himself from all his iniquities which he hath wrought, he shall surely live, and not die.

Responsorial Psalm: Psalms 130: 1-2, 3-4, 5-6, 7-8 R. (3) If you, O Lord, mark iniquities, who can stand?

1 Out of the depths I have cried to thee, O Lord:

2 Lord, hear my voice. Let thy ears be attentive to the voice of my supplication.

R. If you, O Lord, mark iniquities, who can stand?
3 If thou, O Lord, wilt mark iniquities: Lord, who shall stand it.

4 For with thee there is merciful forgiveness: and by reason of thy law, I have waited for thee, O Lord. My soul hath relied on his word:

R. If you, O Lord, mark iniquities, who can stand?

5 My soul hath hoped in the Lord.
6 From the morning watch even until night, let Israel hope in the Lord.
R. If you, O Lord, mark iniquities, who can stand?
7 Because with the Lord there is mercy: and with him plentiful redemption. 8 And he shall redeem Israel from all his iniquities.
R. If you, O Lord, mark iniquities, who can stand?

Verse Before the Gospel: Ezekiel 18: 31
31 Cast away from you all the crimes you have committed, says the LORD, and make for yourselves a new heart and a new spirit.

Gospel: Matthew 5: 20-26
20 For I tell you, that unless your justice abound more than that of the scribes and Pharisees, you shall not enter into the kingdom of heaven.

21 You have heard that it was said to them of old: Thou shalt not kill. And whosoever shall kill shall be in danger of the judgment.

22 But I say to you, that whosoever is angry with his brother, shall be in danger of the judgment. And whosoever shall say to his brother, Raca, shall be in danger of the council. And whosoever shall say, Thou Fool, shall be in danger of hell fire.

23 If therefore thou offer thy gift at the altar, and there thou remember that thy brother hath any thing against thee;

24 Leave there thy offering before the altar, and go first to be reconciled to thy brother: and then coming thou shalt offer thy gift.

25 Be at agreement with thy adversary betimes, whilst thou art in the way with him: lest perhaps the adversary deliver thee to the judge, and the judge deliver thee to the officer, and thou be cast into prison.

26 Amen I say to thee, thou shalt not go out from thence till thou repay the last farthing.

Daily Mass Readings for Saturday, 24 February 2024

Lenten Weekday
First Reading: Deuteronomy 26: 16-19
Responsorial Psalm: Psalms 119: 1-2, 4-5, 7-8
Verse Before the Gospel: Second Corinthians 6: 2b
Gospel: Matthew 5: 43-48
Lectionary: 229
First Reading: Deuteronomy 26: 16-19

16 This day the Lord thy God hath commanded thee to do these commandments and judgments: and to keep and fulfill them with all thy heart, and with all thy soul.

17 Thou hast chosen the Lord this day to be thy God, and to walk in his ways and keep his ceremonies, and precepts, and judgments, and obey his command.

18 And the Lord hath chosen thee this day, to be his peculiar people, as he hath spoken to thee, and to keep all his commandments:

19 And to make thee higher than all nations which he hath created, to his own praise, and name, and glory: that thou mayst be a holy people of the Lord thy God, as he hath spoken.

Responsorial Psalm: Psalms 119: 1-2, 4-5, 7-8
R. (1b) Blessed are they who follow the law of the Lord!

1 Blessed are the undefiled in the way, who walk in the law of the Lord.

2 Blessed are they who search his testimonies: that seek him with their whole heart.

R. Blessed are they who follow the law of the Lord!
4 Thou hast commanded thy commandments to be kept most diligently. 5 O! that my ways may be directed to keep thy justifications.

R. Blessed are they who follow the law of the Lord!

7 I will praise thee with uprightness of heart, when I shall have learned the judgments of thy justice.

8 I will keep thy justifications: O! do not thou utterly forsake me. R. Blessed are they who follow the law of the Lord!

Verse Before the Gospel: Second Corinthians 6: 2b
2b Behold, now is a very acceptable time; behold, now is the day of salvation.

Gospel: Matthew 5: 43-48
43 You have heard that it hath been said, Thou shalt love thy neighbour, and hate thy enemy.

44 But I say to you, Love your enemies: do good to them that hate you: and pray for them that persecute and calumniate you:

45 That you may be the children of your Father who is in heaven, who maketh his sun to rise upon the good, and bad, and raineth upon the just and the unjust.

46 For if you love them that love you, what reward shall you have? do not even the publicans this?

47 And if you salute your brethren only, what do you more? do not also the heathens this?

48 Be you therefore perfect, as also your heavenly Father is perfect

Daily Mass Readings for Sunday, 25 February 2024

Second Sunday Of Lent
First Reading: Genesis 22: 1-2, 9a, 10-13, 15-18
Responsorial Psalm: Psalms 116: 10, 15, 16-17, 18-19
Second Reading: Romans 8: 31b-34
Verse Before the Gospel: Matthew 17: 5
Gospel: Mark 9: 2-10
Lectionary: 26
First Reading: Genesis 22: 1-2, 9a, 10-13, 15-18
1 After these things, God tempted Abraham, and said to him: Abraham, Abraham. And he answered: Here I am.

2 He said to him: Take thy only begotten son Isaac, whom thou lovest, and go into the land of vision: and there thou shalt offer him for an holocaust upon one of the mountains which I will shew thee.

9a And they came to the place which God had shewn him, where he built an altar, and laid the wood in order upon it.

10 And he put forth his hand and took the sword, to sacrifice his son.

11 And behold an angel of the Lord from heaven called to him, saying: Abraham, Abraham. And he answered: Here I am.

12 And he said to him: Lay not thy hand upon the boy, neither do thou any thing to him: now I know that thou fearest God, and hast not spared thy only

begotten son for my sake.

13 Abraham lifted up his eyes, and saw behind his back a ram amongst the briers sticking fast by the horns, which he took and offered for a holocaust instead of his son.

15 And the angel of the Lord called to Abraham a second time from heaven, saying:

16 By my own self have I sworn, saith the Lord: because thou hast done this thing, and hast not spared thy only begotten son for my sake:

17 I will bless thee, and I will multiply thy seed as the stars of heaven, and as the sand that is by the sea shore: thy seed shall possess the gates of their enemies.

18 And in thy seed shall all the nations of the earth be blessed, because thou hast obeyed my voice.

Responsorial Psalm: Psalms 116: 10, 15, 16-17, 18-19
R. (9) I will walk before the Lord, in the land of the living.

10 I have believed, therefore have I spoken; but I have been humbled exceedingly.

15 Precious in the sight of the Lord is the death of his saints. R. I will walk before the Lord, in the land of the living.

16 O Lord, for I am thy servant: I am thy servant, and the son of thy handmaid. Thou hast broken my bonds:

17 I will sacrifice to thee the sacrifice of praise, and I will call upon the name of the Lord.

R. I will walk before the Lord, in the land of the living.

18 I will pay my vows to the Lord in the sight of all his people:

19 In the courts of the house of the Lord, in the midst of thee, O Jerusalem. R. I will walk before the Lord, in the land of the living.

Second Reading: Romans 8: 31b-34 31b If God be for us, who is against us?

32 He that spared not even his own Son, but delivered him up for us all, how hath he not also, with him, given us all things?

33 Who shall accuse against the elect of God? God that justifieth.

34 Who is he that shall condemn? Christ Jesus that died, yea that is risen also again; who is at the right hand of God, who also maketh intercession for us.

Verse Before the Gospel: Matthew 17: 5
5 From the shining cloud the Father's voice is heard: This is my beloved Son, listen to him.

Gospel: Mark 9: 2-10
2 And after six days Jesus taketh with him Peter and James and John, and leadeth them up into an high mountain apart by themselves, and was transfigured before them.

3 And his garments became shining and exceeding white as snow, so as no fuller upon earth can make white.

4 And there appeared to them Elias with Moses; and they were talking with Jesus.

5 And Peter answering, said to Jesus: Rabbi, it is good for us to be here: and let us make three tabernacles, one for thee, and one for Moses, and one for Elias.

6 For he knew not what he said: for they were struck with fear.

7 And there was a cloud overshadowing them: and a voice came out of the cloud, saying: This is my most beloved son; hear ye him.

8 And immediately looking about, they saw no man any more, but Jesus only with them.

9 And as they came down from the mountain, he charged them not to tell any man what things they had seen, till the Son of man shall be risen again from the dead.

10 And they kept the word to themselves; questioning together what that should mean, when he shall be risen from the dead

Daily Mass Readings for Monday, 26 February 2024

Lenten Weekday
First Reading: Daniel 9: 4b-10
Responsorial Psalm: Psalms 79: 8, 9, 11 and 13
Verse Before the Gospel: John 6: 63c, 68c
Gospel: Luke 6: 36-38
Lectionary: 230
First Reading: Daniel 9: 4b-10
4b O Lord God, great and terrible, who keepest the covenant, and mercy to them that love thee, and keep thy commandments.

5 We have sinned, we have committed iniquity, we have done wickedly, and have revolted: and we have gone aside from thy commandments, and thy judgments.

6 We have not hearkened to thy servants the prophets, that have spoken in thy name to our kings, to our princes, to our fathers, and to all the people of the land.

7 To thee, O Lord, justice: but to us confusion of face, as at this day to the men of Juda, and to the inhabitants of Jerusalem, and to all Israel to them that are near, and to them that are far off in all the countries whither thou hast driven them, for their iniquities by which they have sinned against thee.

8 O Lord, to us belongeth confusion of face, to our princes, and to our fathers that have sinned.

9 But to thee, the Lord our God, mercy and forgiveness, for we have departed from thee:

10 And we have not hearkened to the voice of the Lord our God, to walk in his law, which he set before us by his servants the prophets.

Responsorial Psalm: Psalms 79: 8, 9, 11 and 13
R. (103: 10a) Lord, do not deal with us according to our sins.

8 Remember not our former iniquities: let thy mercies speedily prevent us, for we are become exceeding poor.

R. Lord, do not deal with us according to our sins.

9 Help us, O God, our saviour: and for the glory of thy name, O Lord, deliver us: and forgive us our sins for thy name's sake:

R. Lord, do not deal with us according to our sins.

11 Let the sighing of the prisoners come in before thee. According to the greatness of thy arm, take possession of the children of them that have been put to death.

13 But we thy people, and the sheep of thy pasture, will give thanks to thee for ever. We will shew forth thy praise, unto generation and generation.

R. Lord, do not deal with us according to our sins.

Verse Before the Gospel: John 6: 63c, 68c
63c, 68cYour words, Lord, are Spirit and life; you have the words of everlasting life.

Gospel: Luke 6: 36-38
36 Be ye therefore merciful, as your Father also is merciful.

37 Judge not, and you shall not be judged. Condemn not, and you shall not be condemned. Forgive, and you shall be forgiven.

38 Give, and it shall be given to you: good measure and pressed down and shaken together and running over shall they give into your bosom. For with the same measure that you shall mete withal, it shall be measured to you again.

Daily Mass Readings for Tuesday, 27 February 2024

Lenten Weekday
First Reading: Isaiah 1: 10, 16-20
Responsorial Psalm: Psalms 50: 8-9, 16bc-17, 21 and 23
Verse Before the Gospel: Ezekiel 18: 31
Gospel: Matthew 23: 1-12
Lectionary: 231
First Reading: Isaiah 1: 10, 16-20
10 Hear the word of the Lord, ye rulers of Sodom, give ear to the law of our God, ye people of Gomorrha.

16 Wash yourselves, be clean, take away the evil of your devices from my eyes: cease to do perversely,

17 Learn to do well: seek judgment, relieve the oppressed, judge for the fatherless, defend the widow.

18 And then come, and accuse me, saith the Lord: if your sins be as scarlet, they shall be made as white as snow: and if they be red as crimson, they shall be white as wool.

19 If you be willing, and will hearken to me, you shall eat the good things of the land.

20 But if you will not, and will provoke me to wrath: the sword shall devour you because the mouth of the Lord hath spoken it.

Responsorial Psalm: Psalms 50: 8-9, 16bc-17, 21 and 23
R. (23b) To the upright I will show the saving power of God.

8 I will not reprove thee for thy sacrifices: and thy burnt offerings are always in my sight.

9 I will not take calves out of thy house: nor he goats out of thy flocks.

R. To the upright I will show the saving power of God.

16bc Why dost thou declare my justices, and take my covenant in thy mouth?

17 Seeing thou hast hated discipline: and hast cast my words behind thee.

R. To the upright I will show the saving power of God.

21 These things hast thou done, and I was silent. Thou thoughtest unjustly that I should be like to thee: but I will reprove thee, and set before thy face.

23 The sacrifice of praise shall glorify me: and there is the way by which I will shew him the salvation of God.

R. To the upright I will show the saving power of God.

Verse Before the Gospel: Ezekiel 18: 31
31 Cast away from you all the crimes you have committed, says the LORD, and make for yourselves a new heart and a new spirit.

Gospel: Matthew 23: 1-12
1 Then Jesus spoke to the multitudes and to his disciples,

2 Saying: The scribes and the Pharisees have sitten on the chair of Moses.

3 All things therefore whatsoever they shall say to you, observe and do: but according to their works do ye not; for they say, and do not.

4 For they bind heavy and insupportable burdens, and lay them on men's shoulders; but with a finger of their own they will not move them.

5 And all their works they do for to be seen of men. For they make their phylacteries broad, and enlarge their fringes.

6 And they love the first places at feasts, and the first chairs in the synagogues,

7 And salutations in the market place, and to be called by men, Rabbi.

8 But be not you called Rabbi. For one is your master; and all you are brethren.

9 And call none your father upon earth; for one is your father, who is in heaven.

10 Neither be ye called masters; for one is your master, Christ. 11 He that is the greatest among you shall be your servant.

12 And whosoever shall exalt himself shall be humbled: and he that shall humble himself shall be exalted.

Daily Mass Readings for Wednesday, 28 February 2024

Lenten Weekday
First Reading: Jeremiah 18: 18-20

Responsorial Psalm: Psalms 31: 5-6, 14, 15-16 Verse Before the Gospel: John 8: 12
Gospel: Matthew 20: 17-28
Lectionary: 232

First Reading: Jeremiah 18: 18-20
18 And they said: Come, and let us invent devices against Jeremias: for the law shall not perish from the priest, nor counsel from the wise, nor the word from the prophet: come, and let us strike him with the tongue, and let us give no heed to all his words.

19 Give heed to me, O Lord, and hear the voice of my adversaries.

20 Shall evil be rendered for good, because they have digged a pit for my soul? Remember that I have stood in thy sight, so speak good for them, and turn away thy indignation from them.

Responsorial Psalm: Psalms 31: 5-6, 14, 15-16 R. (17b) Save me, O Lord, in your kindness.

5 Thou wilt bring me out of this snare, which they have hidden for me: for thou art my protector.

6 Into thy hands I commend my spirit: thou hast redeemed me, O Lord, the God of truth.

R. Save me, O Lord, in your kindness.

14 For I have heard the blame of many that dwell round about. While they assembled together against me, they consulted to take away my life.

R. Save me, O Lord, in your kindness.
15 But I have put my trust in thee, O Lord: I said: Thou art my God.

16 My lots are in thy hands. Deliver me out of the hands of my enemies; and from them that persecute me.

R. Save me, O Lord, in your kindness.

Verse Before the Gospel: John 8: 12
12 I am the light of the world, says the Lord; whoever follows me will have the light of life.

Gospel: Matthew 20: 17-28
17 And Jesus going up to Jerusalem, took the twelve disciples apart, and said to them:

18 Behold we go up to Jerusalem, and the Son of man shall be betrayed to the chief priests and the scribes, and they shall condemn him to death.

19 And shall deliver him to the Gentiles to be mocked, and scourged, and crucified, and the third day he shall rise again.

20 Then came to him the mother of the sons of Zebedee with her sons, adoring and asking something of him.

21 Who said to her: What wilt thou? She saith to him: Say that these my two sons may sit, the one on thy right hand, and the other on thy left, in thy kingdom.

22 And Jesus answering, said: You know not what you ask. Can you drink the chalice that I shall drink? They say to him: We can.

23 He saith to them: My chalice indeed you shall drink; but to sit on my right or left hand, is not mine to give to you, but to them for whom it is prepared by my Father.

24 And the ten hearing it, were moved with indignation against the two brethren.

25 But Jesus called them to him, and said: You know that the princes of the Gentiles lord it over them; and they that are the greater, exercise power upon

them.

26 It shall not be so among you: but whosoever will be the greater among you, let him be your minister:

27 And he that will be first among you, shall be your servant.

28 Even as the Son of man is not come to be ministered unto, but to minister, and to give his life a redemption for many.

Daily Mass Readings for Thursday, 29 February 2024

Lenten Weekday
First Reading: Jeremiah 17: 5-10
Responsorial Psalm: Psalms 1: 1-2, 3, 4 and 6

Verse Before the Gospel: Luke 8: 15 Gospel: Luke 16: 19-31
Lectionary: 233
First Reading: Jeremiah 17: 5-10

5 Thus saith the Lord: Cursed be the man that trusteth in man, and maketh flesh his arm, and whose heart departeth from the Lord.

6 For he shall be like tamaric in the desert, and he shall not see when good shall come: but he shall dwell in dryness in the desert in a salt land, and not inhabited.

7 Blessed be the man that trusteth in the Lord, and the Lord shall be his confidence.

8 And he shall be as a tree that is planted by the waters, that spreadeth out its roots towards moisture: and it shall not fear when the heat cometh. And the leaf thereof shall be green, and in the time of drought it shall not be solicitous, neither shall it cease at any time to bring forth fruit.

9 The heart is perverse above all things, and unsearchable, who can know it?

10 I am the Lord who search the heart and prove the reins: who give to every one according to his way, and according to the fruit of his devices.

Responsorial Psalm: Psalms 1: 1-2, 3, 4 and 6
R. (40:5a) Blessed is the man whose trust is in the name of the Lord.

1 Blessed is the man who hath not walked in the counsel of the ungodly, nor stood in the way of sinners, nor sat in the chair of pestilence.

2 But his will is in the law of the Lord, and on his law he shall meditate day and night.

R. Blessed is the man whose trust is in the name of the Lord.

3 And he shall be like a tree which is planted near the running waters, which shall bring forth its fruit, in due season. And his leaf shall not fall off: and all whatsoever he shall do shall prosper.

R. Blessed is the man whose trust is in the name of the Lord.

4 Not so the wicked, not so: but like the dust, which the wind driveth from the face of the earth.

6 For the Lord knoweth the way of the just: and the way of the wicked shall perish.

R. Blessed is the man whose trust is in the name of the Lord.

Verse Before the Gospel: Luke 8: 15
15 Blessed are they who in a good and perfect heart, hearing the word, keep it, and bring forth fruit in patience.

Gospel: Luke 16: 19-31
19 There was a certain rich man, who was clothed in purple and fine linen; and feasted sumptuously every day.

20 And there was a certain beggar, named Lazarus, who lay at his gate, full of sores,

21 Desiring to be filled with the crumbs that fell from the rich man's table, and no one did give him; moreover the dogs came, and licked his sores.

22 And it came to pass, that the beggar died, and was carried by the angels into Abraham's bosom. And the rich man also died: and he was buried in hell.

23 And lifting up his eyes when he was in torments, he saw Abraham afar off, and Lazarus in his bosom:

24 And he cried, and said: Father Abraham, have mercy on me, and send Lazarus, that he may dip the tip of his finger in water, to cool my tongue: for I am tormented in this flame.

25 And Abraham said to him: Son, remember that thou didst receive good things in thy lifetime, and likewise Lazareth evil things, but now he is comforted; and thou art tormented.

26 And besides all this, between us and you, there is fixed a great chaos: so that they who would pass from hence to you, cannot, nor from thence come hither.

27 And he said: Then, father, I beseech thee, that thou wouldst send him to my father's house, for I have five brethren,

28 That he may testify unto them, lest they also come into this place of torments.

29 And Abraham said to him: They have Moses and the prophets; let them hear them.

30 But he said: No, father Abraham: but if one went to them from the dead, they will do penance.

31 And he said to him: If they hear not Moses and the prophets, neither will they believe, if one rise again from the dead.

March 2024

Daily Mass Readings for Friday, 1 March 2024

Lenten Weekday, Day of Abstinence from Meat (Age 14 and Up) First Reading: Genesis 37: 3-4, 12-13a, 17b-28
Responsorial Psalm: Psalms 105: 16-17, 18-19, 20-21
Verse Before the Gospel: John 3: 16

Gospel: Matthew 21: 33-43, 45-46
Lectionary: 234
First Reading: Genesis 37: 3-4, 12-13a, 17b-28
3 Now Israel loved Joseph above all his sons, because he had him in his old age: and he made him a coat of divers colors.

4 And his brethren seeing that he was loved by his father, more than all his sons, hated him, and could not speak peaceably to him.

12 And when his brethren abode in Sichem feeding their father's flocks,

13a Israel said to him: Thy brethren feed the sheep in Sichem: come, I will send thee to them.

17b And Joseph went forward after his brethren, and found them in Dothan.

18 And when they saw him afar off, before he came near them, they thought to kill him.

19 And said one to another: Behold the dreamer cometh.

20 Come, let us kill him, and cast him into some old pit: and we will say: Some evil beast hath devoured him: and then it shall appear what his dreams avail him:

21 And Ruben hearing this, endeavored to deliver him out of their hands, and said:

22 Do not take away his life, nor shed his blood: but cast him into this pit, that is in the wilderness, and keep your hands harmless: now he said this, being desirous to deliver him out of their hands and to restore him to his father.

23 And as soon as he came to his brethren, they forthwith stript him of his outside coat, that was of divers colors:

24 And cast him into an old pit, where there was no water.

25 And sitting down to eat bread, they saw some Ismaelites on their way coming from Galaad, with their camels, carrying spices, balm, and myrrh to Egypt.

26 And Juda said to his brethren: What will it profit us to kill our brother, and conceal his blood?

27 It is better that he be sold to the Ismaelites, and that our hands be not defiled: for he is our brother and our flesh. His brethren agreed to his words.

28 And when the Midianite merchants passed by, they drew him out of the pit, and sold him to the Ismaelites, for twenty pieces of silver.

Responsorial Psalm: Psalms 105: 16-17, 18-19, 20-21 R. (5a) Remember the marvels the Lord has done.

16 And he called a famine upon the land: and he broke in pieces all the support of bread.

17 He sent a man before them: Joseph, who was sold for a slave. R. Remember the marvels the Lord has done.
18 They humbled his feet in fetters: the iron pierced his soul,

19 Until his word came. The word of the Lord inflamed him.

R. Remember the marvels the Lord has done.

20 The king sent, and he released him: the ruler of the people, and he set him at liberty.

21 He made him master of his house, and ruler of all his possessions. R. Remember the marvels the Lord has done.

Verse Before the Gospel: John 3: 16
16 God so loved the world that he gave his only-begotten Son; so that everyone who believes in him might have eternal life.

Gospel: Matthew 21: 33-43, 45-46
33 Hear yet another parable. There was a man and householder, who planted a

vineyard, and made a hedge round about it, and dug in it a press, and built a tower, and let it out to husbandmen; and went into a strange country.

34 And when the time of the fruits drew nigh, he sent his servants to the husbandmen that they might receive the fruits thereof.

35 And the husbandmen laying hands on his servants, beat one, and killed another, and stoned another.

36 Again he sent other servants more than the former; and they did to them in a like manner.

37 And last of all he sent to them his son, saying: They will revere my son.

38 But the husbandmen seeing the son, said among themselves: This is the heir: come, let us kill him, and we shall have his inheritance.

39 And taking him, they cast him forth out of the vineyard, and killed him.

40 When therefore the lord of the vineyard shall come, what will he do to those husbands?

41 They say to him: He will bring those evil men to an evil end; and will let out his vineyard to other husbands, that shall render him the fruit in due season.

42 Jesus said to them: Have you never read in the Scriptures: The stone which the builders rejected, the same is becoming the head of the corner? By the Lord this has been done; and it is wonderful in our eyes.

43 Therefore I say to you, that the kingdom of God shall be taken from you, and shall be given to a nation yielding the fruits thereof.

45 And when the chief priests and Pharisees had heard his parables, they knew that he spoke of them.

46 And seeking to lay hands on him, they feared the multitudes: because they held him as a prophet

Daily Mass Readings for Saturday, 2 March 2024

Lenten Weekday
First Reading: Micah 7: 14-15, 18-20
Responsorial Psalm: Psalms 103: 1-2, 3-4, 9-10, 11-12 Verse Before the Gospel: Luke 15: 18

Gospel: Luke 15: 1-3, 11-32
Lectionary: 235
First Reading: Micah 7: 14-15, 18-20
14 Feed thy people with thy rod, the flock of thy inheritance, them that dwell alone in the forest, in the midst of Carmel: they shall feed in Basan and Galaad according to the days of old.

15 According to the days of thy coming out of the land of Egypt I will shew him wonders.

18 Who is a God like thee, who takest away iniquity, and passest by the sin of the remnant of thy inheritance? He will send his fury in no more, because he delighteth in mercy.

19 He will turn again, and have mercy on us: he will put away our iniquities: and he will cast all our sins into the bottom of the sea.

20 Thou wilt perform the truth of Jacob, the mercy to Abraham: which thou hast sworn to our fathers from the days of old.

Responsorial Psalm: Psalms 103: 1-2, 3-4, 9-10, 11-12 R. (8a) The Lord is kind and merciful.

1 For David himself. Bless the Lord, O my soul: and let all that is within me bless his holy name.

2 Bless the Lord, O my soul, and never forget all he hath done for thee.

R. The Lord is kind and merciful.

3 Who forgiveth all thy iniquities: who healeth all thy diseases.

4 Who redeemeth thy life from destruction: who crowneth thee with mercy and compassion.

R. The Lord is kind and merciful.
9 He will not always be angry: nor will he threaten for ever.

10 He hath not dealt with us according to our sins: nor rewarded us according to our iniquities.

R. The Lord is kind and merciful.

11 For according to the height of the heaven above the earth: he hath strengthened his mercy towards them that fear him.

12 As far as the east is from the west, so far hath he removed our iniquities from us.

R. The Lord is kind and merciful.

Verse Before the Gospel: Luke 15: 18
18 I will get up and go to my father and shall say to him, Father, I have sinned against heaven and against you.

Gospel: Luke 15: 1-3, 11-32
1 Now the publicans and sinners drew near unto him to hear him.

2 And the Pharisees and the scribes murmured, saying: This man receiveth sinners, and eateth with them.

3 And he spoke to them this parable, saying: 11 And he said: A certain man had two sons:

12 And the younger of them said to his father: Father, give me the portion of substance that falleth to me. And he divided unto them his substance.

13 And not many days after, the younger son, gathering all together, went abroad into a far country: and there wasted his substance, living riotously.

14 And after he had spent all, there came a mighty famine in that country; and he began to be in want.

15 And he went and cleaved to one of the citizens of that country. And he sent him into his farm to feed swine.

16 And he would fain have filled his belly with the husks the swine did eat; and no man gave unto him.

17 And returning to himself, he said: How many hired servants in my father's house abound with bread, and I here perish with hunger?

18 I will arise, and will go to my father, and say to him: Father, I have sinned against heaven, and before thee:

19 I am not worthy to be called thy son: make me as one of thy hired servants.

20 And rising up he came to his father. And when he was yet a great way off, his father saw him, and was moved with compassion, and running to him fell upon his neck, and kissed him.

21 And the son said to him: Father, I have sinned against heaven, and before thee, I am not now worthy to be called thy son.

22 And the father said to his servants: Bring forth quickly the first robe, and put it on him, and put a ring on his hand, and shoes on his feet:

23 And bring hither the fatted calf, and kill it, and let us eat and make merry:

24 Because this my son was dead, and is come to life again: was lost, and is found. And they began to be merry.

25 Now his elder son was in the field, and when he came and drew nigh to the house, he heard music and dancing:

26 And he called one of the servants, and asked what these things meant.

27 And he said to him: Thy brother is come, and thy father hath killed the fatted calf, because he hath received him safe.

28 And he was angry, and would not go in. His father therefore began to entreat him.

29 And he answering, said to his father: Behold, for so many years do I serve thee, and I have never transgressed thy commandment, and yet thou hast never given me a kid to make merry with my friends:

30 But as soon as this thy son is come, who hath devoured his substance with harlots, thou hast killed for him the fatted calf.

31 But he said to him: Son, thou art always with me, and all I have is thine.

32 But it was fit that we should make merry and be glad, for this thy brother was dead and is come to life again; he was lost, and is found.

Daily Mass Readings for Sunday, 3 March 2024

Lenten; Third Sunday of Lent, First Scrutiny of the Elect/ Lenten First
Reading: Exodus 20: 1-17
Responsorial Psalm: Psalms 19: 8, 9, 10, 11
Second Reading: First Corinthians 1: 22-25

Verse Before the Gospel: John 3: 16 Gospel: John 2: 13-25
Select Mass – Lenten | Scrutiny

Lenten Mass Readings

Lectionary: 29
First Reading: Exodus 20: 1-17
1 And the Lord spoke all these words:

2 I am the Lord thy God, who brought thee out of the land of Egypt, out of the house of bondage.

3 Thou shalt not have strange gods before me.

4 Thou shalt not make to thyself a graven thing, nor the likeness of any thing that is in heaven above, or in the earth beneath, nor of those things that are in the waters under the earth.

5 Thou shalt not adore them, nor serve them: I am the Lord thy God, mighty, jealous, visiting the iniquity of the fathers upon the children, unto the third and fourth generation of them that hate me:

6 And shewing mercy unto thousands to them that love me, and keep my commandments.

7 Thou shalt not take the name of the Lord thy God in vain: for the Lord will not hold him guiltless that shall take the name of the Lord his God in vain.

8 Remember that thou keep holy the sabbath day.
9 Six days shalt thou labor, and shalt do all thy works.

10 But on the seventh day is the sabbath of the Lord thy God: thou shalt do no work on it, thou nor thy son, nor thy daughter, nor thy manservant, nor thy maidservant, nor thy beast, nor the stranger that is within thy gates.

11 For in six days the Lord made heaven and earth, and the sea, and all things that are in them, and rested on the seventh day: therefore the Lord blessed the seventh day, and sanctified it.

12 Honour thy father and thy mother, that thou mayest be long lived upon the land which the Lord thy God will give thee.

13 Thou shalt not kill.
14 Thou shalt not commit adultery.
15 Thou shalt not steal.
16 Thou shalt not bear false witness against thy neighbor.

17 Thou shalt not covet thy neighbor's house: neither shall thou desire his wife, nor his servant, nor his handmaid, nor his ox, nor his ass, nor any thing that is his.

Responsorial Psalm: Psalms 19: 8, 9, 10, 11
R. (John 6: 68c) Lord, you have the words of everlasting life.

8 The law of the Lord is unspotted, converting souls: the testimony of the Lord is faithful, giving wisdom to little ones.

R. Lord, you have the words of everlasting life.

9 The justices of the Lord are right, rejoicing hearts: the commandment of the Lord is lightsome, enlightening the eyes.

R. Lord, you have the words of everlasting life.

10 The fear of the Lord is holy, enduring forever and ever: the judgments of the Lord are true, justified in themselves.

R. Lord, you have the words of everlasting life.

11 More to be desired than gold and many precious stones: and sweeter than honey and the honeycomb.

R. Lord, you have the words of everlasting life.

Second Reading: First Corinthians 1: 22-25
22 For both the Jews require signs, and the Greeks seek after wisdom:

23 But we preach Christ crucified, unto the Jews indeed a stumbling block, and unto the Gentiles foolishness:

24 But unto them that are called, both Jews and Greeks, Christ the power of God, and the wisdom of God.

25 For the foolishness of God is wiser than men; and the weakness of God is stronger than men.

Verse Before the Gospel: John 3: 16
16 God so loved the world that he gave his only Son, so that everyone who believes in him might have eternal life.

Gospel: John 2: 13-25
13 And the pasch of the Jews was at hand, and Jesus went up to Jerusalem.

14 And he found in the temple them that sold oxen and sheep and doves, and the changers of money sitting.

15 And when he had made, as it were, a scourge of little cords, he drove them all out of the temple, the sheep also and the oxen, and the money of the changers he poured out, and the tables he overthrew.

16 And to them that sold doves he said: Take these things hence, and make not the house of my Father a house of traffic.

17 And his disciples remembered, that it was written: The zeal of thy house hath eaten me up.

18 The Jews, therefore, answered, and said to him: What sign dost thou shew unto us, seeing thou dost these things?

19 Jesus answered, and said to them: Destroy this temple, and in three days I will raise it up.

20 The Jews then said: Six and forty years was this temple in building; and wilt thou raise it up in three days?

21 But he spoke of the temple of his body.

22 When therefore he was risen again from the dead, his disciples remembered that he had said this, and they believed the scripture, and the word that Jesus had said.

23 Now when he was at Jerusalem, at the pasch, upon the festival day, many believed in his name, seeing his signs which he did.

24 But Jesus did not trust himself unto them, for that he knew all men,

25 And because he needed not that any should give testimony of man: for he knew what was in man

Daily Mass Readings for Monday, 4 March 2024

Lenten Weekday/ Casimir
First Reading: Second Kings 5: 1-15
Responsorial Psalm: Psalms 42: 2, 3; 43: 3, 4
Verse Before the Gospel: Psalms 130: 5, 7
Gospel: Luke 4: 24-30
Lectionary: 237
First Reading: Second Kings 5: 1-15

1 Naaman, general of the army of the king of Syria, was a great man with his master, and honorable: for by him the Lord gave deliverance to Syria: and he was a valiant man and rich, but a leper.

2 Now there had gone out robbers from Syria, and had led away captive out of the land of Israel a little maid, and she waited upon Naaman's wife.

3 And she said to her mistress: I wish my master had been with the prophet, that is in Samaria: he would certainly have healed him of the leprosy which he hath.

4 Then Naaman went in to his lord, and told him, saying: Thus and thus said tile girl from the land of Israel.

5 And the king of Syria said to him: Go, and I will send a letter to the king of Israel. And he departed, and took with him ten talents of silver, and six thousand pieces of gold, and tell changes of raiment,

6 And brought the letter to the king of Israel, in these words: When thou shalt receive this letter, know that I have sent to thee my servant, that thou mayest

heal him of his leprosy.

7 And when the king of Israel had read the letter, he rented his garments, and said: Am I God, to be able to kill and give life, that this man hath sent to me, to heal a man of his leprosy? mark, and see how he seeketh occasions against me.

8 And when Eliseus the man of God had heard this, to wit, that the king of Israel had rented his garments, he sent to him, saying: Why hast thou rent thy garments? let him come to me, and let him know that there is a prophet in Israel.

9 So Naaman came with his horses and chariots, and stood at the door of the house of Eliseus:

10 And Eliseus sent a messenger to him, saying: Go, and wash seven times in the Jordan, and thy flesh shall recover health, and thee shalt be clean.

11 Naaman was angry and went away, saying: I thought he would have come out to me, and standing would have invoked the name of the Lord his God, and touched with his hand the place of the leprosy, and healed me.

12 Are not the Abana, and the Pharphar, rivers of Damascus, better than all the waters of Israel, that I may wash in them, and be made clean? So as he turned, and was going away with indignation,

13 His servants came to him, and said to him: Father, if the prophet had bid thee do some great thing, surely thou shouldst have done it: how much rather what he now hath said to thee: Wash, and thou shalt he clean?

14 Then he went down, and washed in the Jordan seven times: according to the word of the man of God, and his flesh was restored, like the flesh of a little child, and he was made clean.

15 And returning to the man of God with all his train, became, and stood before him, and said: In truth, I know there is no other God in all the earth, but only in Israel.

Responsorial Psalm: Psalms 42: 2, 3; 43: 3, 4
R. (42:3) Atheist is my soul for the living God. When shall I go and behold the face of God?

2 As the hart panteth after the fountains of water; so my soul panteth after thee, O God.

R. Athirst is my soul for the living God. When shall I go and behold the face of God?

3 My soul hath thirsted after the strong living God; when shall I come and appear before the face of God?

R. Athirst is my soul for the living God. When shall I go and behold the face of God?

43:3 Send forth thy light and thy truth: they have conducted me, and brought me unto thy holy hill, and into thy tabernacles.

R. Athirst is my soul for the living God. When shall I go and behold the face of God?

4 And I will go into the altar of God: to God who giveth joy to my youth. To thee, O God my God, I will give praise upon the harp: why art thou sad, O mysoul?

R. Athirst is my soul for the living God. When shall I go and behold the face of God?

Verse Before the Gospel: Psalms 130: 5, 7
5, 7 I hope in the LORD, I trust in his word; with him there is kindness and plenteous redemption.

Gospel: Luke 4: 24-30

24 And he said: Amen I say to you, that no prophet is accepted in his own country.

25 In truth I say to you, there were many widows in the days of Elias in Israel, when heaven was shut up three years and six months, when there was a great famine throughout all the earth.

26 And to none of them was Elias sent, but to Sarepta of Sidon, to a widow woman.

27 And there were many lepers in Israel in the time of Eliseus the prophet: and none of them was cleansed but Naaman the Syrian.

28 And all they in the synagogue, hearing these things, were filled with anger.

29 And they rose up and thrust him out of the city; and they brought him to the brow of the hill, whereon their city was built, that they might cast him down headlong.

30 But he passed through the midst of them, and went his way.

Daily Mass Readings for Tuesday, 5 March 2024

Lenten Weekday
First Reading: Daniel 3: 25, 34-43
Responsorial Psalm: Psalms 25: 4-5ab, 6 and 7bc, 8-9

Verse Before the Gospel: Joel 2: 12-13 Gospel: Matthew 18: 21-35 Lectionary: 238
First Reading: Daniel 3: 25, 34-43

25 Then Azarias standing up prayed in this manner, and opening his mouth in the midst of the fire, he said:

34 Deliver us not up for ever, we beseech thee, for thy name's sake, and abolish not thy covenant.

35 And take not away thy mercy from us for the sake of Abraham thy beloved, and Isaac thy servant, and Israel thy holy one:

36 To whom thou hast spoken, promising that thou wouldst multiply their seed as the stars of heaven, and as the sand that is on the sea shore.

37 For we, O Lord, are diminished more than any nation, and are brought low in all the earth this day for our sins.

38 Neither is there at this time prince, or leader, or prophet, or holocaust, or sacrifice, or oblation, or incense, or place of firstfruits before thee,

39 That we may find thy mercy: nevertheless in a contrite heart and humble spirit let us be accepted.

40 As in holocausts of rams, and bullocks, and as in thousands of fat lambs: so let our sacrifice be made in thy sight this day, that it may please thee: for there is no confusion to them that trust in thee.

41 And now we follow thee with all our heart, and we fear thee, and seek thy face.

42 Put us not to confusion, but deal. with us according to thy meekness, and according to the multitude of thy mercies.

43 And deliver us according to thy wonderful works, and give glory to thy name, O Lord:

Responsorial Psalm: Psalms 25: 4-5ab, 6 and 7bc, 8-9 R. (6a) Remember your mercies, O Lord.

4 Let all of them be confused and act unjustly without cause. shew, O Lord, thy ways to me, and teach me thy paths.

5ab Direct me in thy truth, and teach me; for thou art God my Savior. R. Remember your mercies, O Lord.

6 Remember, O Lord, thy bowels of compassion; and thy mercies that are from the beginning of the world.

7bc According to thy mercy remember thou me: for thy goodness' sake, O Lord.

R. Remember your mercies, O Lord.

8 The Lord is sweet and righteous: therefore he will give a law to sinners in this way.

9 He will guide the mild in judgment: he will teach the meek his ways.

R. Remember your mercies, O Lord.

Verse Before the Gospel: Joel 2: 12-13
12-13 Even now, says the LORD, return to me with your whole heart; for I am gracious and merciful.

Gospel: Matthew 18: 21-35
21 Then came Peter unto him and said: Lord, how often shall my brother offend against me, and I forgive him? till seven times?

22 Jesus saith to him: I say not to thee, till seven times; but till seventy times seven times.

23 Therefore is the kingdom of heaven likened to a king, who would take an account of his servants.

24 And when he had begun to take the account, one was brought to him, who owed him ten thousand talents.

25 And as he had no wherewith to pay it, his lord commanded that he should be sold, and his wife and children and all that he had, and payment to be made.

26 But that servant falling down, besought him, saying: Have patience with me, and I will pay thee all.

27 And the lord of that servant, being moved with pity, let him go and forgave him the debt.

28 But when that servant was gone out, he found one of his fellow servants that owed him a hundred pence: and laying hold of him, throttled him, saying: Pay what thou owest.

29 And his fellow servant falling down, besought him, saying: Have patience with me, and I will pay thee all.

30 And he would not: but went and cast him into prison, till he paid the debt.

31 Now his fellow servants, seeing what was done, were very much grieved, and they came and told their lord all that was done.

32 Then his lord called him; and said to him: Thou wicked servant, I forgave thee all the debt, because thou besoughtest me:

33 Shouldst not thou then have had compassion also on thy fellow servant, even as I had compassion on thee?

34 And his lord, being angry, delivered him to the torturers until he paid all the debt.

35 So also shall my heavenly Father do to you, if you forgive not every one his brother from your hearts

Daily Mass Readings for Wednesday, 6 March 2024

Lenten Weekday
First Reading: Deuteronomy 4:1, 5-9
Responsorial Psalm: Psalms 147: 12-13, 15-16, 19-20
Verse Before the Gospel: John 6: 63c, 68c
Gospel: Matthew 5: 17-19
Lectionary: 239
First Reading: Deuteronomy 4:1, 5-9

1 And now, O Israel, hear the commandments and judgments which I teach thee: that doing them, thou mayst live, and entering in mayst possess the land which the Lord the God of your fathers will give you.

5 You know that I have taught you statutes and justices, as the Lord my God hath commanded me: so shall you do them in the land which you shall possess:

6 And you shall observe, and fulfill them in practice. For this is your wisdom, and understanding in the sight of nations, that hearing all these precepts, they may say: Behold a wise and understanding people, a great nation.

7 Neither is there any other nation so great, that hath gods so nigh them, as our God is present to all our petitions.

8 For what other nation is there so renowned that hath ceremonies, and just judgments, and all the law, which I will set forth this day before your eyes?

9 Keep thyself therefore, and thy soul carefully. Forget not the words that thy eyes have seen, and let them not go out of thy heart all the days of thy life. Thou shalt teach them to thy sons and to thy grandsons,

Responsorial Psalm: Psalms 147: 12-13, 15-16, 19-20 R. (12a) Praise the Lord, Jerusalem.

12 Praise the Lord, O Jerusalem: praise thy God, O Sion.

13 Because he hath strengthened the bolts of thy gates, he hath blessed thy children within thee.

R. Praise the Lord, Jerusalem.

15 Who sendeth forth his speech to the earth: his word runneth swiftly.

16 Who giveth snow like wool: scattereth mists like ashes.

R. Praise the Lord, Jerusalem.

19 Who declareth his word to Jacob: his justices and his judgments to Israel.

20 He hath not done in like manner to every nation: and his judgments he hath not made manifest to them. Alleluia.

R. Praise the Lord, Jerusalem.

Verse Before the Gospel: John 6: 63c, 68c
63c, 68c Your words, Lord, are Spirit and life; you have the words of everlasting life.

Gospel: Matthew 5: 17-19
17 Do not think that I have come to destroy the law, or the prophets. I am not coming to destroy, but to fulfill.

18 For amen I say unto you, till heaven and earth pass, one jot, or one tittle shall not pass of the law, till all be fulfilled.

19 He therefore that shall break one of these least commandments, and shall so teach men, shall be called the least in the kingdom of heaven. But he that shall do and teach, he shall be called great in the kingdom of heaven.

Daily Mass Readings for Thursday, 7 March 2024

Lenten Weekday/ Perpetua and Felicity, Martyrs First Reading: Jeremiah 7: 23-28

Responsorial Psalm: Psalms 95: 1-2, 6-7, 8-9 Verse Before the Gospel: Joel 2: 12-13

Gospel: Luke 11: 14-23

Lectionary: 240

First Reading: Jeremiah 7: 23-28

23 But this thing I commanded them, saying: Hearken to my voice, and I will be your God, and you shall be my people: and walk ye in all the way that I have commanded you, that it may be well with you.

24 But they hearkened not, nor inclined their ear: but walked in their own will, and in the perversity of their wicked heart: and went backward and not forward,

25 From the day that their fathers came out of the land of Egypt, even to this day. And I have sent to you all my servants the prophets from day to day, rising up early and sending.

26 And they have not hearkened to me: nor inclined their ear: but have hardened their neck, and have done worse than their fathers.

27 And thou shalt speak to them all these words, but they will not hearken to thee: and thou shalt call them, but they will not answer thee.

28 And thou shalt say to them: This is a nation which hath not hearkened to the voice of the Lord their God, nor received instruction: Faith is lost, and is carried away out of their mouth.

Responsorial Psalm: Psalms 95: 1-2, 6-7, 8-9

R. (8) If today you hear his voice, harden not your hearts.

1 Come let us praise the Lord with joy: let us joyfully sing to God our savior.

2 Let us come before his presence with thanksgiving; and make a joyful noise to him with psalms.

R. If today you hear his voice, harden not your hearts.
6 Come let us adore and fall down: and weep before the Lord that made us.

7 For he is the Lord our God: and we are the people of his pasture and the sheep of his hand.

R. If today you hear his voice, harden not your hearts.
8 Today if you shall hear his voice, harden not your hearts:

9 As in the provocation, according to the day of temptation in the wilderness: where your fathers tempted me, they proved me, and saw my works.

R. If today you hear his voice, harden not your hearts.

Verse Before the Gospel: Joel 2: 12-13
12-13 Even now, says the LORD, return to me with your whole heart, for I am gracious and merciful.

Gospel: Luke 11: 14-23
14 And he was casting out a devil, and the same was dumb: and when he had cast out the devil, the dumb spoke: and the multitudes were in admiration at it:

15 But some of them said: He casteth out devils by Beelzebub, the prince of devils.

16 And others, tempting, asked him for a sign from heaven.

17 But he, seeing their thoughts, said to them: Every kingdom divided against itself, shall be brought to desolation, and house upon house shall fall.

18 And if Satan also be divided against himself, how shall his kingdom stand? Because you say that through Beelzebub I cast out devils.

19 Now if I cast out devils by Beelzebub; by whom do your children cast them out? Therefore they shall be your judges.

20 But if I by the finger of God cast out devils; doubtless the kingdom of God will come upon you.

21 When a strong man armed keepeth his court, those things are in peace which he possesseth.

22 But if a stronger person comes upon him, and overcomes him; he will take away all his armor wherein he trusted, and will distribute his spoils.

23 He that is not with me, is against me; and he that gathereth not with me, scattereth.

Daily mass readings for 8th March 2024

Lenten Weekday/ John of God, Religious Founder, Day of Abstinence from Meat (Age 14 and Up)
First Reading: Hosea 14: 2-10
Responsorial Psalm: Psalms 81: 6c-8a, 8bc-9, 10-11ab, 14 and 17

Verse Before the Gospel: Matthew 4: 17 Gospel: Mark 12: 28-34
Lectionary: 241
First Reading: Hosea 14: 2-10

2 Return, O Israel, to the Lord thy God: for thou hast fallen down by thy iniquity.

3 Take with you words, and return to the Lord, and say to him: Take away all iniquity, and receive the good: and we will render the calves of our lips.

4 Assyria shall not save us, we will not ride upon horses, neither will we say any more: The works of our hands are our gods, for thou wilt have mercy on the fatherless that is in thee.

5 I will heal their breaches, I will love them freely: for my wrath is turned away from them.

6 I will be as the dew, Israel shall spring as the lily, and his root shall shoot forth as that of Libanus.

7 His branches shall spread, and his glory shall be as the olive tree: and his smell as that of Libanus.

8 They shall be converted that sit under his shadow: they shall live upon wheat, and they shall blossom as a vine: his memorial shall be as the wine of Libanus.

9 Ephraim shall say, What have I to do any more with idols? I will hear him, and I will make him flourish like a green fir tree: from me is thy fruit found.

10 Who is wise, and he shall understand these things? prudent, and he shall know these things? for the ways of the Lord are right, and the just shall walk in them: but the transgressors shall fall in them.

Responsorial Psalm: Psalms 81: 6c-8a, 8bc-9, 10-11ab, 14 and 17 R. (11, 9a) I am the Lord your God: hear my voice.

6c He heard a tongue which he knew not.
7 He removed his back from the burdens: his hands had served in baskets. 8a Thou calledst upon me in affliction, and I delivered thee.
R. I am the Lord your God: hear my voice.

8bc I heard thee in the secret place of tempest: I proved thee at the waters of contradiction.

9 Hear, O my people, and I will testify to thee: O Israel, if thou wilt hearken to me,

R. I am the Lord your God: hear my voice.

10 There shall be no new god in thee: neither shalt thou adore a strange god.

11ab For I am the Lord thy God, who brought thee out of the land of Egypt.

R. I am the Lord your God: hear my voice.

14 If my people had heard me: if Israel had walked in my ways:

17 And he fed them with the fat of wheat, and filled them with honey out of the rock.

R. I am the Lord your God: hear my voice.

Verse Before the Gospel: Matthew 4: 17
17 Repent, says the Lord; the Kingdom of heaven is at hand.

Gospel: Mark 12: 28-34
28 And there came one of the scribes that had heard them reasoning together, and seeing that he had answered them well, asked him which was the first commandment of all.

29 And Jesus answered him: The first commandment of all is, Hear, O Israel: the Lord thy God is one God.

30 And thou shalt love the Lord thy God, with thy whole heart, and with thy whole soul, and with thy whole mind, and with thy whole strength. This is the first commandment.

31 And the second is like it: Thou shalt love thy neighbor as thyself. There is no other commandment greater than these.

32 And the scribe said to him: Well, Master, thou hast said in truth, that there is one God, and there is no other besides him.

33 And that he should be loved with the whole heart, and with the whole understanding, and with the whole soul, and with the whole strength; and to love one's neighbor as one's self, is a greater thing than all holocausts and sacrifices.

34 And Jesus, seeing that he had answered wisely, said to him: Thou art not far from the kingdom of God. And no man after that durst asked him any question.

Daily Mass Readings for Saturday, 9 March 2024

Lenten Weekday/ Frances of Rome, Married Woman, Religious Founder First Reading: Hosea 6: 1-6
Responsorial Psalm: Psalms 51: 3-4, 18-19, 20-21ab
Verse Before the Gospel: Psalms 95: 8

Gospel: Luke 18: 9-14
Lectionary: 242
First Reading: Hosea 6: 1-6
1 In their affliction they will rise early to me: Come, and let us return to the Lord:

2 For he hath taken us, and he will heal us: he will strike, and he will cure us.

3 He will revive us after two days: on the third day he will raise us up, and we shall live in his sight. We shall know, and we shall follow on, that we may know the Lord. His going forth is prepared as the morning light, and he will come to us as the early and the latter rain to the earth.

4 What shall I do to thee, O Ephraim? what shall I do to thee, O Juda? Your mercy is as a morning cloud, and as the dew that goeth away in the morning.

5 For this reason have I hewed them by the prophets, I have slain them by the words of my mouth: and thy judgments shall go forth as the light.

6 For I desired mercy, and not sacrifice: and the knowledge of God more than holocausts.

Responsorial Psalm: Psalms 51: 3-4, 18-19, 20-21ab R. (Hosea 6:6) It is mercy I desire, and not sacrifice.

3 Have mercy on me, O God, according to thy great mercy. And according to the multitude of thy tender mercies blot out my iniquity.

4 Wash me yet more from my iniquity, and cleanse me from my sin. R. It is mercy I desire, and not sacrifice.

18 For if thou hadst desired sacrifice, I would indeed have given it: with burnt offerings thou wilt not be delighted.

19 A sacrifice to God is an afflicted spirit: a contrite and humbled heart, O God, thou wilt not despise.

R. It is mercy I desire, and not sacrifice.

20 Deal favorably, O Lord, in thy good will with Sion; that the walls of Jerusalem may be built up.

21ab Then shalt thou accept the sacrifice of justice, oblations and whole burnt offerings.

R. It is mercy I desire, and not sacrifice.

Verse Before the Gospel: Psalms 95: 8
8 If today you hear his voice, harden not your hearts.

Gospel: Luke 18: 9-14
9 And to some who trusted in themselves as just, and despised others, he spoke also this parable:

10 Two men went up into the temple to pray: the one a Pharisee, and the other a publican.

11 The Pharisee standing, prayed thus with himself: O God, I give thee thanks that I am not as the rest of men, extortioners, unjust, adulterers, as also is this publican.

12 I fast twice in a week: I give tithes of all that I possess.

13 And the publican, standing afar off, would not so much as lift up his eyes towards heaven; but struck his breast, saying: O God, be merciful to me a sinner.

14 I say to you, this man went down into his house justified rather than the other: because every one that exalteth himself, shall be humbled: and he that humbleth himself, shall be exalted.

Daily Mass Readings for Sunday, 10 March 2024

Lenten; Fourth Sunday Of Lent, Second Scrutiny of the Elect/ Lenten First Reading: Second Chronicles 36: 14-16, 19-23 Responsorial Psalm: Psalms 137: 1-2, 3, 4-5, 6
Second Reading: Ephesians 2: 4-10

Verse Before the Gospel: John 3: 16 Gospel: John 3: 14-21
Select Mass – Lenten | Scrutiny

Lenten Mass Readings

Lectionary: 32
First Reading: Second Chronicles 36: 14-16, 19-23
14 Moreover all the chief priests, and the people wickedly transgressed according to all the abominations of the Gentiles: and they defiled the house of the Lord, which he had sanctified to himself in Jerusalem.

15 And the Lord the God of their fathers sent to them, by the hand of his messengers, rising early, and daily admonishing them: because he spared his people and his dwelling place.

16 But they mocked the messengers of God, and despised his words, and misused the prophets, until the wrath of the Lord arose against his people, and there was no remedy.

19 And the enemies set fire to the house of God, and broke down the wall of Jerusalem, burnt all the towers, and whatever was precious they destroyed.

20 Whosoever escaped the sword, was led into Babylon, and there served the king and his sons till the reign of the king of Persia.

21 That the word of the Lord by the mouth of Jeremias might be fulfilled, and the land might keep her sabbaths: for all the days of the desolation she kept a sabbath, till the seventy years were expired.

22 But in the first year of Cyrus king of the Persians, to fulfill the word of the Lord, which he had spoken by the mouth of Jeremias, the Lord stirred up the heart of Cyrus king of the Persians who commanded it to be proclaimed through all his kingdom, and by writing also, saying:

23 Thus saith Cyrus king of the Persians: All the kingdoms of the earth hath the Lord the God of heaven given to me, and he hath charged me to build him a house in Jerusalem, which is in Judea: who is there among you of all his people? The Lord his God be with him, and let him go up.

Responsorial Psalm: Psalms 137: 1-2, 3, 4-5, 6
R. (6ab) Let my tongue be silenced, if I ever forget you!

1 Upon the rivers of Babylon, there we sat and wept: when we remembered Zion:

2 On the willows in the midst thereof we hung up our instruments. R. Let my tongue be silenced, if I ever forget you!

3 For there they that led us into captivity required of us the words of songs. And they that carried us away, said: Sing ye to us a hymn of the songs of Sion.

R. Let my tongue be silenced, if I ever forget you!
4 How shall we sing the song of the Lord in a strange land? 5 If I forget thee, O Jerusalem, let my right hand be forgotten. R. Let my tongue be silenced, if I ever forget you!

6 Let my tongue cleave to my jaws, if I do not remember thee: If I make not Jerusalem the beginning of my joy.

R. Let my tongue be silenced, if I ever forget you!

Second Reading: Ephesians 2: 4-10
4 But God, (who is rich in mercy,) for his exceeding charity wherewith he loved us,

5 Even when we were dead in sins, hath quickened us together in Christ, (by whose grace you are saved,)

6 And hath raised us up together, and hath made us sit together in the heavenly places, through Christ Jesus.

7 That he might shew in the ages to come the abundant riches of his grace, in his bounty towards us in Christ Jesus.

8 For by grace you are saved through faith, and that not of yourselves, for it is the gift of God;

9 Not of works, that no man may glory.

10 For we are his workmanship, created in Christ Jesus in good works, which God hath prepared that we should walk in them.

Verse Before the Gospel: John 3: 16
16 God so loved the world that he gave his only Son, so everyone who believes in him might have eternal life.

Gospel: John 3: 14-21
14 And as Moses lifted up the serpent in the desert, so must the Son of man be lifted up:

15 That whosoever believeth in him, may not perish; but may have life everlasting.

16 For God so loved the world, as to give his only begotten Son; that whosoever believeth in him, may not perish, but may have life everlasting.

17 For God sent not his Son into the world, to judge the world, but that the world may be saved by him.

18 He that believeth in him is not judged. But he that doth not believe, is already judged: because he believeth not in the name of the only begotten Son of God.

19 And this is the judgment: because the light has come into the world, and men loved darkness rather than the light: for their works were evil.

20 For everyone that doeth evil hateth the light, and cometh not to the light, that his works may not be reproved.

21 But he that doth truth, cometh to the light, that his works may be made manifest, because they are done in God.

Daily Mass Readings for Monday, 11 March 2024

Lenten Weekday
First Reading: Isaiah 65: 17-21
Responsorial Psalm: Psalms 30: 2 and 4, 5-6, 11-12a and 13b
Verse Before the Gospel: Amos 5: 14
Gospel: John 4: 43-54
Lectionary: 244
First Reading: Isaiah 65: 17-21

17 For behold I create new heavens, and a new earth: and the former things shall not be in remembrance, and they shall not come upon the heart.

18 But you shall be glad and rejoice forever in these things, which I create: for behold I create Jerusalem a rejoicing, and the people thereof joy.

19 And I will rejoice in Jerusalem, and joy in my people, and the voice of weeping shall no more be heard in her, nor the voice of crying.

20 There shall no more be an infant of days there, nor an old man that shall not fill up his days: for the child shall die a hundred years old, and the sinner being a hundred years old shall be accursed.

21 And they shall build houses, and inhabit them; and they shall plant vineyards, and eat the fruits of them.

Responsorial Psalm: Psalms 30: 2 and 4, 5-6, 11-12a and 13b R. (2a) I will praise you, Lord, for you have rescued me.

2 I will extol thee, O Lord, for thou hast upheld me: and hast not made my enemies to rejoice over me.

4 Thou hast brought forth, O Lord, my soul from hell: thou hast saved me from them that go down into the pit.

R. I will praise you, Lord, for you have rescued me.

5 Sing to the Lord, O ye his saints: and give praise to the memory of his holiness.

6 For wrath is in his indignation; and life in his good will. In the evening weeping shall take place, and in the morning gladness.

R. I will praise you, Lord, for you have rescued me.

11 The Lord hath heard, and hath had mercy on me: the Lord became my helper.

12 Thou hast turned for me my mourning into joy:
13b O Lord my God, I will give praise to thee for ever. R. I will praise you, Lord, for you have rescued me.

Verse Before the Gospel: Amos 5: 14
14 Seek good and not evil so that you may live, and the LORD will be with you.

Gospel: John 4: 43-54
43 Now after two days, he departed thence, and went into Galilee.

44 For Jesus himself gave testimony that a prophet hath no honor in his own country.

45 And when he came into Galilee, the Galileans received him, having seen all the things he had done at Jerusalem on the festival day; for they also went to the festival day.

46 He came again therefore into Cana of Galilee, where he made the water wine. And there was a certain ruler, whose son was sick at Capharnaum.

47 He, having heard that Jesus was from Judea and Galilee, went to him, and prayed for him to come down, and heal his son; for he was at the point of

death.

48 Jesus therefore said to him: Unless you see signs and wonders, you believe not.

49 The ruler saith to him: Lord, come down before my son dies.

50 Jesus saith to him: Go thy way; thy son liveth. The man believed the word which Jesus said to him, and went his way.

51 And as he was going down, his servants met him; and they brought word, saying that his son lived.

52 He asked therefore of them the hour wherein he grew better. And they said to him: Yesterday, at the seventh hour, the fever left him.

53 The father therefore knew, that it was at the same hour that Jesus said to him, Thy son liveth; and himself believed, and his whole house.

54 This is again the second miracle that Jesus did, when he came out of Judea into Galilee.

Daily Mass Readings for Tuesday, 12 March 2024

Lenten Weekday
First Reading: Ezekiel 47: 1-9, 12
Responsorial Psalm: Psalms 46: 2-3, 5-6, 8-9
Verse Before the Gospel: Psalms 51: 12a, 14a
Gospel: John 5: 1-16
Lectionary: 245
First Reading: Ezekiel 47: 1-9, 12

1 And he brought me again to the gate of the house, and behold waters issued out from under the threshold of the house toward the east: for the forefront, the house looked toward the east: but the waters came down to the right side of the temple to the south part of the altar.

2 And he led me out by the way of the north gate, and he caused me to turn to the way without the outward gate to the way that looked toward the east: and behold there ran out waters on the right side.

3 And when the man that had the line in his hand went out towards the east, he measured a thousand cubits: and he brought me through the water up to the ankles.

4 And again he measured a thousand, and he brought me through the water up to my knees.

5 And he measured a thousand, and he brought me through the water up to the loins. And he measured a thousand, and it was a torrent, which I could not pass over: for the waters were risen so as to make a deep torrent, which could not be passed over.

6 And he said to me: Surely thou hast seen, O son of man. And he brought me out, and he caused me to turn to the bank of the torrent.

7 And when I had turned myself, behold on the bank of the torrent were very many trees on both sides.

8 And he said to me: These waters that issue forth toward the hillocks of sand to the east, and go down to the plains of the desert, shall go into the sea, and shall go out, and the waters shall be healed.

9 And every living creature that creepeth through the torrent shall come, shall live: and there shall be fishes in abundance after these waters shall come thither, and they shall be healed, and all things shall live to which the torrent shall come.

12 And by the torrent on the banks thereof on both sides shall grow all trees that bear fruit: their leaf shall not fall off, and their fruit shall not fail: every month shall they bring forth firstfruits, because the waters thereof shall issue out of the sanctuary: and the fruits thereof shall be for food, and the leaves thereof for medicine.

Responsorial Psalm: Psalms 46: 2-3, 5-6, 8-9
R. (8) The Lord of hosts is with us; our stronghold is the God of Jacob.

2 Our God is our refuge and strength: a helper in troubles, which have found us exceedingly.

3 Therefore we will not fear, when the earth shall be troubled; and the mountains shall be removed into the heart of the sea.

R. The Lord of hosts is with us; our stronghold is the God of Jacob.

5 The stream of the river maketh the city of God joyful: the most High hath sanctified his own tabernacle.

6 God is in the midst thereof, it shall not be moved: God will help it in the morning early.

R. The Lord of hosts is with us; our stronghold is the God of Jacob.

8 The Lord of armies is with us: the God of Jacob is our protector.

9 Come and behold ye the works of the Lord: what wonders he hath done upon earth,

R. The Lord of hosts is with us; our stronghold is the God of Jacob.

Verse Before the Gospel: Psalms 51: 12a, 14a
12a, 14a A clean heart created for me, O God; give me back the joy of your salvation.

Gospel: John 5: 1-16

1 After these things was a festival day of the Jews, and Jesus went up to Jerusalem.

2 Now there is in Jerusalem a pond, called Probatica, which in Hebrew is named Bethsaida, having five porches.

3 In these lay a great multitude of sick, of blind, of lame, of withered; waiting for the moving of the water.

4 And an angel of the Lord descended at certain times into the pond; and the water was moved. And he that went down first into the pond after the motion of the water, was made whole, of whatsoever infirmity he lay under.

5 And there was a certain man there, that had been eight and thirty years under his infirmity.

6 Him when Jesus had seen lying, and knew that he had been now a long time, he said to him: Wilt thou be made whole?

7 The infirm man answered him: Sir, I have no man, when the water is troubled, to put me into the pond. While I am coming, another goeth down before me.

8 Jesus saith to him: Arise, take up thy bed, and walk.

9 And immediately the man was made whole: and he took up his bed, and walked. And it was the sabbath that day.

10 The Jews therefore said to him that was healed: It is the sabbath; it is not lawful for thee to take up thy bed.

11 He answered them: He that made me whole, he said to me, Take up thy bed, and walk.

12 They asked him therefore: Who is that man who said to thee, Take up thy bed, and walk?

13 But he who was healed, knew not who it was; for Jesus went aside from the multitude standing in the place.

14 Afterwards, Jesus findeth him in the temple, and saith to him: Behold thou art made whole: sin no more, lest some worse thing happen to thee.

15 The man went his way, and told the Jews, that it was Jesus who had made him whole.

16 Therefore did the Jews persecute Jesus, because he did these things on the sabbath

Daily Mass Readings for Wednesday, 13 March 2024

Lenten Weekday
First Reading: Isaiah 49: 8-15
Responsorial Psalm: Psalms 145: 8-9, 13cd-14, 17-18
Verse Before the Gospel: John 11: 25a, 26
Gospel: John 5: 17-30
Lectionary: 246
First Reading: Isaiah 49: 8-15

8 Thus saith the Lord: In an acceptable time I have heard thee, and in the day of salvation I have helped thee: and I have preserved thee, and given thee to be a covenant of the people, that thou mightest raise up the earth, and possess the inheritances that were destroyed:

9 That thou mightest say to them that are bound: Come forth: and to them that are in darkness: shew yourselves. They shall feed in the ways, and their pastures shall be in every plain.

10 They shall not hunger, nor thirst, neither shall the heat nor the sun strike them: for he that is merciful to them, shall be their shepherd, and at the fountains of waters he shall give them drink.

11 And I will make all my mountains a way, and my paths shall be exalted.

12 Behold these shall come from afar, and behold these from the north and from the sea, and these from the south country.

13 Give praise, O ye heavens, and rejoice, O earth, ye mountains, give praise with jubilation: because the Lord hath comforted his people, and will have mercy on his poor ones.

14 And Sion said: The Lord hath forsaken me, and the Lord hath forgotten me.

15 Can a woman forget her infant, so as not to have pity on the son of her womb? and if she should forget, yet will not I forget thee.

Responsorial Psalm: Psalms 145: 8-9, 13cd-14, 17-18 R. (8a) The Lord is gracious and merciful.

8 The Lord is gracious and merciful: patient and plenteous in mercy.

9 The Lord is sweet to all: and his tender mercies are over all his works.

R. The Lord is gracious and merciful.

13cd The Lord is faithful in all his words: and holy in all his works.

14 The Lord lifteth up all that fall: and setteth up all that are cast down.

R. The Lord is gracious and merciful.

17 The Lord is just in all his ways: and holy in all his works.

18 The Lord is nigh unto all them that call upon him: to all that call upon him in truth.

R. The Lord is gracious and merciful.

Verse Before the Gospel: John 11: 25a, 26
25a, 26 I am the resurrection and the life, says the Lord; whoever believes in me will never die.

Gospel: John 5: 17-30
17 But Jesus answered them: My Father worketh until now; and I work.

18 Hereupon therefore the Jews sought the most to kill him, because he did not only break the sabbath, but also said God was his Father, making himself equal to God.

19 Then Jesus answered, and said to them: Amen, amen, I say unto you, the Son cannot do anything of himself, but what he seeth the Father doing: for what things soever he doth, these the Son also doth in like manner.

20 For the Father loveth the Son, and sheweth him all things which himself doth: and greater works than these will he shew him, that you may wonder.

21 For as the Father raiseth up the dead, and giveth life: so the Son also giveth life to whom he will.

22 For neither doth the Father judge any man, but hath given all judgment to the Son.

23 That all men may honor the Son, as they honor the Father. He who honoureth not the Son, honoureth not the Father, who hath sent him.

24 Amen, amen I say unto you, that he who heareth my word, and believeth him that sent me, hath life everlasting; and cometh not into judgment, but is passed from death to life.

25 Amen, amen I say unto you, that the hour cometh, and now is, when the dead shall hear the voice of the Son of God, and they that hear shall live.

26 For as the Father hath life in himself, so he hath given the Son also to have life in himself:

27 And he hath given him power to do judgment, because he is the Son of man.

28 Wonder not at this; for the hour cometh, wherein all that are in the graves shall hear the voice of the Son of God.

29 And they that have done good things, shall come forth unto the resurrection of life; but they that have done evil, unto the resurrection of judgment.

30 I cannot do anything by myself. As I hear, so I judge: and my judgment is just; because I seek not my own will, but the will of him that sent me

Daily Mass Readings for Thursday, 14 March 2024

Lenten Weekday
First Reading: Exodus 32: 7-14
Responsorial Psalm: Psalms 106: 19-20, 21-22, 23
Verse Before the Gospel: John 3: 16
Gospel: John 5: 31-47
Lectionary: 247
First Reading: Exodus 32: 7-14

7 And the Lord spoke to Moses, saying: Go, get thee down: thy people, which thou hast brought out of the land of Egypt, hath sinned.

8 They have quickly strayed from the way which thou didst shew them: and they have made to themselves a molten calf, and have adored it, and

sacrificing victims to it, have said: These are thy gods, O Israel, that have brought thee out of the land of Egypt.

9 And again the Lord said to Moses: See that this people is stiff necked:

10 Let me alone, that my wrath may be kindled against them, and that I may destroy them, and I will make a great nation.

11 But Moses besought the Lord his God, saying: Why, O Lord, is thy indignation kindled against thy people, whom thou hast brought out of the land of Egypt, with great power, and with a mighty hand?

12 Let not the Egyptians say, I beseech thee: He craftily brought them out, that he might kill them in the mountains, and destroy them from the earth: let thy anger cease, and be appeased upon the wickedness of thy people.

13 Remember Abraham, Isaac, and Israel, thy servants, to whom thou sworest by thy own self, saying: I will multiply your seed as the stars of heaven: and this whole land that I have spoken of, I will give to you seed, and you shall possess it for ever.

14 And the Lord was appeased from doing the evil which he had spoken against his people.

Responsorial Psalm: Psalms 106: 19-20, 21-22, 23
R. (4a) Remember us, O Lord, as you favor your people.

19 They also made a calf in Horeb: and they adored the graven thing.
20 And they changed their glory into the likeness of a calf that eateth grass. R.
Remember us, O Lord, as you favor your people.
21 They forgot God, who saved them, who had done great things in Egypt, 22 Wondrous works in the land of Cham: terrible things in the Red Sea.

R. Remember us, O Lord, as you favor your people.

23 And he said that he would destroy them: had not Moses his chosen stood before him in the breach: To turn away his wrath, lest he should destroy them.

R. Remember us, O Lord, as you favor your people.

Verse Before the Gospel: John 3: 16
16 God so loved the world that he gave his only-begotten Son, so that everyone who believes in him might have eternal life.

Gospel: John 5: 31-47
31 If I bear witness of myself, my witness is not true.

32 There is another that beareth witness of me; and I know that the witness which he witnesseth of me is true.

33 You sent to John, and he gave testimony to the truth.

34 But I receive no testimony from man: but I say these things, that you may be saved.

35 He was a burning and a shining light: and you were willing for a time to rejoice in his light.

36 But I have a greater testimony than that of John: for the works which the Father hath given me to perfect; the works themselves, which I do, give testimony of me, that the Father hath sent me.

37 And the Father himself who hath sent me, hath given testimony of me: neither have you heard his voice at any time, nor seen his shape.

38 And you have not his word abiding in you: for whom he hath sent, him you believe not.

39 Search the scriptures, for you think in them to have life everlasting; and the same are they that give testimony of me.

40 And you will not come to me so that you may have life.
41 I receive glory not from men.
42 But I know you, that you do not have the love of God in you.

43 I come in the name of my Father, and you receive me not: if another shall come in his own name, he you will receive.

44 How can you believe, who receives glory one from another: and the glory which is from God alone, you do not seek?

45 Think not that I will accuse you of the Father. There is one that accuses you, Moses, in whom you trust.

46 For if you did believe Moses, you would perhaps believe me also; for he wrote of me.

47 But if you do not believe his writings, how will you believe my words?

Daily Mass Readings for Friday, 15 March 2024

Lenten Weekday, Day of Abstinence from Meat (Age 14 and Up) First Reading: Wisdom 2: 1a, 12-22
Responsorial Psalm: Psalms 34: 17-18, 19-20, 21 and 23
Verse Before the Gospel: Matthew 4: 4b

Gospel: John 7: 1-2, 10, 25-30

Lectionary: 248
First Reading: Wisdom 2: 1a, 12-22
1a For they have said, reasoning with themselves, but not right.

12 Let us therefore lie in wait for the just, because he is not for our turn, and he is contrary to our doings, and upbraideth us with transgressions of the law, and divulged against us the sins of our way of life.

13 He boasted that he had the knowledge of God, and calleth himself the son of God.

14 He has become a censor of our thoughts.

15 He is grievous unto us, even to behold: for his life is not like other men's, and his ways are very different.

16 We are esteemed by him as triflers, and he abstained from our ways as from filthiness, and he preferred the latter end of the just, and glorieth that he hath God for his father.

17 Let us see then if his words are true, and let us prove what shall happen to him, and we shall know what his end shall be.

18 For if he be the true son of God, he will defend him, and will deliver him from the hands of his enemies.

19 Let us examine him by outrages and tortures, that we may know his meekness and try his patience.

20 Let us condemn him to a most shameful death: for there shall be respect given unto him by his words.

21 These things they thought, and were deceived: for their own malice blinded them.

22 And they knew not the secrets of God, nor hoped for the wages of justice, nor esteemed the honor of holy souls.

Responsorial Psalm: Psalms 34: 17-18, 19-20, 21 and 23 R. (19a) The Lord is close to the brokenhearted.

17 But the countenance of the Lord is against them that do evil things: to cut off the remembrance of them from the earth.

18 They just cried, and the Lord heard them: and delivered them out of all their troubles.

R. The Lord is close to the brokenhearted.

19 The Lord is nigh unto them that are of a contrite heart: and he will save the humble of spirit.

20 Many are the afflictions of the just; but out of them all will the Lord deliver them.

R. The Lord is close to the brokenhearted.
21 The Lord keepeth all their bones, not one of them shall be broken.

23 The Lord will redeem the souls of his servants: and none of them that trust in him shall offend.

R. The Lord is close to the brokenhearted.

Verse Before the Gospel: Matthew 4: 4b
4b One does not live on bread alone, but on every word that comes forth from the mouth of God.

Gospel: John 7: 1-2, 10, 25-30
1 After these things Jesus walked in Galilee; for he would not walk in Judea, because the Jews sought to kill him.

2 Now the Jews' feast of tabernacles was at hand.

10 But after his brethren were gone up, then he also went up to the feast, not openly, but, as it were, in secret.

25 Some therefore of Jerusalem said: Is not this he whom they seek to kill?

26 And behold, he speaketh openly, and they say nothing to him. Have the rulers known for a truth that this is Christ?

27 But we know this man, whence he is: but when the Christ cometh, no man knoweth whence he is.

28 Jesus therefore cried out in the temple, teaching, and saying: You both know me, and you know whence I am: and I am not come of myself; but he that sent me, is true, whom you know not.

29 I know him, because I am from him, and he hath sent me.

30 They sought therefore to apprehend him: and no man laid hands on him, because his hour had not yet come.

Daily Mass Readings for Saturday, 16 March 2024

Lenten Weekday
First Reading: Jeremiah 11: 18-20
Responsorial Psalm: Psalms 7: 2-3, 9bc-10, 11-12 Verse Before the Gospel: Luke 8: 15
Gospel: John 7: 40-53

Lectionary: 249
First Reading: Jeremiah 11: 18-20
18 But thou, O Lord, hast shewn me, and I have known: then thou shewedst me their doings.

19 And I was as a meek lamb, that is carried to be a victim: and I knew not that they had devised counsels against me, saying: Let us put wood on his bread, and cut him off from the land of the living, and let his name be remembered no more.

20 But thou, O Lord of Sabaoth, who judges justly, and triest the reins and hearts, let me see thy revenge on them: for to thee I have revealed my cause.

Responsorial Psalm: Psalms 7: 2-3, 9bc-10, 11-12 R. (2a) O Lord, my God, in you I take refuge.

2 O Lord my God, in thee have I put my trust: save me from all them that persecute me, and deliver me.

3 Lest at any time he seize upon my soul like a lion, while there is no one to redeem me, nor to save.

R. O Lord, my God, in you I take refuge.

9bc Judge me, O Lord, according to my justice, and according to my innocence in me.

10 The wickedness of sinners shall be brought to nought: and thou shalt direct the just: the searcher of hearts and reins is God.

R. O Lord, my God, in you I take refuge.
11 Just is my help from the Lord: who saveth the upright of heart. 12 God is a just judge, strong and patient: is he angry every day?

R. O Lord, my God, in you I take refuge.

Verse Before the Gospel: Luke 8: 15
15 Blessed are those who have kept the word with a generous heart and yield a harvest through perseverance.

Gospel: John 7: 40-53
40 Of that multitude therefore, when they had heard these words of his, some said: This is the prophet indeed.

41 Others said: This is Christ. But some said: Doth the Christ come out of Galilee?

42 Doth not the scripture say: That Christ cometh of the seed of David, and from Bethlehem the town where David was?

43 So there arose a dissension among the people because of him.

44 And some of them would have apprehended him: but no man laid hands on him.

45 The ministers therefore came to the chief priests and the Pharisees. And they said to them: Why have you not brought him?

46 The ministers answered: Never did man speak like this man. 47 The Pharisees therefore answered them: Are you also seduced? 48 Hath any one of the rulers believed in him, or of the Pharisees? 49 But this multitude, that knoweth not the law, are accursed.

50 Nicodemus said to them, (he that came to him by night, who was one of them:)

51 Doth our law judge any man, unless it first hears him, and knows what he doth?

52 They answered, and said to him: Art thou also a Galilean? Search the scriptures, and see, that out of Galilee a prophet riseth not.

53 And every man returned to his own house

Daily Mass Readings for Sunday, 17 March 2024

Lenten; Fifth Sunday of Lent, Third Scrutiny of the Elect/ Lenten First Reading: Jeremiah 31: 31-34
Responsorial Psalm: Psalms 51: 3-4, 12-13, 14-15 Second Reading: Hebrews 5: 7-9

Verse Before the Gospel: John 12: 26 Gospel: John 12: 20-33
Select Mass – Lenten | Scrutiny

Lenten Mass Readings

Lectionary: 35
First Reading: Jeremiah 31: 31-34
31 Behold the days shall come, saith the Lord, and I will make a new covenant with the house of Israel, and with the house of Judah:

32 Not according to the covenant which I made with their fathers, on the day that I took them by the hand to bring them out of the land of Egypt: the covenant which they made void, and I had dominion over them, saith the Lord.

33 But this shall be the covenant that I will make with the house of Israel, after those days, saith the Lord: I will give my law in their bowels, and I will write it in their heart: and I will be their God, and they shall be my people.

34 And they shall teach no more every man his neighbor, and every man his brother, saying: Know the Lord: for all shall know me from the least of them even to the greatest, saith the Lord: for I will forgive their iniquity, and I will remember their sin no more.

Responsorial Psalm: Psalms 51: 3-4, 12-13, 14-15 R. (12a) Create a clean heart in me, O God.

3 Have mercy on me, O God, according to thy great mercy. And according to the multitude of thy tender mercies blot out my iniquity.

4 Wash me yet more from my iniquity, and cleanse me from my sin. R. Create a clean heart in me, O God.

12 Create a clean heart in me, O God: and renew a right spirit within my bowels.

13 Cast me not away from thy face; and take not thy holy spirit from me. R. Create a clean heart in me, O God.

14 Restore unto me the joy of thy salvation, and strengthen me with a perfect spirit.

15 I will teach the unjust thy ways: and the wicked shall be converted to thee. R. Create a clean heart in me, O God.

Second Reading: Hebrews 5: 7-9
7 Who in the days of his flesh, with a strong cry and tears, offering up prayers and supplications to him that was able to save him from death, was heard for his reverence.

8 And whereas indeed he was the Son of God, he learned obedience by the things which he suffered:

9 And being consummated, he became, to all that obey him, the cause of eternal salvation.

Verse Before the Gospel: John 12: 26
26 Whoever serves me must follow me, says the Lord; and where I am, there also will my servant be.

Gospel: John 12: 20-33
20 Now there were certain Gentiles among them, who came up to adore on the festival day.

21 These therefore came to Philip, who was of Bethsaida of Galilee, and desired him, saying: Sir, we would see Jesus.

22 Philip cometh, and telleth Andrew. Again Andrew and Philip told Jesus.

23 But Jesus answered them, saying: The hour has come, that the Son of man should be glorified.

24 Amen, amen I say to you, unless the grain of wheat falling into the ground die,

25 Itself remaineth alone. But if it dies, it bringeth forth much fruit. He that loveth his life shall lose it; and he that hateth his life in this world, keepeth it unto life eternal.

26 If any man minister to me, let him follow me; and where I am, there also shall my minister be. If any man ministers to me, he will honor my Father honor.

27 Now my soul is troubled. And what shall I say? Father, save me from this hour. But for this reason I came at this hour.

28 Father, glorify thy name. A voice therefore came from heaven: I have both glorified it, and will glorify it again.

29 The multitude therefore that stood and heard, said that it thundered. Others said: An angel spoke to him.

30 Jesus answered, and said: This voice came not because of me, but for your sake.

31 Now is the judgment of the world: now shall the prince of this world be cast out.

32 And I, if I be lifted up from the earth, will draw all things to myself. 33 (Now this he said, signifying what death he should die.)

Daily Mass Readings for Monday, 18 March 2024

Lenten Weekday/ Cyril of Jerusalem, Bishop, Doctor
First Reading: Daniel 13: 1-9, 15-17, 19-30, 33-62 or Daniel 13: 41c-62
Responsorial Psalm: Psalms 23: 1-3a, 3b-4, 5, 6
Verse Before the Gospel: Ezekiel 33: 11

Gospel: John 8: 1-11
Lectionary: 251
First Reading: Daniel 13: 1-9, 15-17, 19-30, 33-62 or Daniel 13: 41c-62 1 Now there was a man that dwelt in Babylon, and his name was Joakim:

2 And he took a wife whose name was Susanna, the daughter of Helcias, a very beautiful woman, and one that feared God.

3 For her parents, being just, had instructed their daughter according to the law of Moses.

4 Now Joakim was very rich, and had an orchard near his house: and the Jews resorted to him, because he was the most honorable of them all.

5 And there were two of the ancients of the people appointed judges that year, of whom the Lord said: Iniquity came out from Babylon from the ancient judges, that seemed to govern the people.

6 These men frequented the house of Joakim, and all that had any matters of judgment came to them.

7 And when the people departed at noon, Susanna went in, and walked in her husband's orchard.

8 And the old men saw her going in every day, and walking: and they were inflamed with lust towards her:

9 And they perverted their own mind and turned away their eyes so that they might not look unto heaven, nor remember just judgments.

15 And it fell out, as they watched a fit day, she went in on a time, as yesterday and the day before, with two maids only, and was desirous to wash herself in the orchard: for it was hot weather.

16 And there was nobody there, but the two old men that had hid themselves and were beholding her.

17 So she said to the maids: Bring me oil, and washing balls, and shut the doors of the orchard, that I may wash me.

19 Now when the maids were gone forth, the two elders arose, and ran to her, and said:

20 Behold the doors of the orchard are shut, and nobody seeth us, and we are in love with thee: wherefore consent to us, and lie with us.

21 But if thou wilt not, we will bear witness against thee, that a young man was with thee, and therefore thou didst send away thy maids from thee.

22 Susanna sighed, and said: I am straitened on every side: for if I do this thing, it is death to me: and if I do it not, I shall not escape your hands.

23 But it is better for me to fall into your hands without doing it, than to sin in the sight of the Lord.

24 With that Susanna cried out with a loud voice: and the elders also cried out against her.

25 And one of them ran to the door of the orchard, and opened it.

26 So when the servants of the house heard the cry in the orchard, they rushed in by the back door to see what was the matter.

27 But after the old men had spoken, the servants were greatly ashamed: for never had there been any such word said of Susanna. And on the next day,

28 When the people were to come to Joakim her husband, the two elders also came full of wicked devices against Susanna, to put her to death.

29 And they said before the people: Send to Susanna daughter of Helcias the wife of Joakim. And presently they sent.

30 And she came with her parents, and children, and all her kindred.

33 Therefore her friends and all her acquaintances wept.

34 But the two elders rising up in the midst of the people, laid their hands upon her head.

35 And she weeping looked up to heaven, for her heart had confidence in the Lord.

36 And the elders said: As we walked in the orchard alone, this woman came in with two maids, and shut the doors of the orchard, and sent away the maids from her.

37 Then a young man that was there hid came to her, and lay with her.

38 But we that were in a corner of the orchard, seeing this wickedness, ran up to them, and we saw them lie together.

39 And him indeed we could not take, because he was stronger than us, and opening the doors he leaped out:

40 But having taken this woman, we asked who the young man was, but she would not tell us: of this thing we are witnesses.

41 The multitude believed them as being the elders and the judges of the people, and they condemned her to death.

42 Then Susanna cried out with a loud voice, and said: O eternal God, who knowest hidden things, who knowest all things before they come to pass,

43 Thou knowest that they have borne false witness against me: and behold I must die, whereas I have done none of these things, which these men have maliciously forged against me.

44 And the Lord heard her voice.

45 And when she was led to be put to death, the Lord raised up the holy spirit of a young boy, whose name was Daniel.

46 And he cried out with a loud voice. I am clear from the blood of this woman.

47 Then all the people turning themselves towards him, said: What meaneth this word that thou hast spoken?

48 But he standing in the midst of them, said: Are ye so foolish, ye children of Israel, that without examination or knowledge of the truth, you have condemned a daughter of Israel?

49 Return to judgment, for they have borne false witness against her.

50 So all the people turned again in haste, and the old men said to him: Come, and sit thou down among us, and shew it us: seeing God hath given thee the honor of old age.

51 And Daniel said to the people: Separate these two far from one another, and I will examine them.

52 So when they were put asunder one from the other, he called one of them, and said to him: O thou that art grown old in evil days, now are thy sins come out, which thou hast committed before:

53 In judging unjust judgments, oppressing the innocent, and letting the guilty go free, whereas the Lord saith: The innocent and the just thou shalt not kill.

54 Now then, if thou sawest her, tell me under what tree thou sawest them conversing together. He said: Under a mastic tree.

55 And Daniel said: Well hast thou lied against thy own head: for behold the angel of God having received the sentence of him, shall cut thee in two.

56 And having put him aside, he commanded that the other should come, and he said to him: O thou seed of Chanaan, and not of Judah, beauty hath

deceived thee, and lust hath perverted thy heart:

57 Thus did you do to the daughters of Israel, and they for fear conversed with you: but a daughter of Judah would not abide your wickedness.

58 Now therefore tell me, under what tree didst thou take them conversing together. And he answered: Under a holm tree.

59 And Daniel said to him: Well hast thou also lied against thy own head: for the angel of the Lord waiteth with a sword to cut thee in two, and to destroy you.

60 With that all the assembly cried out with a loud voice, and they blessed God, who saveth them that trust in him.

61 And they rose up against the two elders, (for Daniel had convicted them of false witness by their own mouth,) and they did to them as they had maliciously dealt against their neighbor,

62 To fulfill the law of Moses: and they put them to death, and innocent blood was saved on that day.

Or
41c The multitude condemned Susanna to death.

42 Then Susanna cried out with a loud voice, and said: O eternal God, who knowest hidden things, who knowest all things before they come to pass,

43 Thou knowest that they have borne false witness against me: and behold I must die, whereas I have done none of these things, which these men have maliciously forged against me.

44 And the Lord heard her voice.

45 And when she was led to be put to death, the Lord raised up the holy spirit of a young boy, whose name was Daniel.

46 And he cried out with a loud voice. I am clear from the blood of this woman.

47 Then all the people turning themselves towards him, said: What meaneth this word that thou hast spoken?

48 But he standing in the midst of them, said: Are ye so foolish, ye children of Israel, that without examination or knowledge of the truth, you have condemned a daughter of Israel?

49 Return to judgment, for they have borne false witness against her.

50 So all the people turned again in haste, and the old men said to him: Come, and sit thou down among us, and shew it us: seeing God hath given thee the honor of old age.

51 And Daniel said to the people: Separate these two far from one another, and I will examine them.

52 So when they were put asunder one from the other, he called one of them, and said to him: O thou that art grown old in evil days, now are thy sins come out, which thou hast committed before:

53 In judging unjust judgments, oppressing the innocent, and letting the guilty go free, whereas the Lord saith: The innocent and the just thou shalt not kill.

54 Now then, if thou sawest her, tell me under what tree thou sawest them conversing together. He said: Under a mastic tree.

55 And Daniel said: Well hast thou lied against thy own head: for behold the angel of God having received the sentence of him, shall cut thee in two.

56 And having put him aside, he commanded that the other should come, and he said to him: O thou seed of Chanaan, and not of Judah, beauty hath

deceived thee, and lust hath perverted thy heart:

57 Thus did you do to the daughters of Israel, and they for fear conversed with you: but a daughter of Judah would not abide your wickedness.

58 Now therefore tell me, under what tree didst thou take them conversing together. And he answered: Under a holm tree.

59 And Daniel said to him: Well hast thou also lied against thy own head: for the angel of the Lord waiteth with a sword to cut thee in two, and to destroy you.

60 With that all the assembly cried out with a loud voice, and they blessed God, who saveth them that trust in him.

61 And they rose up against the two elders, (for Daniel had convicted them of false witness by their own mouth,) and they did to them as they had maliciously dealt against their neighbor,

62 To fulfill the law of Moses: and they put them to death, and innocent blood was saved on that day.

Responsorial Psalm: Psalms 23: 1-3a, 3b-4, 5, 6
R. (4ab) Even though I walk in the dark valley I fear no evil; for you are at myside.

1 A psalm for David. The Lord ruleth me: and I shall want nothing.

2 He hath set me in a place of pasture. He hath brought me up, on the water of refreshment:

3a He hath converted my soul.
R. Even though I walk in the dark valley I fear no evil; for you are at my side.
3b He hath led me on the paths of justice, for his own name's sake.

4 For though I should walk in the midst of the shadow of death, I will fear no evils, for thou art with me. Thy rod and thy staff, they have comforted me.

R. Even though I walk in the dark valley I fear no evil; for you are at my side.

5 Thou hast prepared a table before me against them that afflict me. Thou hast anointed my head with oil; and my chalice which inebriated me, how goodly is it!

R. Even though I walk in the dark valley I fear no evil; for you are at my side.

6 And thy mercy will follow me all the days of my life. And that I may dwell in the house of the Lord unto length of days.

R. Even though I walk in the dark valley I fear no evil; for you are at my side.

Verse Before the Gospel: Ezekiel 33: 11
11 I take no pleasure in the death of the wicked man, says the Lord, but rather in his conversion, that he may live.

Gospel: John 8: 1-11
1 And Jesus went unto mount Olivet.

2 And early in the morning he came again into the temple, and all the people came to him, and sitting down he taught them.

3 And the scribes and the Pharisees bring unto him a woman taken in adultery: and they set her in the midst,

4 And said to him: Master, this woman was even now taken in adultery.

5 Now Moses in the law commanded us to stone such a one. But what sayest thou?

6 And this they said, tempting him, that they might accuse him. But Jesus bowing himself down, wrote with his finger on the ground.

7 When they continued asking him, he lifted himself up, and said to them: He that is without sin among you, let him first cast a stone at her.

8 And again stooping down, he wrote on the ground.

9 But hearing this, they went out one by one, beginning at the eldest. And Jesus alone remained, and the woman standing in the midst.

10 Then Jesus lifting up himself, said to her: Woman, where are they that accused thee? Hath no man condemned thee?

11 Who said: No man, Lord. And Jesus said: Neither will I condemn thee. Go, and now sin no more.

Daily Mass Readings for Tuesday, 19 March 2024

Joseph, Husband of Mary Solemnity
First Reading: Second Samuel 7: 4-5a, 12-14a, 16
Responsorial Psalm: Psalms 89: 2-3, 4-5, 27 and 29
Second Reading: Romans 4: 13, 16-18, 22
Verse Before the Gospel: Psalms 84: 5
Gospel: Matthew 1: 16, 18-21, 24 or Luke 2: 41-51a
Lectionary: 543
First Reading: Second Samuel 7: 4-5a, 12-14a, 16
4 But it came to pass that night, that the word of the Lord came to Nathan, saying:

5a Go, and say to my servant David,

12 And when thy days shall be fulfilled, and thou shalt sleep with thy fathers, I will raise up thy seed after thee, which shall proceed out of thy bowels, and I will establish his kingdom.

13 He shall build a house to my name, and I will establish the throne of his kingdom for ever.

14a I will be to him a father, and he shall be to me a son.

16 And thy house shall be faithful, and thy kingdom for ever before thy face, and thy throne shall be firm for ever.

Responsorial Psalm: Psalms 89: 2-3, 4-5, 27 and 29 R. (37) The son of David will live forever.

2 The mercies of the Lord I will sing forever. I will shew forth thy truth with my mouth to generation and generation.

3 For thou hast said: Mercy shall be built up for ever in the heavens: thy truth shall be prepared in them.

R. The son of David will live forever.
4 I have made a covenant with my elect: I have sworn to David my servant:

5 Thy seed will I settle for ever. And I will build up thy throne unto generation and generation.

R. The son of David will live forever.

27 He shall cry out to me: Thou art my father: my God, and the support of my salvation.

29 I will keep my mercy for him for ever: and my covenant faithful to him.

R. The son of David will live forever.

Second Reading: Romans 4: 13, 16-18, 22
13 For not through the law was the promise to Abraham, or to his seed, that he should be heir of the world; but through the justice of faith.

16 Therefore is it of faith, that according to grace the promise might be firm to all the seed; not to that only which is of the law, but to that also which is of the faith of Abraham, who is the father of us all,

17 (As it is written: I have made thee a father of many nations,) before God, whom he believed, who quickeneth the dead; and calleth those things that are not, as those that are.

18 Who against hope believed in hope; that he might be made the father of many nations, according to that which was said to him: So shall thy seed be.

22 And therefore it was reputed to him unto justice.

Verse Before the Gospel: Psalms 84: 5
5 Blessed are those who dwell in your house, O Lord; they never cease to praise you.

Gospel: Matthew 1: 16, 18-21, 24 or Luke 2: 41-51a
16 And Jacob begot Joseph the husband of Mary, of whom was born Jesus, who is called Christ.

18 Now the generation of Christ was this wise. When his mother Mary was espoused to Joseph, before they came together, she was found with the child of the Holy Ghost.

19 Whereupon Joseph her husband, being a just man, and not willing publicly to expose her, was minded to put her away privately.

20 But while he thought on these things, behold the angel of the Lord appeared to him in his sleep, saying: Joseph, son of David, fear not to take

unto thee Mary thy wife, for that which is conceived in her, is of the Holy Ghost.

21 And she shall bring forth a son: and thou shalt call his name JESUS. For he shall save his people from their sins.

24 And Joseph rising up from sleep, did as the angel of the Lord had commanded him, and took unto him his wife.

Or

41 And his parents went every year to Jerusalem, at the solemn day of the pasch,

42 And when he was twelve years old, they going up into Jerusalem, according to the custom of the feast,

43 And having fulfilled the days, when they returned, the child Jesus remained in Jerusalem; and his parents knew it not.

44 And thinking that he was in the company, they came on a day's journey, and sought him among their kinsfolks and acquaintances.

45 And not finding him, they returned into Jerusalem, seeking him.

46 And it came to pass, that, after three days, they found him in the temple, sitting in the midst of the doctors, hearing them, and asking them questions.

47 And all that heard him were astonished at his wisdom and his answers.

48 And seeing him, they wondered. And his mother said to him: Son, why hast thou done so to us? behold thy father and I have sought thee sorrowing.

49 And he said to them: How is it that you sought me? did you not know that I must be about my father's business?

50 And they understood not the word that he spoke unto them.

51a And he went down with them, and came to Nazareth, and was subject to them.

Daily Mass Readings for Wednesday, 20 March 2024

Lenten Weekday
First Reading: Daniel 3: 14-20, 91-92, 95 Responsorial Psalm: Daniel 3: 52, 53, 54, 55, 56 Verse Before the Gospel: Luke 8: 15

Gospel: John 8: 31-42
Lectionary: 253
First Reading: Daniel 3: 14-20, 91-92, 95
14 And Nabuchodonosor the king spoke to them, and said: Is it true, O Sidrach, Misach, and Abdenago, that you do not worship my gods, nor adore the golden statue that I have set up?

15 Now therefore if you be ready at what hour soever you shall hear the sound of the trumpet, flute, harp, sackbut, and psaltery, and symphony, and of all kind of music, prostrate yourselves, and adore the statue which I have made: but if you do not adore, you shall be cast the same hour into the

furnace of burning fire: and who is the God that shall deliver you out of my hand?

16 Sidrach, Misach, and Abdenago answered and said to king Nabuchodonosor: We have no occasion to answer thee concerning this matter.

17 For behold our God, whom we worship, is able to save us from the furnace of burning fire, and to deliver us out of thy hands, O king.

18 But if he will not, be it known to thee, O king, that we will not worship thy gods, nor adore the golden statue which thou hast set up.

19 Then was Nabuchodonosor filled with fury: and the countenance of his face was changed against Sidrach, Misach, and Abdenago, and he commanded that the furnace should be heated seven times more than it had been accustomed to be heated.

20 And he commanded the strongest men that were in his army, to bind the feet of Sidrach, Misach, and Abdenago, and to cast them into the furnace of burning fire.

91 Then Nabuchodonosor the king was astonished, and rose up in haste, and said to his nobles: Did we not cast three men bound into the midst of the fire? They answered the king, and said: True, O king.

92 He answered, and said: Behold I see four men loose, and walking in the midst of the fire, and there is no hurt in them, and the form of the fourth is like the Son of God.

95 Then Nabuchodonosor breaking forth, said: Blessed be the God of them, to wit, of Sidrach, Misach, and Abdenago, who hath sent his angel, and delivered his servants that believed in him: and they changed the king's word, and delivered up their bodies that they might not serve, nor adore any god, except their own God.

Responsorial Psalm: Daniel 3: 52, 53, 54, 55, 56 R. (52b) Glory and praise for ever!

52 Blessed art thou, O Lord the God of our fathers: and worthy to be praised, and glorified, and exalted above all for ever: and blessed is the holy name of thy glory: and worthy to be praised, and exalted above all in all ages.

R. Glory and praise for ever!

53 Blessed art thou in the holy temple of thy glory: and exceedingly to be praised, and exceeding glorious forever.

R. Glory and praise for ever!

54 Blessed art thou on the throne of thy kingdom, and exceedingly to be praised, and exalted above all for ever.

R. Glory and praise for ever!

55 Blessed art thou, that beholdest the depths, and sittest upon the cherubims: and worthy to be praised and exalted above all for ever.

R. Glory and praise for ever!

56 Blessed art thou in the firmament of heaven: and worthy of praise, and glorious forever.

R. Glory and praise for ever!

Verse Before the Gospel: Luke 8: 15
15 Blessed are those who have kept the word with a generous heart and yield a harvest through perseverance.

Gospel: John 8: 31-42
31 Then Jesus said to those Jews, who believed him: If you continue in my word, you shall be my disciples indeed.

32 And you shall know the truth, and the truth shall make you free.

33 They answered him: We are the seed of Abraham, and we have never been slaves to any man: how sayest thou: you shall be free?

34 Jesus answered them: Amen, amen I say unto you: that whosoever committeth sin, is the servant of sin.

35 Now the servant abideth not in the house for ever; but the son abideth forever.

36 If therefore the son shall make you free, you shall be free indeed.

37 I know that you are the children of Abraham: but you seek to kill me, because my word hath no place in you.

38 I speak that which I have seen with my Father: and you do the things that you have seen with your father.

39 They answered, and said to him: Abraham is our father. Jesus saith to them: If you be the children of Abraham, do the works of Abraham.

40 But now you seek to kill me, a man who has spoken the truth to you, which I have heard of God. Abraham did not.

41 You do the work of your father. They said therefore to him: We are not born of fornication: we have one Father, even God.

42 Jesus therefore said to them: If God were your Father, you would indeed love me. For from God I proceeded, and came; for I came not of myself, but he sent me:

Daily Mass Readings for Thursday, 21 March 2024

Lenten Weekday
First Reading: Genesis 17: 3-9
Responsorial Psalm: Psalms 105: 4-5, 6-7, 8-9 Verse Before the Gospel: Psalms 95: 8 Gospel: John 8: 51-59
Lectionary: 254
First Reading: Genesis 17: 3-9
3 Abram fell flat on his face.

4 And God said to him: I AM, and my covenant is with thee, and thou shalt be a father of many nations.

5 Neither shall thy name be called any more Abram: but thou shalt be called Abraham: because I have made thee a father of many nations.

6 And I will make thee increase, exceedingly, and I will make nations of thee, and kings shall come out of thee.

7 And I will establish my covenant between me and thee, and between thy seed after thee in their generations, by a perpetual covenant: to be a God to thee, and to thy seed after thee.

8 And I will give to thee, and to thy seed, the land of thy sojournment, all the land of Canaan for a perpetual possession, and I will be their God.

9 Again God said to Abraham: And thou therefore shalt keep my covenant, and thy seed after thee in their generations.

Responsorial Psalm: Psalms 105: 4-5, 6-7, 8-9
R. (8a) The Lord remembers his covenant forever.

4 Seek ye the Lord, and be strengthened: seek his face evermore.

5 Remember his marvelous works which he hath done; his wonders, and the judgments of his mouth.

R. The Lord remembers his covenant forever.

6 O ye seed of Abraham his servant; ye sons of Jacob his chosen.

7 He is the Lord our God: his judgments are in all the earth.

R. The Lord remembers his covenant forever.

8 He hath remembered his covenant forever: the word which he commanded to a thousand generations.

9 Which he made to Abraham; and his oath to Isaac: R. The Lord remembers his covenant forever.

Verse Before the Gospel: Psalms 95: 8
8 If today you hear his voice, harden not your hearts.

Gospel: John 8: 51-59
51 Amen, amen I say to you: If any man keeps my word, he shall not see death for ever.

52 The Jews therefore said: Now we know that thou hast a devil. Abraham is dead, and the prophets; and thou sayest: If any man keeps my word, he shall not taste death for ever.

53 Art thou greater than our father Abraham, who is dead? and the prophets are dead. Whom dost thou make thyself?

54 Jesus answered: If I glorify myself, my glory is nothing. It is my Father that glorifieth me, of whom you say that he is your God.

55 And you have not known him, but I know him. And if I shall say that I know him not, I shall be like you, a liar. But I do know him, and do keep his word.

56 Abraham your father rejoiced that he might see my day: he saw it, and was glad.

57 The Jews therefore said to him: Thou art not yet fifty years old, and hast thou seen Abraham?

58 Jesus said to them: Amen, amen I say to you, before Abraham was made, I am.

59 They took up stones to cast at him. But Jesus hid himself, and went out of the temple.

Daily Mass Readings for Friday, 22 March 2024

Lenten Weekday, Day of Abstinence from Meat (Age 14 and Up) First Reading: Jeremiah 20: 10-13
Responsorial Psalm: Psalms 18: 2-3a, 3bc-4, 5-6, 7
Verse Before the Gospel: John 6: 63c, 68c

Gospel: John 10: 31-42
Lectionary: 255
First Reading: Jeremiah 20: 10-13
10 For I heard the reproaches of many, and terror on every side: Persecute him, and let us persecute him: from all the men that were my familiars, and continued at my side: if by any means he may be deceived, and we may prevail against him, and be revenged on him.

11 But the Lord is with me as a strong warrior: therefore they that persecute me shall fall, and shall be weak: they shall be greatly confounded, because they have not understood the everlasting reproach, which never shall be effaced.

12 And thou, O Lord of hosts, prover of the just, who seest the reins and the heart: let me see, I beseech thee, thy vengeance on them: for to thee I have laid open my cause.

13 Sing ye to the Lord, praise the Lord: because he hath delivered the soul of the poor out of the hand of the wicked.

Responsorial Psalm: Psalms 18: 2-3a, 3bc-4, 5-6, 7
R. (7) In my distress I called upon the Lord, and he heard my voice.

2 I will love thee, O Lord, my strength:

3a The Lord is my firmament, my refuge, and my deliverer.

R. In my distress I called upon the Lord, and he heard my voice.

3bc My God is my helper, and in him will I put my trust. My protector and the horn of my salvation, and my support.

4 Praising I will call upon the Lord: and I shall be saved from my enemies. R. In my distress I called upon the Lord, and he heard my voice.

5 The sorrows of death surrounded me: and the torrents of iniquity troubled me.

6 The sorrows of hell encompassed me: and the snares of death prevented me.

R. In my distress I called upon the Lord, and he heard my voice.

7 In my affliction I called upon the Lord, and I cried to my God: And he heard my voice from his holy temple: and my cry before him came into his ears.

R. In my distress I called upon the Lord, and he heard my voice.

Verse Before the Gospel: John 6: 63c, 68c
63c, 68cYour words, Lord, are Spirit and life; you have the words of everlasting life.

Gospel: John 10: 31-42
31 The Jews then took up stones to stone him.

32 Jesus answered them: Many good works I have shewed you from my Father; for which of these works do you stone me?

33 The Jews answered him: For a good work we stone thee not, but for blasphemy; and because that thou, being a man, makest thyself God.

34 Jesus answered them: Is it not written in your law: I said you are gods?

35 If he called them gods, to whom the word of God was spoken, and the scripture cannot be broken;

36 Do you say of him whom the Father hath sanctified and sent into the world: Thou blasphemous, because I said, I am the Son of God?

37 If I do not the works of my Father, believe me not.

38 But if I do, though you will not believe me, believe the works: that you may know and believe that the Father is in me, and I in the Father.

39 They sought therefore to take him; and he escaped out of their hands.

40 And he went again beyond the Jordan, into that place where John was baptizing first; and there he abdicated.

41 And many resorted to him, and they said: John indeed did not sign.

42 But all things whatsoever John said of this man were true. And many believed in him.

Daily Mass Readings for Saturday, 23 March 2024

Lenten Weekday/ Toribio De Mogrovejo, Bishop First Reading: Ezekiel 37: 21-28

Responsorial Psalm: Jeremiah 31: 10, 11-12, 13 Verse Before the Gospel: Ezekiel 18: 31 Gospel: John 11: 45-56

Lectionary: 256

First Reading: Ezekiel 37: 21-28

21 And thou shalt say to them: Thus saith the Lord God: Behold, I will take the children of Israel from the midst of the nations whither they are gone: and I will gather them on every side, and will bring them to their own land.

22 And I will make them one nation in the land on the mountains of Israel, and one king shall be king over them all: and they shall no more be two nations, neither shall they be divided any more into two kingdoms.

23 Nor shall they be defiled any more with their idols, nor with their abominations, nor with all their iniquities: and I will save them out of all the places in which they have sinned, and I will cleanse them: and they shall be my people, and I will be their God.

24 And my servant David shall be king over them, and they shall have one shepherd: they shall walk in my judgments, and shall keep my commandments, and shall do them.

25 And they shall dwell in the land which I gave to my servant Jacob, wherein your fathers dwelt, and they shall dwell in it, they and their children, and their children's children, for ever: and David my servant shall be their prince for ever.

26 And I will make a covenant of peace with them, it shall be an everlasting covenant with them: and I will establish them, and will multiply them, and will set my sanctuary in the midst of them for ever.

27 And my tabernacle shall be with them: and I will be their God, and they shall be my people.

28 And the nations shall know that I am the Lord the sanctifier of Israel, when my sanctuary shall be in the midst of them for ever.

Responsorial Psalm: Jeremiah 31: 10, 11-12, 13
R. (see 10d) The Lord will guard us, as a shepherd guards his flock.

10 Hear the word of the Lord, O ye nations, and declare it in the islands that are afar off, and say: He that scattered Israel will gather him: and he will keep him as the shepherd doth his flock.

R. The Lord will guard us, as a shepherd guards his flock.

11 For the Lord hath redeemed Jacob, and delivered him out of the hand of one that was mightier than he.

12 And they shall come, and shall give praise in mount Sion: and they shall flow together to the good things of the Lord, for the corn, and wine, and oil, and the increase of cattle and herds.

R. The Lord will guard us, as a shepherd guards his flock.

13 Then shall the virgin rejoice in the dance, the young men and old men together: and I will turn their mourning into joy, and will comfort them, and make them joyful after their sorrow.

R. The Lord will guard us, as a shepherd guards his flock.

Verse Before the Gospel: Ezekiel 18: 31
31 Cast away from you all the crimes you have committed, says the LORD, and make for yourselves a new heart and a new spirit.

Gospel: John 11: 45-56
45 Many therefore of the Jews, who had come to Mary and Martha, and had seen the things that Jesus did, believed in him.

46 But some of them went to the Pharisees, and told them the things that Jesus had done.

47 The chief priests therefore, and the Pharisees, gathered a council, and said: What do we, for this man do many miracles?

48 If we let him alone so, all will believe in him; and the Romans will come, and take away our place and nation.

49 But one of them, named Caiphas, being the high priest that year, said to them: You know nothing.

50 Neither do you consider that it is expedient for you that one man should die for the people, and that the whole nation perish not.

51 And this he spoke not of himself: but being the high priest of that year, he prophesied that Jesus should die for the nation.

52 And not only for the nation, but to gather together in one the children of God, that were dispersed.

53 From that day therefore they devised to put him to death.

54 Wherefore Jesus walked no more openly among the Jews; but he went into a country near the desert, unto a city that is called Ephrem, and there he abode with his disciples.

55 And the pasch of the Jews was at hand; and many from the country went up to Jerusalem, before the pasch to purify themselves.

56 They sought therefore for Jesus; and they discoursed one with another, standing in the temple: What do you think that he is not coming to the festival day?

Daily Mass Readings for Sunday, 24 March 2024

Palm Sunday of the Lord' Solemnity Passion
Procession: Mark 11: 1-10 or John 12: 12-16
First Reading: Isaiah 50: 4-7
Responsorial Psalm: Psalms 22: 8-9, 17-18, 19-20, 23-24 Second Reading: Philippians 2: 6-11

Verse Before the Gospel: Philippians 2: 8-9
Gospel: Mark 14: 1 – 15: 47
Lectionary: 37/38
Procession: Mark 11: 1-10 or John 12: 12-16

1 And when they were drawing near to Jerusalem and to Bethania at the mount of Olives, he sendeth two of his disciples,

2 And saith to them: Go into the village that is over against you, and immediately at your coming in thither, you shall find a colt tied, upon which no man yet hath sat: loose him, and bring him.

3 And if any man shall say to you, What are you doing? say ye that the Lord hath need of him: and immediately he will let him come hither.

4 And going their way, they found the colt tied before the gate without, in the meeting of two ways: and they lost him.

5 And some of them that stood there, said to them: What are you losing the colt?

6 Who said to them as Jesus had commanded them; and they let him go with them.

7 And they brought the colt to Jesus; and they laid their garments on him, and he sat upon him.

8 And many spread their garments in the way: and others cut down boughs from the trees, and strewed them in the way.

9 And they that went before and they that followed, cried, saying: Hosanna, blessed is he that cometh in the name of the Lord.

10 Blessed be the kingdom of our father David that cometh: Hosanna in the highest.

Or

12 And on the next day, a great multitude that was to come to the festival day, when they had heard that Jesus was coming to Jerusalem,

13 Took branches of palm trees, and went forth to meet him, and cried: Hosanna, blessed is he that cometh in the name of the Lord, the king of Israel.

14 And Jesus found a young ass, and sat upon it, as it is written:

15 Fear not, daughter of Sion: behold, thy king cometh, sitting on an ass's colt.

16 These things his disciples did not know at the first; but when Jesus was glorified, then they remembered that these things were written of him, and that they had done these things to him.

First Reading: Isaiah 50: 4-7
4 The Lord hath given me a learned tongue, that I should know how to uphold by word him that is weary: he wakeneth in the morning, in the morning he wakeneth my ear, that I may hear him as a master.

5 The Lord God hath opened my ear, and I do not resist: I have not gone back.

6 I have given my body to the strikers, and my cheeks to them that plucked them: I have not turned away my face from them that rebuked me, and spit upon me.

7 The Lord God is my helper, therefore am I not confounded: therefore have I set my face as a most hard rock, and I know that I shall not be confounded.

Responsorial Psalm: Psalms 22: 8-9, 17-18, 19-20, 23-24 R. (2a) My God, my God, why have you abandoned me?

8 All they that saw me have laughed me to scorn: they have spoken with the lips, and wagged their heads.

9 He hoped in the Lord, let him deliver him: let him save him, seeing he delighteth in him.

R. My God, my God, why have you abandoned me?

17 For many dogs have encompassed me: the council of the malignant hath besieged me. They have dug my hands and feet.

18 They have numbered all my bones. And they have looked and stared upon me.

R. My God, my God, why have you abandoned me?

19 They parted my garments amongst them; and upon my vesture they cast lots.

20 But thou, O Lord, remove not thy help to a distance from me; look towards my defense.

R. My God, my God, why have you abandoned me?

23 I will declare thy name to my brethren: in the midst of the church will I praise thee.

24 Ye that fear the Lord, praise him: all ye the seed of Jacob, glorify him. R. My God, my God, why have you abandoned me?

Second Reading: Philippians 2: 6-11
6 Who being in the form of God, thought it not robbery to be equal with God:

7 But emptied himself, taking the form of a servant, being made in the likeness of men, and in habit found as a man.

8 He humbled himself, becoming obedient unto death, even to the death of the cross.

9 For which cause God also hath exalted him, and hath given him a name which is above all names:

10 That in the name of Jesus every knee should bow, of those that are in heaven, on earth, and under the earth:

11 And that every tongue should confess that the Lord Jesus Christ is in the glory of God the Father.

Verse Before the Gospel: Philippians 2: 8-9

8-9 Christ became obedient to the point of death, even death on a cross. Because of this, God greatly exalted him and bestowed on him the name which is above every name.

Gospel: Mark 14: 1 – 15: 47

1 Now the feast of the pasch, and of the Azymes was after two days; and the chief priests and the scribes sought how they might by some wile lay hold on him, and kill him.

2 But they said: Not on the festival day, lest there should be a tumult among the people.

3 And when he was in Bethania, in the house of Simon the leper, and was at meat, there came a woman having an alabaster box of ointment of precious spikenard: and breaking the alabaster box, she poured it out upon his head.

4 Now there were some that had indignation within themselves, and said: Why was this waste of the ointment made?

5 For this ointment might have been sold for more than three hundred pence, and given to the poor. And they murmured against her.

6 But Jesus said: Let her alone, why do you molest her? She hath wrought a good work upon me.

7 For the poor you have always with you: and whensoever you will, you may do them good: but me you have not always.

8 She hath done what she could: she came beforehand to anoint my body for burial.

9 Amen, I say to you, wheresoever this gospel shall be preached in the whole world, that also which she hath done, shall be told for a memorial of her.

10 And Judas Iscariot, one of the twelve, went to the chief priests, to betray him to them.

11 Who heard it were glad; and they promised him they would give him money. And he sought how he might conveniently betray him.

12 Now on the first day of the unleavened bread, when they sacrificed the pasch, the disciples say to him: Whither wilt thou that we go, and prepare for thee to eat the pasch?

13 And he sendeth two of his disciples, and saith to them: Go ye into the city; and there shall meet you a man carrying a pitcher of water, follow him;

14 And whichever he shall go in, say to the master of the house, The master saith, Where is my refectory, where I may eat the pasch with my disciples?

15 And he will shew you a large dining room furnished; and there prepare ye for us.

16 And his disciples went their way, and came into the city; and they found as he had told them, and they prepared the pasch.

17 And when evening came, he cometh with the twelve.

18 And when they were at table and eating, Jesus saith: Amen I say to you, one of you that eateth with me shall betray me.

19 But they began to be sorrowful, and to say to him one by one: Is it I?

20 Who saith to them: One of the twelve, who dippeth with me his hand in the dish.

21 And the Son of man indeed goeth, as it is written of him: but woe to that man by whom the Son of man shall be betrayed. It would be better for him, if that man had not been born.

22 And whilst they were eating, Jesus took bread; and blessing, broke, and gave to them, and said: Take ye. This is my body.

23 And having taken the chalice, giving thanks, he gave it to them. And they all drank of it.

24 And he said to them: This is my blood of the new testament, which shall be shed for many.

25 Amen I say to you, that I will drink no more of the fruit of the vine, until that day when I shall drink it again in the kingdom of God.

26 And when they had said a hymn, they went forth to the mount of Olives.

27 And Jesus saith to them: You will all be scandalized in my regard this night; for it is written, I will strike the shepherd, and the sheep shall be dispersed.

28 But after I shall be risen again, I will go before you into Galilee.
29 But Peter saith to him: Although all shall be scandalized in thee, yet not I.

30 And Jesus saith to him: Amen I say to thee, today, even in this night, before the cock crow twice, thou shall deny me thrice.

31 But he spoke the more vehemently: Although I should die together with thee, I will not deny thee. And in like manner also said them all.

32 And they came to a farm called Gethsemani. And he said to his disciples: Sit you here, while I pray.

33 And he taketh Peter and James and John with him; and he began to fear and to be heavy.

34 And he saith to them: My soul is sorrowful even unto death; stay you here, and watch.

35 And when he went forward a little, he fell flat on the ground; and he prayed, that if it might be, the hour might pass from him.

36 And he saith: Abba, Father, all things are possible to thee: remove this chalice from me; but not what I will, but what thou wilt.

37 And he cometh, and findeth them sleeping. And he saith to Peter: Simon, sleepest thou? couldst thou not watch one hour?

38 Watch ye, and pray that you enter not into temptation. The spirit indeed is willing, but the flesh is weak.

39 And going away again, he prayed, saying the same words.

40 And when he returned, he found them again asleep, (for their eyes were heavy,) and they knew not what to answer him.

41 And he cometh the third time, and saith to them: Sleep ye now, and take your rest. It is enough: the hour has come: behold the Son of man shall be betrayed into the hands of sinners.

42 Rise up, let us go. Behold, he that will betray me is at hand.

43 And while he was yet speaking, cometh Judas Iscariot, one of the twelve: and with him a great multitude with swords and staves, from the chief priests and the scribes and the ancients.

44 And he that betrayed him, had given them a sign, saying: Whomsoever I shall kiss, that is he; lay hold on him, and lead him away carefully.

45 And when he came, immediately going up to him, he said: Hail, Rabbi; and he kissed him.

46 But they laid hands on him, and held him.

47 And one of them that stood by, drawing a sword, struck a servant of the chief priest, and cut off his ear.

48 And Jesus, answering, said to them: Are you coming out as a robber, with swords and staves to apprehend me?

49 I was daily with you in the temple teaching, and you did not lay hands on me. But that the scriptures may be fulfilled.

50 Then his disciples leaving him, all fled away.

51 And a certain young man followed him, having a linen cloth cast about his naked body; and they laid hold on him.

52 But he, casting off the linen cloth, fled from them naked.

53 And they brought Jesus to the high priest; and all the priests and the scribes and the ancients assembled together.

54 And Peter followed him from afar off, even into the court of the high priest; and he sat with the servants at the fire, and warmed himself.

55 And the chief priests and all the council sought for evidence against Jesus, that they might put him to death, and found none.

56 For many bore false witness against him, and their evidence was not agreeing.

57 And some rising up, bore false witness against him, saying:

58 We heard him say, I will destroy this temple made with hands, and within three days I will build another not made with hands.

59 And their witness did not agree.

60 And the high priest rising up in the midst, asked Jesus, saying: Answerest thou nothing to the things that are laid to thy charge by these men?

61 But he held his peace, and answered nothing. Again the high priest asked him, and said to him: Art thou the Christ the Son of the blessed God?

62 And Jesus said to him: I am. And you shall see the Son of man sitting on the right hand of the power of God, and coming with the clouds of heaven.

63 Then the high priest rending his garments, saith: What need we any further witnesses?

64 You have heard the blasphemy. What think you? Who all condemned him to be guilty of death.

65 And some began to spit on him, and to cover his face, and to buffet him, and to say unto him: Prophesy: and the servants struck him with the palms of their hands.

66 Now when Peter was in the court below, there cometh one of the maidservants of the high priest.

67 And when she had seen Peter warming himself, looking at him she said: Thou also wast with Jesus of Nazareth.

68 But he denied, saying: I neither know nor understand what thou sayest. And he went forth before the court; and the cock crew.

69 And again a maidservant seeing him, began to say to the standers: This is one of them.

70 But he denied again. And after a while they that stood by said again to Peter: Surely thou art one of them; for thou art also a Galilean.

71 But he began to curse and to swear, saying; I know not this man of whom you speak.

72 And immediately the cock crew again. And Peter remembered the word that Jesus had said unto him: Before the cock crow twice, thou shalt thrice deny me. And he began to weep.

15:1 And straightway in the morning, the chief priests held a consultation with the ancients and the scribes and the whole council, binding Jesus, led him away, and delivered him to Pilate.

2 And Pilate asked him: Art thou the king of the Jews? But he answered, saith to him: Thou sayest it.

3 And the chief priests accused him of many things.

4 And Pilate again asked him, saying: Answerest thou nothing? behold in how many things they accuse thee.

5 But Jesus still answered nothing; so Pilate wondered.

6 Now on the festival day he was wont to release unto them one of the prisoners, whomsoever they demanded.

7 And there was one called Barabbas, who was put in prison with some seditious men, who in the sedition had committed murder.

8 And when the multitude came up, they began to desire that he would do, as he had ever done unto them.

9 And Pilate answered them, and said: Will you release to you the king of the Jews?

10 For he knew that the chief priests had delivered him up out of envy.

11 But the chief priests moved the people, that he should rather release Barabbas to them.

12 And Pilate again answered, saith to them: What will you then do to the king of the Jews?

13 But they again cried out: Crucify him.

14 And Pilate saith to them: Why, what evil hath he done? But they cried out the more: Crucify him.

15 And so Pilate, being willing to satisfy the people, released to them Barabbas, and delivered up Jesus, when he had scourged him, to be crucified.

16 And the soldiers led him away into the court of the palace, and they called together the whole band:

17 And they clothe him with purple, and by platting a crown of thorns, they put it upon him.

18 And they began to salute him: Hail, king of the Jews.

19 And they struck his head with a reed: and they spit on him. And bowing their knees, they adored him.

20 And after they had mocked him, they took off the purple from him, and put his own garments on him, and they led him out to crucify him.

21 And they forced one Simon, a Cyrenian who passed by, coming out of the country, the father of Alexander and of Rufus, to take up his cross.

22 And they bring him into the place called Golgotha, which being interpreted is, The place of Calvary.

23 And they gave him to drink wine mingled with myrrh; but he took it not.

24 And crucifying him, they divided his garments, casting lots upon them, what every man should take.

25 And it was the third hour, and they crucified him.

26 And the inscription of his cause was written over: THE KING OF THE JEWS.

27 And with him they crucify two thieves; the one on his right hand, and the other on his left.

28 And the scripture was fulfilled, which saith: And with the wicked he was reputed.

29 And they that passed by blasphemed him, wagging their heads, and saying: Vah, thou that destroyed the temple of God, and in three days buildest it up again;

30 Save thyself, coming down from the cross.

31 In like manner also the chief priests mocking, said with the scribes one to another: He saved others; himself he cannot save.

32 Let Christ the king of Israel come down now from the cross, that we may see and believe. And they that were crucified with him reviled him.

33 And when the sixth hour came, there was darkness over the whole earth until the ninth hour.

34 And at the ninth hour, Jesus cried out with a loud voice, saying: Eloi, Eloi, ? Which is, being interpreted, My God, my God, why hast thou forsaken me?

35 And some of the standers by hearing, said: Behold he calleth Elias.

36 And one running and filling a sponge with vinegar, and putting it upon a reed, gave him to drink, saying: Stay, let us see if Elias comes to take him down.

37 And Jesus, having cried out with a loud voice, gave up the ghost.

38 And the veil of the temple was rented in two, from the top to the bottom.

39 And the centurion who stood over against him, seeing that crying out in this manner he had given up the ghost, said: Indeed this man was the son of God.

40 And there were also women looking on afar off: among whom was Mary Magdalene, and Mary the mother of James the less and of Joseph, and Salome:

41 Who also when he was in Galilee followed him, and ministered to him, and many other women that came up with him to Jerusalem.

42 And when evening was now come, (because it was the Parasceve, that is, the day before the sabbath,)

43 Joseph of Arimathea, a noble counselor, who was also himself looking for the kingdom of God, came and went in boldly to Pilate, and begged the body of Jesus.

44 But Pilate wondered that he should be already dead. And sending for the centurion, he asked him if he were already dead.

45 And when he had understood it by the centurion, he gave the body to Joseph.

46 And Joseph bought fine linen, and took him down, wrapped him up in the fine linen, and laid him in a sepulcher which was hewed out of a rock. And he rolled a stone to the door of the sepulcher.

47 And Mary Magdalen, and Mary the mother of Joseph, beheld where he was laid.

Daily Mass Readings for Monday, 25 March 2024

Monday of Holy Week
First Reading: Isaiah 42: 1-7
Responsorial Psalm: Psalms 27: 1, 2, 3, 13-14
Gospel: John 12: 1-11
Lectionary: 257

First Reading: Isaiah 42: 1-7

1 Behold my servant, I will uphold him: my elect, my soul delighteth in him: I have given my spirit upon him, he shall bring forth judgment to the Gentiles.

2 He shall not cry, nor have respect for anyone, nor shall his voice be heard abroad.

3 The bruised reed he shall not break, and smoking flax he shall not quench: he shall bring forth judgment unto truth.

4 He shall not be sad, nor troublesome, till he set judgment in the earth: and the islands shall wait for his law.

5 Thus saith the Lord God that created the heavens, and stretched them out: that established the earth, and the things that spring out of it: that giveth breath to the people upon it, and spirit to them that tread thereon.

6 I the Lord have called thee in justice, and taken thee by the hand, and preserved thee. And I have given thee for a covenant of the people, for a light

of the Gentiles:

7 That thou mightest open the eyes of the blind, and bring forth the prisoner out of prison, and them that sit in darkness out of the prison house.

Responsorial Psalm: Psalms 27: 1, 2, 3, 13-14 R. (1a) The Lord is my light and my salvation.

1 The psalm of David before he was anointed. The Lord is my light and my salvation, whom shall I fear? The Lord is the protector of my life: of whom shall I be afraid?

R. The Lord is my light and my salvation.

2 Whilst the wicked draw near against me, to eat my flesh. My enemies that trouble me, have themselves been weakened, and have fallen.

R. The Lord is my light and my salvation.

3 If armies in camp should stand together against me, my heart shall not fear. If a battle should rise up against me, I will be confident in this.

R. The Lord is my light and my salvation.
13 I believe to see the good things of the Lord in the land of the living.

14 Expect the Lord, do manfully, and let thy heart take courage, and wait thou for the Lord.

R. The Lord is my light and my salvation.

Verse Before the Gospel
Hail to you, our King; you alone are compassionate with our faults.

Gospel: John 12: 1-11

1 Jesus therefore, six days before the pasch, came to Bethania, where Lazarus had been dead, whom Jesus raised to life.

2 And they made him a supper there: and Martha served: but Lazarus was one of them that were at table with him.

3 Mary therefore took a pound of ointment of right spikenard, of great price, and anointed the feet of Jesus, and wiped his feet with her hair; and the house was filled with the odor of the ointment.

4 Then one of his disciples, Judas Iscariot, he that was about to betray him, said:

5 Why was not this ointment sold for three hundred pence, and given to the poor?

6 Now he said this, not because he cared for the poor; but because he was a thief, and having the purse, carried the things that were put therein.

7 Jesus therefore said: Let her alone, that she may keep it against the day of my burial.

8 For the poor you have always with you; but me you have not always.

9 A great multitude therefore of the Jews knew that he was there; and they came, not for Jesus' sake only, but that they might see Lazarus, whom he had raised from the dead.

10 But the chief priests thought to kill Lazarus also:

11 Because many of the Jews, by reason of him, went away, and believed in Jesus.

Daily Mass Readings for Tuesday, 26 March 2024

Tuesday of Holy Week
First Reading: Isaiah 49: 1-6
Responsorial Psalm: Psalms 71: 1-2, 3-4a, 5ab-6ab, 15 and 17 Gospel: John 13: 21-33, 36-38
Lectionary: 258
First Reading: Isaiah 49: 1-6

1 Give ear, ye islands, and hearken, ye people from afar. The Lord hath called me from the womb, from the bowels of my mother he hath been mindful of my name.

2 And he hath made my mouth like a sharp sword: in the shadow of his hand he hath protected me, and hath made me as a chosen arrow: in his quiver he hath hidden me.

3 And he said to me: Thou art my servant Israel, for in thee will I glory.

4 And I said: I have labored in vain, I have spent my strength without cause and in vain: therefore my judgment is with the Lord, and my work with my God.

5 And now saith the Lord, that formed me from the womb to be his servant, that I may bring back Jacob unto him, and Israel will not be gathered together: and I am glorified in the eyes of the Lord, and my God is made my strength.

6 And he said: It is a small thing that thou shouldst be my servant to raise up the tribes of Jacob, and to convert the dregs of Israel. Behold, I have given thee to be the light of the Gentiles, that thou mayst be my salvation even to the farthest part of the earth.

Responsorial Psalm: Psalms 71: 1-2, 3-4a, 5ab-6ab, 15 and 17 R. (15ab) I will sing of your salvation.

1 A psalm for David. Of the sons of Jonadab, and the former captives. In thee, O Lord, I have hoped, let me never be put to confusion:

2 Deliver me in thy justice, and rescue me. Incline thy ear unto me, and save me.

R. I will sing of your salvation.

3 Be thou unto me a God, a protector, and a place of strength: that thou mayst make me safe. For thou art my firmament and my refuge.

4a Deliver me, O my God, out of the hand of the sinner.

R. I will sing of your salvation.

5ab For thou art my patience, O Lord: my hope, O Lord, from my youth;

6ab By thee have I been confirmed from the womb: from my mother's womb thou art my protector.

R. I will sing of your salvation.

15 My mouth shall shew forth thy justice; thy salvation all the day long. Because I have not known learning,

17 Thou hast taught me, O God, from my youth: and till now I will declare thy wonderful works.

R. I will sing of your salvation.

Verse Before the Gospel
Hail to you, our King, obedient to the Father; you were led to your crucifixion like a gentle lamb to the slaughter.

Gospel: John 13: 21-33, 36-38
21 When Jesus had said these things, he was troubled in spirit; and he testified, and said: Amen, amen I say to you, one of you shall betray me.

22 The disciples therefore looked one upon another, doubting whom he spoke.

23 Now there was leaning on Jesus' bosom one of his disciples, whom Jesus loved.

24 Simon Peter therefore beckoned to him, and said to him: Who is it of whom he speaketh?

25 He therefore, leaning on the breast of Jesus, saith to him: Lord, who is it?

26 Jesus answered: He is to whom I shall reach bread dipped. And when he had dipped the bread, he gave it to Judas Iscariot, the son of Simon.

27 And after the morsel, Satan entered into him. And Jesus said to him: That which thou dost, do quickly.

28 Now no man at the table knew to what purpose he said this unto him.

29 For some thought, because Judas had the purse, that Jesus had said to him: Buy those things which we need for the festival day: or that he should give something to the poor.

30 He therefore, having received the morsel, went out immediately. And it was night.

31 When he therefore was gone out, Jesus said: Now is the Son of man glorified, and God is glorified in him.

32 If God be glorified in him, God also will glorify him in himself; and immediately will he glorify him.

33 Little children, yet a little while I am with you. You shall seek me; and as I said to the Jews: Whither I go you cannot come; so I say to you now.

36 Simon Peter saith to him: Lord, whither goest thou? Jesus answered: Whither I go, thou canst not follow me now; but thou shalt follow hereafter.

37 Peter said to him: Why can't I follow thee now? I will lay down my life for thee.

38 Jesus answered him: Will thou lay down thy life for me? Amen, amen I say to thee, the cock shall not crow, till thou deny me thrice

Daily Mass Readings for Wednesday, 27 March 2024

Wednesday of Holy Week
First Reading: Isaiah 50: 4-9a
Responsorial Psalm: Psalms 69: 8-10, 21-22, 31 and 33-34
Gospel: Matthew 26: 14-25
Lectionary: 259

First Reading: Isaiah 50: 4-9a

4 The Lord hath given me a learned tongue, that I should know how to uphold by word him that is weary: he wakeneth in the morning, in the morning he wakeneth my ear, that I may hear him as a master.

5 The Lord God hath opened my ear, and I do not resist: I have not gone back.

6 I have given my body to the strikers, and my cheeks to them that plucked them: I have not turned away my face from them that rebuked me, and spit upon me.

7 The Lord God is my helper, therefore am I not confounded: therefore have I set my face as a most hard rock, and I know that I shall not be confounded.

8 He is near that justifieth me, who will contend with me? Let us stand together, who is my adversary? let him come near to me.

9a Behold the Lord God is my helper: who is he that shall condemn me?

Responsorial Psalm: Psalms 69: 8-10, 21-22, 31 and 33-34 R. (14c) Lord, in your great love, answer me.

8 Because for thy sake I have borne reproach; shame has covered my face.

9 I have become a stranger to my brethren, and an alien to the sons of my mother.

10 For the zeal of thy house hath eaten me up: and the reproaches of them that reproached thee are fallen upon me.

R. Lord, in your great love, answer me.

21 In thy sight are all they that afflict me; my heart hath expected reproach and misery. And I looked for one that would grieve together with me, but there was none: and for one that would comfort me, and I found none.

22 And they gave me gall for my food, and in my thirst they gave me vinegar to drink.

R. Lord, in your great love, answer me.

31 I will praise the name of God with a canticle: and I will magnify him with praise.

33 Let the poor see and rejoice: seek ye God, and your soul shall live. 34 For the Lord hath heard the poor: and hath not despised his prisoners.

R. Lord, in your great love, answer me.

Verse Before the Gospel
Hail to you, our King; you alone are compassionate with our errors.

Or

Hail to you, our King, obedient to the Father; you were led to your crucifixion like a gentle lamb to the slaughter.

Gospel: Matthew 26: 14-25
14 Then went one of the twelve, who was called Judas Iscariot, to the chief priests,

15 And said to them: What will you give me, and I will deliver him unto you? But they appointed him thirty pieces of silver.

16 And from thenceforth he sought an opportunity to betray him.

17 And on the first day of the Azymes, the disciples came to Jesus, saying: Where wilt thou that we prepare for thee to eat the pasch?

18 But Jesus said: Go ye into the city to a certain man, and say to him: the master saith, My time is near at hand, with thee I make the pasch with my disciples.

19 And the disciples did as Jesus appointed them, and they prepared the pasch.

20 But when it was evening, he sat down with his twelve disciples.

21 And whilst they were eating, he said: Amen I say to you, that one of you is about to betray me.

22 And they, being very much troubled, began every one to say: Is it I, Lord?

23 But he answered, said: He that dippeth his hand with me in the dish, he shall betray me.

24 The Son of man indeed goeth, as it is written of him: but woe to that man by whom the Son of man shall be betrayed: it were better for him, if that man had not been born.

25 And Judas that betrayed him, answering, said: Is it I, Rabbi? He said to him: Thou hast said it.

Daily Mass Readings for Thursday, 28 March 2024

Holy Thursday, At Evening, Begin Easter Triduum of the Lord' Solemnity Passion, Death and Resurrection
First Reading: Exodus 12: 1-8, 11-14
Responsorial Psalm: Psalms 116: 12-13, 15-16 bc, 17-18

Second Reading: First Corinthians 11: 23-26 Verse Before the Gospel: John 13: 34 Gospel: John 13: 1-15
Evening Mass of the Lord' Solemnity Supper

Lectionary: 39
First Reading: Exodus 12: 1-8, 11-14
1 And the Lord said to Moses and Aaron in the land of Egypt:

2 This month shall be to you the beginning of months: it shall be the first in the months of the year.

3 Speak ye to the whole assembly of the children of Israel, and say to them: On the tenth day of this month let every man take a lamb from their families and houses.

4 But if the number be less than may suffice to eat the lamb, he shall take unto him his neighbor that joined to his house, according to the number of souls which may be enough to eat the lamb.

5 And it shall be a lamb without blemish, a male, of one year: according to which rite also you shall take a kid.

6 And you shall keep it until the fourteenth day of this month: and the whole multitude of the children of Israel shall sacrifice it in the evening.

7 And they shall take of the blood thereof, and put it upon both the side posts, and on the upper door posts of the houses, wherein they shall eat it.

8 And they shall eat the flesh that night roasted at the fire, and unleavened bread with wild lettuce.

11 And thus you shall eat it: you shall gird your reins, and you shall have shoes on your feet, holding staves in your hands, and you shall eat in haste: for it is the Phase (that is the Passage) of the Lord.

12 And I will pass through the land of Egypt that night, and will kill every firstborn in the land of Egypt, both man and beast: and against all the gods of Egypt I will execute judgments: I am the Lord.

13 And the blood shall be unto you for a sign in the houses where you shall be: and I shall see the blood, and shall pass over you: and the plague shall not be upon you to destroy you, when I shall strike the land of Egypt.

14 And this day shall be for a memorial to you: and you shall keep it a feast to the Lord in your generations with an everlasting observance.

Responsorial Psalm: Psalms 116: 12-13, 15-16 bc, 17-18
R. (1 Cor 10:16) Our blessing-cup is a communion with the Blood of Christ.

12 What shall I render to the Lord, for all the things he hath rendered unto me?

13 I will take the chalice of salvation; and I will call upon the name of the Lord.

R. Our blessing-cup is a communion with the Blood of Christ. 15 Precious in the sight of the Lord is the death of his saints.

16bc I am thy servant: I am thy servant, and the son of thy handmaid. Thou hast broken my bonds:

R. Our blessing-cup is a communion with the Blood of Christ.

17 I will sacrifice to thee the sacrifice of praise, and I will call upon the name of the Lord.

18 I will pay my vows to the Lord in the sight of all his people:

R. Our blessing-cup is a communion with the Blood of Christ.

Second Reading: First Corinthians 11: 23-26
23 For I have received from the Lord that which also I delivered unto you, that the Lord Jesus, the same night in which he was betrayed, took bread.

24 And giving thanks, broke, and said: Take ye, and eat: this is my body, which shall be delivered for you: this do for the commemoration of me.

25 In like manner also the chalice, after he had supped, saying: This chalice is the new testament in my blood: this do ye, as often as you shall drink, for the commemoration of me.

26 For as often as you shall eat this bread, and drink the chalice, you shall shew the death of the Lord, until he comes.

Verse Before the Gospel: John 13: 34
34 I give you a new commandment, says the Lord: love one another as I have loved you.

Gospel: John 13: 1-15
1 Before the festival day of the pasch, Jesus knew that his hour had come, that he should pass out of this world to the Father: having loved his own who were in the world, he loved them unto the end.

2 And when supper was done, (the devil having now put into the heart of Judas Iscariot, the son of Simon, to betray him,)

3 Knowing that the Father had given him all things into his hands, and that he came from God, and goeth to God;

4 He riseth from supper, and layeth aside his garments, and having taken a towel, girded himself.

5 After that, he putteth water into a basin, and began to wash the feet of the disciples, and to wipe them with the towel wherewith he was girded.

6 He cometh therefore to Simon Peter. And Peter saith to him: Lord, dost thou wash my feet?

7 Jesus answered, and said to him: What I do thou knowest not now; but thou shalt know hereafter.

8 Peter said to him: Thou shalt never wash my feet. Jesus answered him: If I wash thee not, thou shalt have no part with me.

9 Simon Peter saith to him: Lord, not only my feet, but also my hands and my head.

10 Jesus saith to him: He that is washed, needeth not but to wash his feet, but is clean wholly. And you are clean, but not all.

11 For he knew who he was that would betray him; therefore he said: You are not all clean.

12 Then after he had washed their feet, and taken his garments, being set down again, he said to them: Know you what I have done to you?

13 You call me Master, and Lord; and you say well, for so I am.

14 If then I, being your Lord and Master, have washed your feet; you also ought to wash one another's feet.

15 For I have given you an example, that as I have done to you, so you do also.

Daily Mass Readings for Friday, 29 March 2024

Good Friday, Day of Fast (Ages 18-59) and Abstinence from Meat (Age 14 and Up)
First Reading: Isaiah 52: 13 – 53: 12
Responsorial Psalm: Psalms 31: 2, 6, 12-13, 15-16, 17, 25

Second Reading: Hebrews 4: 14-16; 5: 7-9 Verse Before the Gospel: Philippians 2: 8-9 Gospel: John 18: 1 – 19: 42

Mass Isaiah not celebrated today, Celebration of the Lord' Solemnity Passion

Lectionary: 40
First Reading: Isaiah 52: 13 – 53: 12
13 Behold my servant shall understand, he shall be exalted, and extolled, and shall be exceeding high.

14 As many have been astonished at thee, so shall his visage be inglorious among men, and his form among the sons of men.

15 He shall sprinkle many nations, kings shall shut their mouth at him: for they to whom it was not told of him, have seen: and they that heard not, have beheld.

53:1 Who hath believed our report? and to whom is the arm of the Lord revealed?

2 And he shall grow up as a tender plant before him, and as a root out of a thirsty ground: there is no beauty in him, nor comeliness: and we have seen him, and there was no sightliness, that we should be desirous of him:

3 Despised, and the most abject of men, a man of sorrows, and acquainted with infirmity: and his look was as it were hidden and despised, whereupon we esteemed him not.

4 Surely he hath borne our infirmities and carried our sorrows: and we have thought him as if he were a leper, and as one struck by God and afflicted.

5 But he was wounded for our iniquities, he was bruised for our sins: the chastisement of our peace was upon him, and by his bruises we are healed.

6 All we like sheep have gone astray, every one hath turned aside into his own way: and the Lord hath laid on him the iniquity of us all.

7 He was offered because it was his own will, and he opened not his mouth: he shall be led as a sheep to the slaughter, and shall be dumb as a lamb

before his shearer, and he shall not open his mouth.

8 He was taken away from distress, and from judgment: who shall declare his generation? because he is cut off from the land of the living: for the wickedness of my people have I struck him.

9 And he shall give the ungodly for his burial, and the rich for his death: because he hath done no iniquity, neither was there deceit in his mouth.

10 And the Lord was pleased to bruise him in infirmity: if he shall lay down his life for sin, he shall see a long-lived seed, and the will of the Lord shall be prosperous in his hand.

11 Because his soul hath labored, he shall see and be filled: by his knowledge shall this my just servant justify many, and he shall bear their iniquities.

12 Therefore will I distribute to him very many, and he shall divide the spoils of the strong, because he hath delivered his soul unto death, and was reputed with the wicked: and he hath borne the sins of many, and hath prayed for the transgressors.

Responsorial Psalm: Psalms 31: 2, 6, 12-13, 15-16, 17, 25 R. (Luke 23:46) Father, into your hands I commend my spirit.

2 In thee, O Lord, have I hoped, let me never be confused: deliver me in thy justice.

6 Into thy hands I commend my spirit: thou hast redeemed me, O Lord, the God of truth.

R. Father, into your hands I commend my spirit.

12 I have become a reproach among all my enemies, and very much to my neighbors; and a fear to my acquaintance. They saw me without fleeing from me.

13 I am forgotten as one dead from the heart. I am becoming a vessel that is destroyed.

R. Father, into your hands I commend my spirit.
15 But I have put my trust in thee, O Lord: I said: Thou art my God.

16 My lots are in thy hands. Deliver me out of the hands of my enemies; and from them that persecute me.

R. Father, into your hands I commend my spirit.
17 Make thy face shine upon thy servant; save me in thy mercy.

25 Do ye manfully, and let your heart be strengthened, all ye that hope in the Lord.

R. Father, into your hands I commend my spirit.

Second Reading: Hebrews 4: 14-16; 5: 7-9
14 Having therefore a great high priest that hath passed into the heavens, Jesus the Son of God: let us hold fast our confession.

15 For we have not a high priest, who can not have compassion on our infirmities: but one tempted in all things like as we are, without sin.

16 Let us go therefore with confidence to the throne of grace: that we may obtain mercy, and find grace in seasonable aid.

5:7 Who in the days of his flesh, with a strong cry and tears, offering up prayers and supplications to him that was able to save him from death, was heard for his reverence.

8 And whereas indeed he was the Son of God, he learned obedience by the things which he suffered:

9 And being consummated, he became, to all that obey him, the cause of eternal salvation.

Verse Before the Gospel: Philippians 2: 8-9
8-9 Christ became obedient to the point of death, even death on a cross. Because of this, God greatly exalted him and bestowed on him the name which is above every other name.

Gospel: John 18: 1 – 19: 42

1 When Jesus had said these things, he went forth with his disciples over the brook Cedron, where there was a garden, into which he entered with his disciples.

2 And Judas also, who betrayed him, knew the place; because Jesus had often resorted thither together with his disciples.

3 Judas therefore having received a band of soldiers and servants from the chief priests and the Pharisees, cometh thither with lanterns and torches and weapons.

4 Jesus therefore, knowing all things that should come upon him, went forth, and said to them: Whom seek ye?

5 They answered him: Jesus of Nazareth. Jesus saith to them: I am he. And Judas also, who betrayed him, stood with them.

6 As soon as he had said to them: I am he; they went backward, and fell to the ground.

7 Again therefore he asked them: Whom seek ye? And they said, Jesus of Nazareth.

8 Jesus answered, I have told you that I am he. If therefore you seek me, let these go their way.

9 That the word might be fulfilled which he said: Of them whom thou hast given me, I have not lost any one.

10 Then Simon Peter, having a sword, drew it, and struck the servant of the high priest, and cut off his right ear. And the name of the servant was Malchus.

11 Jesus therefore said to Peter: Put up thy sword into the scabbard. The chalice which my Father hath given me, shall I not drink it?

12 Then the band and the tribune, and the servants of the Jews, took Jesus, and bound him:

13 And they led him away to Annas first, for he was father in law to Caiphas, who was the high priest of that year.

14 Now Caiphas was he who had given counsel to the Jews: That it was expedient that one man should die for the people.

15 And Simon Peter followed Jesus, and so did another disciple. And that disciple was known to the high priest, and went in with Jesus into the court of the high priest.

16 But Peter stood at the door without. The other disciple therefore, who was known to the high priest, went out, and spoke to the portress, and brought in Peter.

17 The maid therefore that was portress, saith to Peter: Art not thou also one of this man's disciples? He said: I am not.

18 Now the servants and ministers stood at a fire of coals, because it was cold, and warmed themselves. And with them was Peter also, standing, and warming himself.

19 The high priest therefore asked Jesus of his disciples, and of his doctrine.

20 Jesus answered him: I have spoken openly to the world: I have always taught in the synagogue, and in the temple, whither all the Jews resort; and in secret I have spoken nothing.

21 Why asketh thou me? ask them who have heard what I have spoken unto them: behold they know what things I have said.

22 And when he had said these things, one of the servants standing by, gave Jesus a blow, saying: Answerest thou the high priest so?

23 Jesus answered him: If I have spoken evil, give testimony of the evil; but if well, why strikest thou me?

24 And Annas sent him bound to Caiphas the high priest.

25 And Simon Peter was standing, and warming himself. They said therefore to him: Art not thou also one of his disciples? He denied it, and said: I am not.

26 One of the servants of the high priest (a kinsman to him whose ear Peter cut off) said to him: Did I not see thee in the garden with him?

27 Again therefore Peter denied; and immediately the cock crew.

28 Then they led Jesus from Caiphas to the governor's hall. And it was morning; and they went not into the hall, that they might not be defiled, but that they might eat the pasch.

29 Pilate therefore went out to them, and said: What accusation brings you against this man?

30 They answered, and said to him: If he were not a malefactor, we would not have delivered him up to thee.

31 Pilate therefore said to them: Take him you, and judge him according to your law. The Jews therefore said to him: It is not lawful for us to put any man to death;

32 That the word of Jesus might be fulfilled, which he said, signifying what death he should die.

33 Pilate therefore went into the hall again, and called Jesus, and said to him: Art thou the king of the Jews?

34 Jesus answered: Sayest thou this thing of thyself, or have others told it thee of me?

35 Pilate answered: Am I a Jew? Thy own nation, and the chief priests, have delivered thee up to me: what hast thou done?

36 Jesus answered: My kingdom is not of this world. If my kingdom were of this world, my servants would certainly strive that I should not be delivered to the Jews: but now my kingdom is not from hence.

37 Pilate therefore said to him: Art thou a king then? Jesus answered: Thou sayest that I am a king. For this was I born, and for this came I into the world; that I should give testimony to the truth. Every one that is of the truth, heareth my voice.

38 Pilate saith to him: What is truth? And when he said this, he went out again to the Jews, and said to them: I find no cause in him.

39 But you have a custom that I should release one unto you at the pasch: will you, therefore, that I release unto you the king of the Jews?

40 Then they cried all again, saying: Not this man, but Barabbas. Now Barabbas was a robber.

19:1 Then therefore, Pilate took Jesus, and scourged him.

2 And the soldiers, with a crown of thorns, put it upon his head; and they put on him a purple garment.

3 And they came to him, and said: Hail, king of the Jews; and they gave him blows.

4 Pilate therefore went forth again, and saith to them: Behold, I bring him forth unto you, that you may know that I find no cause in him.

5 (Jesus therefore came forth, bearing the crown of thorns and the purple garment.) And he saith to them: Behold the Man.

6 When the chief priests, therefore, and the servants, had seen him, they cried out, saying: Crucify him, crucify him. Pilate saith to them: Take him you, and crucify him: for I find no cause in him.

7 The Jews answered him: We have a law; and according to the law he ought to die, because he made himself the Son of God.

8 When Pilate therefore had heard this saying, he feared the more.

9 And he entered into the hall again, and he said to Jesus: Whence art thou? But Jesus gave him no answer.

10 Pilate therefore saith to him: Speakest thou not to me? knowest thou not that I have power to crucify thee, and I have power to release thee?

11 Jesus answered: Thou shouldst not have any power against me, unless it were given thee from above. Therefore, he that hath delivered me to thee, hath the greater sin.

12 And from henceforth Pilate sought to release him. But the Jews cried out, saying: If thou release this man, thou art not Caesar's friend. For whosoever maketh himself a king, speaketh against Caesar.

13 Now when Pilate had heard these words, he brought Jesus forth, and sat down in the judgment seat, in the place that is called Lithostrotos, and in Hebrew Gabbatha.

14 And it was the parasceve of the pasch, about the sixth hour, and he saith to the Jews: Behold your king.

15 But they cried out: Away with him; away with him; crucify him. Pilate saith to them: Shall I crucify your king? The chief priests answered: We have no king but Caesar.

16 Then therefore he delivered him to them to be crucified. And they took Jesus, and led him forth.

17 And bearing his own cross, he went forth to that place which is called Calvary, but in Hebrew Golgotha.

18 Where they crucified him, and with him two others, one on each side, and Jesus in the midst.

19 And Pilate wrote a title also, and he put it upon the cross. And the writing was: JESUS OF NAZARETH, THE KING OF THE JEWS.

20 This title therefore many of the Jews did read: because the place where Jesus was crucified was adjacent to the city: and it was written in Hebrew, in Greek, and in Latin.

21 Then the chief priests of the Jews said to Pilate: Write not, The King of the Jews; but that he said, I am the King of the Jews.

22 Pilate answered: What I have written, I have written.

23 The soldiers therefore, when they had crucified him, took his garments, (and they made four parts, to every soldier a part,) and also his coat. Now the coat was without seam, woven from the top throughout.

24 They said then one to another: Let us not cut it, but let us cast lots for it, whose it shall be; that the scripture might be fulfilled, saying: They have parted my garments among them, and upon my vesture they have cast lots. And the soldiers indeed did these things.

25 Now there stood by the cross of Jesus, his mother, and his mother's sister, Mary of Cleophas, and Mary Magdalen.

26 When Jesus therefore had seen his mother and the disciple standing whom he loved, he saith to his mother: Woman, behold thy son.

27 After that, he saith to the disciple: Behold thy mother. And from that hour, the disciple took her to his own.

28 Afterwards, Jesus knowing that all things were now accomplished, that the scripture might be fulfilled, said: I thirst.

29 Now there was a vessel set there full of vinegar. And they, putting a sponge full of vinegar and hyssop, put it to his mouth.

30 Jesus therefore, when he had taken the vinegar, said: It is consummated. And bowing his head, he gave up the ghost.

31 Then the Jews, (because it was the parasceve,) that the bodies might not remain on the cross on the sabbath day, (for that was a great sabbath day,) besought Pilate that their legs might be broken, and that they might be taken away.

32 The soldiers therefore came; and they broke the legs of the first, and of the other that was crucified with him.

33 But after they came to Jesus, when they saw that he was already dead, they did not break his legs.

34 But one of the soldiers with a spear opened his side, and immediately there came out blood and water.

35 And he that saw it, hath given testimony, and his testimony is true. And he knoweth that he saith true; that you also may believe.

36 For these things were done, that the scripture might be fulfilled: You shall not break a bone of him.

37 And again another scripture saith: They shall look on him whom they pierced.

38 And after these things, Joseph of Arimathea (because he was a disciple of Jesus, but secretly for fear of the Jews) besought Pilate that he might take away the body of Jesus. And Pilate gave leave. He came therefore, and took the body of Jesus.

39 And Nicodemus also came, (he who at the first came to Jesus by night,) bringing a mixture of myrrh and aloes, about a hundred pound weight.

40 They took therefore the body of Jesus, and bound it in linen cloth, with the spices, as the manner of the Jews is to bury.

41 Now there was in the place where he was crucified, a garden; and in the garden a new sepulcher, wherein no man yet had been laid.

42 There, therefore, because of the parasceve of the Jews, they laid Jesus, because the sepulcher was nigh at hand.

Daily Mass Readings for Saturday, 30 March 2024

Holy Saturday
First Reading: Genesis 1: 1 – 2: 2 or 1: 1, 26-31a
Responsorial Psalm: Psalms 104: 1-2, 5-6, 10, 12, 13-14, 24, 35 or Psalms 33: 4-5, 6-7, 12-13, 20 and 22
Second Reading: Genesis 22: 1-18 or 22: 1-2, 9a, 10-13, 15-18 Responsorial Psalm: Psalms 16: 5, 8, 9-10, 11
Third Reading: Exodus 14: 15 – 15: 1
Responsorial Psalm: Exodus 15: 1-2, 3-4, 5-6, 17-18
Fourth Reading: Isaiah 54: 5-14
Responsorial Psalm: Psalms 30: 2, 4, 5-6, 11-12, 13
Fifth Reading: Isaiah 55: 1-11
Responsorial Psalm: Isaiah 12: 2-3, 4, 5-6
Sixth Reading: Baruch 3: 9-15, 32 – 4: 4
Responsorial Psalm: Psalms 19: 8, 9, 10, 11

Seventh Reading: Ezekiel 36: 16-17a, 18-28
Responsorial Psalm: Psalms 42: 3, 5; 43: 3, 4 or Isaiah 12: 2-3, 4bcd, 5-6 or Psalms 51:12-13, 14-15, 18-19
Epistle Reading: Romans 6: 3-11
Responsorial Psalm: Psalms 118: 1-2, 16-17, 22-23
Gospel: Mark 16: 1-7
Lectionary: 41
Quick Navigation – Reading 1, 2, 3, 4, 5, 6, 7, Epistle, Gospel

First Reading: Genesis 1: 1 – 2: 2 or 1: 1, 26-31a 1 In the beginning, God created heaven and earth.

2 And the earth was void and empty, and darkness was upon the face of the deep; and the spirit of God moved over the waters.

3 And God said: Be light made. And light was made.

4 And God saw the light that it was good; and he divided the light from the darkness.

5 And he called the light Day, and the darkness Night; and there was evening and morning one day.

6 And God said: Let there be a firmament made amidst the waters: and let it divide the waters from the waters.

7 And God made a firmament, and divided the waters that were under the firmament, from those that were above the firmament, and it was so.

8 And God called the firmament, Heaven; and the evening and morning were the second day.

9 God also said: Let the waters that are under heaven, be gathered together into one place: and let the dry land appear. And it was so done.

10 And God called the dry land, Earth; and the gathering together of the waters, he called Seas. And God saw that it was good.

11 And he said: Let the earth bring forth the green herb, and such as may seed, and the fruit tree yielding fruit after its kind, which may have seed in itself upon the earth. And it was so done.

12 And the earth brought forth the green herb, and such as yieldeth seed according to its kind, and the tree that beareth fruit, having seed each one according to its kind. And God saw that it was good.

13 And the evening and the morning were the third day.

14 And God said: Let there be lights made in the firmament of heaven, to divide the day and the night, and let them be for signs, and for seasons, and for days and years:

15 To shine in the firmament of heaven, and to give light upon the earth. And it was so done.

16 And God made two great lights: a greater light to rule the day; and a lesser light to rule the night: and the stars.

17 And he set them in the firmament of heaven to shine upon the earth.

18 And to rule the day and the night, and to divide the light and the darkness. And God saw that it was good.

19 And the evening and morning were the fourth day.

20 God also said: Let the waters bring forth the creeping creature having life, and the fowl that may fly over the earth under the firmament of heaven.

21 And God created the great whales, and every living and moving creature, which the waters brought forth, according to their kinds, and every winged fowl according to its kind. And God saw that it was good.

22 And he blessed them, saying: Increase and multiply, and fill the waters of the sea: and let the birds be multiplied upon the earth.

23 And the evening and morning were the fifth day.

24 And God said: Let the earth bring forth the living creature in its kind, cattle and creeping things, and beasts of the earth, according to their kinds. And it was so done.

25 And God made the beasts of the earth according to their kinds, and cattle, and every thing that creepeth on the earth after its kind. And God saw that it was good.

26 And he said: Let us make man to our image and likeness: and let him have dominion over the fishes of the sea, and the fowls of the air, and the beasts, and the whole earth, and every creeping creature that moveth upon the earth.

27 And God created man to his own image: to the image of God he created him: male and female he created them.

28 And God blessed them, saying: Increase and multiply, and fill the earth, and subdue it, and rule over the fishes of the sea, and the fowls of the air, and all living creatures that move upon the earth.

29 And God said: Behold I have given you every herb bearing seed upon the earth, and all trees that have in themselves seed of their own kind, to be your meat:

30 And to all beasts of the earth, and to every fowl of the air, and to all that move upon the earth, and wherein there is life, that they may have to feed upon. And it was so done.

31 And God saw all the things that he had made, and they were very good. And the evening and morning were the sixth day.

2:1 So the heavens and the earth were finished, and all the furniture of them.

2 And on the seventh day God ended his work which he had made: and he rested on the seventh day from all his work which he had done.

Or
1 In the beginning, God created heaven and earth.

26 And he said: Let us make man to our image and likeness: and let him have dominion over the fishes of the sea, and the fowls of the air, and the beasts, and the whole earth, and every creeping creature that moveth upon the earth.

27 And God created man to his own image: to the image of God he created him: male and female he created them.

28 And God blessed them, saying: Increase and multiply, and fill the earth, and subdue it, and rule over the fishes of the sea, and the fowls of the air, and all living creatures that move upon the earth.

29 And God said: Behold I have given you every herb bearing seed upon the earth, and all trees that have in themselves seed of their own kind, to be your meat:

30 And to all beasts of the earth, and to every fowl of the air, and to all that move upon the earth, and wherein there is life, that they may have to feed upon. And it was so done.

31a And God saw all the things that he had made, and they were very good.

Responsorial Psalm: Psalms 104: 1-2, 5-6, 10, 12, 13-14, 24, 35 or Psalms 33: 4-5, 6-7, 12-13, 20 and 22
R. (30) Lord, send out your Spirit, and renew the face of the earth.

1 Bless the Lord, O my soul: O Lord my God, thou art exceedingly great. Thou hast put on praise and beauty:

2 And art clothed with light as with a garment. Who stretches out the heaven like a pavilion:

R. Lord, send out your Spirit, and renew the face of the earth.

5 Who has founded the earth upon its own bases: it shall not be moved for ever and ever.

6 The deep like a garment is its clothing: above the mountains shall the waters stand.

R. Lord, send out your Spirit, and renew the face of the earth.

10 Thou sendest forth springs in the vales: between the midst of the hills the waters shall pass.

12 Over them the birds of the air shall dwell: from the midst of the rocks they shall give forth their voices.

R. Lord, send out your Spirit, and renew the face of the earth.

13 Thou waterest the hills from thy upper rooms: the earth shall be filled with the fruit of thy works:

14 Bringing forth grass for cattle, and herbs for the service of men. That thou mayst bring bread out of the earth:

R. Lord, send out your Spirit, and renew the face of the earth.

24 How great are thy works, O Lord? thou hast made all things in wisdom: the earth is filled with thy riches.

35 Let sinners be consumed out of the earth, and the unjust, so that they be no more: O my soul, bless thou the Lord.

R. Lord, send out your Spirit, and renew the face of the earth. Or

R. (5b) The earth is full of the goodness of the Lord.

4 For the word of the Lord is right, and all his works are done with faithfulness.

5 He loveth mercy and judgment; the earth is full of the mercy of the Lord. R. The earth is full of the goodness of the Lord.

6 By the word of the Lord the heavens were established; and all the power of them by the spirit of his mouth:

7 Gathering together the waters of the sea, as in a vessel; laying up the depths in storehouses.

R. The earth is full of the goodness of the Lord.

12 Blessed is the nation whose God is the Lord: the people whom he hath chosen for his inheritance.

13 The Lord hath looked from heaven: he hath be held all the sons of men. R. The earth is full of the goodness of the Lord.
20 Our soul waiteth for the Lord: for he is our helper and protector.
22 Let thy mercy, O Lord, be upon us, as we have hoped in thee.

R. The earth is full of the goodness of the Lord.

Second Reading: Genesis 22: 1-18 or 22: 1-2, 9a, 10-13, 15-18
1 After these things, God tempted Abraham, and said to him: Abraham, Abraham. And he answered: Here I am.

2 He said to him: Take thy only begotten son Isaac, whom thou lovest, and go into the land of vision: and there thou shalt offer him for an holocaust upon one of the mountains which I will shew thee.

3 So Abraham rising up in the night, saddled his ass: and took with him two young men, and Isaac his son: and when he had cut wood for the holocaust he went his way to the place which God had commanded him.

4 And on the third day, lifting up his eyes, he saw the place afar off.

5 And he said to his young men: Stay here with the ass: I and the boy will go with speed as far as yonder, and after we have worshiped, will return to you.

6 And he took the wood for the holocaust, and laid it upon Isaac his son: and he himself carried in his hands fire and a sword. And as they two went on together,

7 Isaac said to his father: My father. And he answered: What wilt thou, son? Behold, saith he, fire and wood: where is the victim of the holocaust?

8 And Abraham said: God will provide himself a victim for an holocaust, my son. So they went on together.

9 And they came to the place which God had shewn him, where he built an altar, and laid the wood in order upon it: and when he had bound Isaac his son, he laid him on the altar upon the pile of wood.

10 And he put forth his hand and took the sword, to sacrifice his son.

11 And behold an angel of the Lord from heaven called to him, saying: Abraham, Abraham. And he answered: Here I am.

12 And he said to him: Lay not thy hand upon the boy, neither do thou any thing to him: now I know that thou fearest God, and hast not spared thy only begotten son for my sake.

13 Abraham lifted up his eyes, and saw behind his back a ram amongst the briers sticking fast by the horns, which he took and offered for a holocaust instead of his son.

14 And he called the name of that place, The Lord seeth. Whereupon even to this day it is said: In the mountain the Lord will see.

15 And the angel of the Lord called to Abraham a second time from heaven, saying:

16 By my own self have I sworn, saith the Lord: because thou hast done this thing, and hast not spared thy only begotten son for my sake:

17 I will bless thee, and I will multiply thy seed as the stars of heaven, and as the sand that is by the sea shore: thy seed shall possess the gates of their enemies.

18 And in thy seed shall all the nations of the earth be blessed, because thou hast obeyed my voice.

Or

1 After these things, God tempted Abraham, and said to him: Abraham, Abraham. And he answered: Here I am.

2 He said to him: Take thy only begotten son Isaac, whom thou lovest, and go into the land of vision: and there thou shalt offer him for an holocaust upon one of the mountains which I will shew thee.

9a And they came to the place which God had shewn him, where he built an altar, and laid the wood in order upon it.

10 And he put forth his hand and took the sword, to sacrifice his son.

11 And behold an angel of the Lord from heaven called to him, saying: Abraham, Abraham. And he answered: Here I am.

12 And he said to him: Lay not thy hand upon the boy, neither do thou any thing to him: now I know that thou fearest God, and hast not spared thy only begotten son for my sake.

13 Abraham lifted up his eyes, and saw behind his back a ram amongst the briers sticking fast by the horns, which he took and offered for a holocaust instead of his son.

15 And the angel of the Lord called to Abraham a second time from heaven, saying:

16 By my own self have I sworn, saith the Lord: because thou hast done this thing, and hast not spared thy only begotten son for my sake:

17 I will bless thee, and I will multiply thy seed as the stars of heaven, and as the sand that is by the sea shore: thy seed shall possess the gates of their enemies.

18 And in thy seed shall all the nations of the earth be blessed, because thou hast obeyed my voice.

Responsorial Psalm: Psalms 16: 5, 8, 9-10, 11 R. (1) You are my inheritance, O Lord.

5 The Lord is the portion of my inheritance and of my cup: it is thou that wilt restore my inheritance to me.

8 I set the Lord always in my sight: for he is at my right hand, that I be not moved.

R. You are my inheritance, O Lord.

9 Therefore my heart hath been glad, and my tongue hath rejoiced: moreover my flesh also shall rest in hope.

10 Because thou wilt not leave my soul in hell; nor wilt then give thy holy one to see corruption.

R. You are my inheritance, O Lord.

11 Thou hast made known to me the ways of life, thou shalt fill me with joy with thy countenance: at thy right hand are delights even to the end.

R. You are my inheritance, O Lord.

Third Reading: Exodus 14: 15 – 15: 1
15 And the Lord said to Moses: Why criest thou to me? Speak to the children of Israel to go forward.

16 But lift thou up thy rod, and stretch forth thy hand over the sea, and divide it: that the children of Israel may go through the midst of the sea on dry ground.

17 And I will harden the heart of the Egyptians to pursue you: and I will be glorified in Pharaoh, and in all his host, and in his chariots, and in his horsemen.

18 And the Egyptians shall know that I am the Lord, when I shall be glorified in Pharaoh, and in his chariots and in his horsemen.

19 And the angel of God, who went before the camp of Israel, removing, went behind them: and together with him the pillar of the cloud, leaving the forepart,

20 Stood behind, between the Egyptians' camp and the camp of Israel: and it was a dark cloud, and enlightening the night, so that they could not come at one another all the night.

21 And when Moses had stretched forth his hand over the sea, the Lord took it away by a strong and burning wind blowing all the night, and turned it into dry ground: and the water was divided.

22 And the children of Israel went in through the midst of the sea dried up: for the water was as a wall on their right hand and on their left.

23 And the Egyptians pursuing went in after them, and all Pharaoh's horses, his chariots and horsemen through the midst of the sea,

24 And now the morning watch has come, and behold the Lord looking upon the Egyptian army through the pillar of fire and of the cloud, slew their host.

25 And overthrew the wheels of the chariots, and they were carried into the deep. And the Egyptians said: Let us flee from Israel: for the Lord fighteth for them against us.

26 And the Lord said to Moses: Stretch forth thy hand over the sea, that the waters may come again upon the Egyptians, upon their chariots and horsemen.

27 And when Moses had stretched forth his hand towards the sea, it returned at the first break of day to the former place: and as the Egyptians were fleeing away, the waters came upon them, and the Lord shut them up in the middle of the waves.

28 And the waters returned, and covered the chariots and the horsemen of all the army of Pharaoh, who had come into the sea after them, neither did there so much as one of them remain.

29 But the children of Israel marched through the midst of the sea upon dry land, and the waters were to them as a wall on the right hand and on the left:

30 And the Lord delivered Israel on that day out of the hands of the Egyptians.

31 And they saw the Egyptians dead upon the seashore, and the mighty hand that the Lord had used against them: and the people feared the Lord, and they believed the Lord, and Moses his servant.

15:1 Then Moses and the children of Israel sung this canticle to the Lord: and said: Let us sing to the Lord: for he is gloriously magnified, the horse and the rider he hath thrown into the sea.

Responsorial Psalm: Exodus 15: 1-2, 3-4, 5-6, 17-18
R. (1b) Let us sing to the Lord; he has covered himself in glory.

1 Then Moses and the children of Israel sung this canticle to the Lord: and said: Let us sing to the Lord: for he is gloriously magnified, the horse and the rider he hath thrown into the sea.

2 The Lord is my strength and my praise, and he has become salvation to me: he is my God and I will glorify him: the God of my father, and I will exalt him.

R. Let us sing to the Lord; he has covered himself in glory. 3 The Lord is as a man of war, Almighty is his name.

4 Pharaoh's chariots and his army he hath cast into the sea: his chosen captains are drowned in the Red Sea.

R. Let us sing to the Lord; he has covered himself in glory.
5 The depths have covered them, they are sunk to the bottom like a stone.

6 Thy right hand, O Lord, is magnified in strength: thy right hand, O Lord, hath slain the enemy.

R. Let us sing to the Lord; he has covered himself in glory.

17 Thou shalt bring them in, and plant them in the mountain of thy inheritance, in thy most firm habitation which thou hast made, O Lord; thy sanctuary, O Lord, which thy hands have established.

18 The Lord shall reign for ever and ever.
R. Let us sing to the Lord; he has covered himself in glory.

Fourth Reading: Isaiah 54: 5-14
5 For he that made thee shall rule over thee, the Lord of hosts is his name: and thy Redeemer, the Holy One of Israel, shall be called the God of all the earth.

6 For the Lord hath called thee as woman forsaken and mourning in spirit, and as a wife cast off from her youth, said thy God.

7 For a small moment have I forsaken thee, but with great mercies will I gather thee.

8 In a moment of indignation have I hid my face a little while from thee, but with everlasting kindness have I had mercy on thee, said the Lord thy Redeemer.

9 This thing is to me as in the days of Noe, to whom I swore, that I would no more bring in the waters of Noe upon the earth: so have I sworn not to be angry with thee, and not to rebuke thee.

10 For the mountains shall be moved, and the hills shall tremble; but my mercy shall not depart from thee, and the covenant of my peace shall not be moved: said the Lord that hath mercy on thee.

11 O poor little one, tossed with tempest, without all comfort, behold I will lay thy stones in order, and will lay thy foundations with sapphires,

12 And I will make thy bulwarks of jasper: and thy gates of graven stones, and all thy borders of desirable stones.

13 All thy children shall be taught of the Lord: and great shall be the peace of thy children.

14 And thou shalt be founded in justice: depart far from oppression, for thou shalt not fear; and from terror, for it shall not come near thee.

Responsorial Psalm: Psalms 30: 2, 4, 5-6, 11-12, 13
R. (2a) I will praise you, Lord, for you have rescued me.

2 I will extol thee, O Lord, for thou hast upheld me: and hast not made my enemies to rejoice over me.

4 Thou hast brought forth, O Lord, my soul from hell: thou hast saved me from them that go down into the pit.

R. I will praise you, Lord, for you have rescued me.

5 Sing to the Lord, O ye his saints: and give praise to the memory of his holiness.

6 For wrath is in his indignation; and life in his good will. In the evening weeping shall take place, and in the morning gladness.

R. I will praise you, Lord, for you have rescued me.

11 The Lord hath heard, and hath had mercy on me: the Lord became my helper.

12 Thou hast turned my mourning into joy.
13 O Lord my God, I will give praise to thee for ever. R. I will praise you, Lord, for you have rescued me.

Fifth Reading: Isaiah 55: 1-11

1 All you that thirst, come to the waters: and you that have no money make haste, buy, and eat: come ye, buy wine and milk without money, and without any price.

2 Why do you spend money for those which do not breed, and your labor for those which do not satisfy you? Hearken diligently to me, and eat that which is good, and your soul shall be delighted in fatness.

3 Incline your ear and come to me: hear and your soul shall live, and I will make an everlasting covenant with you, the faithful mercies of David.

4 Behold I have given him for a witness to the people, for a leader and a master to the Gentiles.

5 Behold thou shalt call a nation, which thou knewest not: and the nations that knew not thee shall run to thee, because of the Lord thy God, and for the Holy One of Israel, for he hath glorified thee.

6 Seek ye the Lord, while he may be found: call upon him, while he is near.

7 Let the wicked forsake his way, and the unjust man his thoughts, and let him return to the Lord, and he will have mercy on him, and to our God: for he is bountiful to forgive.

8 For my thoughts are not your thoughts: nor your ways my ways, saith the Lord.

9 For as the heavens are exalted above the earth, so are my ways exalted above your ways, and my thoughts above your thoughts.

10 And as the rain and the snow come down from heaven, and return no more thither, but soak the earth, and water it, and make it to spring, and give seed to the sower, and bread to the eater:

11 So shall my word be, which shall go forth from my mouth: it shall not return to me void, but it shall do whatsoever I please, and shall prosper in the things for which I sent it.

Responsorial Psalm: Isaiah 12: 2-3, 4, 5-6
R. (3) You will draw water joyfully from the springs of salvation.

2 Behold, God is my savior, I will deal confidently, and will not fear: O because the Lord is my strength, and my praise, and he has become my salvation.

3 You shall draw waters with joy out of the savior's fountains: R. You will draw water joyfully from the springs of salvation.

4 And you shall say on that day: Praise ye the Lord, and call upon his name: make his works known among the people: remember that his name is high.

R. You will draw water joyfully from the springs of salvation.

5 Sing ye to the Lord, for he hath done great things: shew this forth in all the earth.

6 Rejoice, and praise, O thou habitation of Sion: for great is he that is in the midst of thee, the Holy One of Israel.

R. You will draw water joyfully from the springs of salvation.

Sixth Reading: Baruch 3: 9-15, 32 – 4: 4
9 Hear, O Israel, the commandments of life: give ear, that thou mayst learn wisdom.

10 How happeneth it happen, O Israel, that thou art in thy enemies' land?

11 Thou art grown old in a strange country, thou art defiled with the dead: thou art counted with them that go down into hell.

12 Thou hast forsaken the fountain of wisdom:

13 For if thou hadst walked in the way of God, thou hadst surely dwelt in peace for ever.

14 Learn where is wisdom, where is strength, where is understanding: that thou mayst know also where is length of days and life, where is the light of the eyes, and peace.

15 Who hath found out her place? and who hath gone into her treasures?

32 But he that knoweth all things, knoweth her, and hath found her out with his understanding: he that prepared the earth for evermore, and filled it with cattle and four footed beasts:

33 He that sendeth forth light, and it goeth: and hath called it, and it obeyeth him with trembling.

34 And the stars have given light in their watches, and rejoiced:

35 They were called, and they said: Here we are: and with cheerfulness they have shined forth to him that made them.

36 This is our God, and there shall no other be accounted for in comparison to him.

37 He found out all the way of knowledge, and gave it to Jacob his servant, and to Israel his beloved.

38 Afterwards he was seen upon earth, and conversed with men.

4:1 This is the book of the commandments of God, and the law, that is forever: all they that keep it, shall come to life: but they that have forsaken it, to death.

2 Return, O Jacob, and take hold of it, walk in the way by its brightness, in the presence of the light thereof.

3 Give not thy honor to another, nor thy dignity to a strange nation.

4 We are happy, O Israel: because the things that are pleasing to God are made known to us.

Responsorial Psalm: Psalms 19: 8, 9, 10, 11
R. (John 6:68c) Lord, you have the words of everlasting life.

8 The law of the Lord is unspotted, converting souls: the testimony of the Lord is faithful, giving wisdom to little ones.

R. Lord, you have the words of everlasting life.

9 The justices of the Lord are right, rejoicing hearts: the commandment of the Lord is lightsome, enlightening the eyes.

R. Lord, you have the words of everlasting life.

10 The fear of the Lord is holy, enduring forever and ever: the judgments of the Lord are true, justified in themselves.

R. Lord, you have the words of everlasting life.

11 More to be desired than gold and many precious stones: and sweeter than honey and the honeycomb.

R. Lord, you have the words of everlasting life.

Seventh Reading: Ezekiel 36: 16-17a, 18-28
16 And the word of the Lord came to me, saying:

17a Son of man, when the house of Israel dwelt in their own land, they defiled it with their ways, and with their doings.

18 And I poured out my indignation upon them for the blood which they had shed upon the land, and with their idols they defiled it.

19 And I scattered them among the nations, and they are dispersed through the countries: I have judged them according to their ways, and their devices.

20 And when they entered among the nations whither they went, they profaned my holy name, when it was said of them: This is the people of the Lord, and they come forth out of his land.

21 And I have regarded my own holy name, which the house of Israel hath profaned among the nations to which they went in.

22 Therefore thou shalt say to the house of Israel: Thus saith the Lord God: It is not for your sake that I will do this, O house of Israel, but for my holy name's sake, which you have profaned among the nations whither you went.

23 And I will sanctify my great name, which was profaned among the Gentiles, which you have profaned in the midst of them: that the Gentiles may

know that I am the Lord, saith the Lord of hosts, when I shall be sanctified in you before their eyes.

24 For I will take you from among the Gentiles, and will gather you together out of all the countries, and will bring you into your own land.

25 And I will pour upon you clean water, and you shall be cleansed from all your filthiness, and I will cleanse you from all your idols.

26 And I will give you a new heart, and put a new spirit within you: and I will take away the stony heart out of your flesh, and will give you a heart of flesh.

27 And I will put my spirit in the midst of you: and I will cause you to walk in my commandments, and to keep my judgments, and do them.

28 And you shall dwell in the land which I gave to your fathers, and you shall be my people, and I will be your God.

Responsorial Psalm: Psalms 42: 3, 5; 43: 3, 4 or Isaiah 12: 2-3, 4bcd, 5-6 or Psalms 51:12-13, 14-15, 18-19
R. (2) Like a deer that longs for running streams, my soul longs for you, my God.

3 My soul hath thirsted after the strong living God; when shall I come and appear before the face of God?

R. Like a deer that longs for running streams, my soul longs for you, my God.

5 These things I remembered, and poured out my soul in me: for I shall go over into the place of the wonderful tabernacle, even to the house of God: With the voice of joy and praise; the noise of one feasting.

R. Like a deer that longs for running streams, my soul longs for you, my God.

43:3 Send forth thy light and thy truth: they have conducted me, and brought me unto thy holy hill, and into thy tabernacles.

R. Like a deer that longs for running streams, my soul longs for you, my God.
4 And I will go into the altar of God: to God who giveth joy to my youth.
R. Like a deer that longs for running streams, my soul longs for you, my God.
Or

R. (3) You will draw water joyfully from the springs of salvation.

2 Behold, God is my savior, I will deal confidently, and will not fear: O because the Lord is my strength, and my praise, and he has become my salvation.

3 You shall draw waters with joy out of the savior's fountains: R. You will draw water joyfully from the springs of salvation.

4bcd Praise ye the Lord, and call upon his name: make his works known among the people: remember that his name is high.

R. You will draw water joyfully from the springs of salvation.

5 Sing ye to the Lord, for he hath done great things: shew this forth in all the earth.

6 Rejoice, and praise, O thou habitation of Sion: for great is he that is in the midst of thee, the Holy One of Israel.

R. You will draw water joyfully from the springs of salvation. Or
R. (12a) Create a clean heart in me, O God.

12 Create a clean heart in me, O God: and renew a right spirit within my bowels.

13 Cast me not away from thy face; and take not thy holy spirit from me. R. Create a clean heart in me, O God.

14 Restore unto me the joy of thy salvation, and strengthen me with a perfect spirit.

15 I will teach the unjust thy ways: and the wicked shall be converted to thee. R. Create a clean heart in me, O God.

18 For if thou hadst desired sacrifice, I would indeed have given it: with burnt offerings thou wilt not be delighted.

19 A sacrifice to God is an afflicted spirit: a contrite and humbled heart, O God, thou wilt not despise.

R. Create a clean heart in me, O God.

Epistle Reading: Romans 6: 3-11

3 Know you not that all we, who are baptized in Christ Jesus, are baptized in his death?

4 For we are buried together with him by baptism into death; that as Christ is risen from the dead by the glory of the Father, so we also may walk in the newness of life.

5 For if we have been planted together in the likeness of his death, we shall be also in the likeness of his resurrection.

6 Knowing this, that our old man is crucified with him, that the body of sin may be destroyed, to the end that we may serve sin no longer.

7 For he that is dead is justified from sin.

8 Now if we be dead with Christ, we believe that we shall live also together with Christ:

9 Knowing that Christ rising again from the dead, dieth now no more, death shall no more have dominion over him.

10 For in that he died to sin, he died once; but in that he liveth, he liveth unto God:

11 So do you also reckon, that you are dead to sin, but alive unto God, in Christ Jesus our Lord.

Responsorial Psalm: Psalms 118: 1-2, 16-17, 22-23 R. Alleluia, alleluia, alleluia.

1 Give praise to the Lord, for he is good: for his mercy endureth for ever.

2 Let Israel now say that he is good: that his mercy endureth forever.

R. Alleluia, alleluia, alleluia.

16 The right hand of the Lord hath wrought strength: the right hand of the Lord hath exalted me: the right hand of the Lord hath wrought strength.

17 I shall not die, but live: and shall declare the works of the Lord. R. Alleluia, alleluia, alleluia.

22 The stone which the builders rejected; the same has become the head of the corner.

23 This is the Lord's doing: and it is wonderful in our eyes. R. Alleluia, alleluia, alleluia.
Gospel: Mark 16: 1-7

1 And when the sabbath was past, Mary Magdalen, and Mary the mother of James, and Salome, bought sweet spices, that coming, they might anoint Jesus.

2 And very early in the morning, the first day of the week, they come to the sepulcher, the sun being now risen.

3 And they said one to another: Who shall roll us back the stone from the door of the sepulcher?

4 And looking, they saw the stone rolled back. For it was very great.

5 And entering into the sepulcher, they saw a young man sitting on the right side, clothed with a white robe: and they were astonished.

6 Who saith to them: Be not affrighted; you seek Jesus of Nazareth, who was crucified: he is risen, he is not here, behold the place where they laid him.

7 But go, tell his disciples and Peter that he goeth before you into Galilee; there you shall see him, as he told you.

Daily Mass Readings for Sunday, 31 March 2024

Easter Sunday, The Resurrection of Our Lord and Savior Jesus Christ First Reading: Acts 10: 34a, 37-43
Responsorial Psalm: Psalms 118: 1-2, 16-17, 22-23
Second Reading: Colossians 3: 1-4 or First Corinthians 5: 6b-8

Alleluia: First Corinthians 5: 7b-8a
Gospel: John 20: 1-9 or Mark 16: 1-7 or, at an afternoon or evening Mass, Luke 24: 13-35
Lectionary: 42
First Reading: Acts 10: 34a, 37-43
34a And Peter opening his mouth, said:

37 You know the word which hath been published through all Judea: for it began from Galilee, after the baptism which John preached,

38 Jesus of Nazareth: how God anointed him with the Holy Ghost, and with power, who went about doing good, and healing all that were oppressed by the devil, for God was with him.

39 And we are witnesses of all things that he did in the land of the Jews and in Jerusalem, whom they killed, hanging him upon a tree.

40 Him God raised up the third day, and gave him to be made manifest,

41 Not to all the people, but to witnesses preordained by God, even to us, who did eat and drink with him after he arose again from the dead;

42 And he commanded us to preach to the people, and to testify that it is he who was appointed by God, to be judge of the living and of the dead.

43 To him all the prophets give testimony, that by his name all receive remission of sins, who believe in him.

Responsorial Psalm: Psalms 118: 1-2, 16-17, 22-23
R. (24) This is the day the Lord has made; let us rejoice and be glad.

or
R. Alleluia.
1 Give praise to the Lord, for he is good: for his mercy endureth for ever.

2 Let Israel now say that he is good: that his mercy endureth forever. R. This is the day the Lord has made; let us rejoice and be glad.
or
R. Alleluia.

16 The right hand of the Lord hath wrought strength: the right hand of the Lord hath exalted me: the right hand of the Lord hath wrought strength.

17 I shall not die, but live: and shall declare the works of the Lord. R. This is the day the Lord has made; let us rejoice and be glad.
or
R. Alleluia.

22 The stone which the builders rejected; the same has become the head of the corner.

23 This is the Lord's doing: and it is wonderful in our eyes.
R. This is the day the Lord has made; let us rejoice and be glad. or
R. Alleluia.

Second Reading: Colossians 3: 1-4 or First Corinthians 5: 6b-8
1 Therefore, if you be risen with Christ, seek the things that are above; where Christ is sitting at the right hand of God:

2 Mind the things that are above, not the things that are upon the earth.

3 For you are dead; and your life is hidden with Christ in God.

4 When Christ shall appear, who is your life, then you also shall appear with him in glory.

Or
6b Do you know that a little leaven corrupted the whole lump?

7 Purge out the old leaven, that you may be a new paste, as you are unleavened. For Christ our pasch is sacrificed.

8 Therefore let us feast, not with the old leaven, nor with the leaven of malice and wickedness; but with the unleavened bread of sincerity and truth.

Alleluia: First Corinthians 5: 7b-8a R. Alleluia, alleluia.

7b-8a Christ, our paschal lamb, has been sacrificed; let us then feast with joy in the Lord.

R. Alleluia, alleluia.

Gospel: John 20: 1-9 or Mark 16: 1-7 or, at an afternoon or evening Mass, Luke 24: 13-35

1 And on the first day of the week, Mary Magdalen cometh early, when it was yet dark, unto the sepulcher; and she saw the stone taken away from the sepulcher.

2 She ran, therefore, and cometh to Simon Peter, and to the other disciple whom Jesus loved, and saith to them: They have taken away the Lord out of the sepulcher, and we know not where they have laid him.

3 Peter therefore went out, and that other disciple, and they came to the sepulcher.

4 And they both ran together, and that other disciple did outrun Peter, and came first to the sepulcher.

5 And when he stooped down, he saw the linen cloths lying; but yet he went not in.

6 Then cometh Simon Peter, following him, and went into the sepulcher, and saw the linen cloths lying,

7 And the napkin that had been about his head, not lying with the linen cloths, but apart, wrapped up into one place.

8 Then that other disciple also went in, who came first to the sepulcher: and he saw, and believed.

9 For as yet they knew not the scripture, that he must rise again from the dead.

Or

1 And when the sabbath was past, Mary Magdalen, and Mary the mother of James, and Salome, bought sweet spices, that coming, they might anoint Jesus.

2 And very early in the morning, the first day of the week, they come to the sepulcher, the sun being now risen.

3 And they said one to another: Who shall roll us back the stone from the door of the sepulcher?

4 And looking, they saw the stone rolled back. For it was very great.

5 And entering into the sepulcher, they saw a young man sitting on the right side, clothed with a white robe: and they were astonished.

6 Who saith to them: Be not affrighted; you seek Jesus of Nazareth, who was crucified: he is risen, he is not here, behold the place where they laid him.

7 But go, tell his disciples and Peter that he goeth before you into Galilee; there you shall see him, as he told you.

or at an afternoon or evening Mass

13 And behold, two of them went, the same day, to a town which was sixty furlongs from Jerusalem, named Emmaus.

14 And they talked together of all these things which had happened.

15 And it came to pass, that while they talked and reasoned with themselves, Jesus himself, also drawing near, went with them.

16 But their eyes were held, that they should not know him.

17 And he said to them: What are these discourses that you hold one with another as you walk, and are sad?

18 And the one of them, whose name was Cleophas, answering, said to him: Art thou only a stranger to Jerusalem, and hast not known the things that have been done there in these days?

19 To whom he said: What things? And they said: Concerning Jesus of Nazareth, who was a prophet, mighty in work and word before God and all the people;

20 And how our chief priests and princes delivered him to be condemned to death, and crucified him.

21 But we hoped that it was he that should have redeemed Israel: and now besides all this, today is the third day since these things were done.

22 Yea and certain women also of our company affrighted us, who before it was light, were at the sepulcher,

23 And not finding his body, came, saying that they had also seen a vision of angels, who say that he is alive.

24 And some of our people went to the sepulcher, and found it so as the women had said, but him they found it not.

25 Then he said to them: O foolish, and slow of heart to believe in all things which the prophets have spoken.

26 Ought not Christ to have suffered these things, and so to enter into his glory?

27 And beginning at Moses and all the prophets, he expounded to them in all the scriptures, the things that were concerning him.

28 And they drew nigh to the town, whither they were going: and he made as though he would go farther.

29 But they constrained him; saying: Stay with us, because it is towards evening, and the day is now far away. And he went in with them.

30 And it came to pass, whilst he was at table with them, he took bread, and blessed, and brake, and gave to them.

31 And their eyes were opened, and they knew him: and he vanished out of their sight.

32 And they said one to the other: Was not our heart burning within us, whilst he spoke in this way, and opened to us the scriptures?

33 And rising up, the same hour, they went back to Jerusalem: and they found the eleven gathered together, and those that were staying with them,

34 Saying: The Lord is risen indeed, and hath appeared to Simon.

35 And they told what things were done in the way; and how they knew him in the breaking of the bread.

Easter Triduum ends after Evening Prayer

BOOK 2 IS NOW AVAILABLE

Made in United States
North Haven, CT
14 April 2024

51316684R00176